The White Moth

Sept. 2021

To Rina,
Spero che ti piace
questo memoriale di
3 generazioni —
Auguri,
Camilla

THE
WHITE
MOTH

THREE GENERATIONS
AT A TUSCAN VILLA

CAMILLA CALHOUN

Matador
9 Priory Business Park,
Wistow Road, Kibworth Beauchamp,
Leicestershire, LE8 0RX
Tel: 0116 279 2299
Email: books@troubador.co.uk
Web: www.troubador.co.uk/matador
Twitter: @matadorbooks

ISBN 978 1789015 652

British Library Cataloguing in Publication Data.
A catalogue record for this book is available from the British Library.

Printed and bound by CPI Group (UK) Ltd, Croydon, CR0 4YY
Typeset in 11pt Gill Sans by Troubador Publishing Ltd, Leicester, UK

Matador is an imprint of Troubador Publishing Ltd

In memory of beloved Aldo, who shared his family, his friends and the beauty of rural life in Tuscany with me, and who, throughout our years in America, always reminded me to celebrate simple pleasures. I am forever grateful for his love, his generous spirit, his insight and wit. And for Alda, his mother, whose courage, resilience and optimism inspired this book.

AUTHOR'S NOTE

Before this work expanded into a three generational saga that includes my own years in Italy, the intention was (and remains) to honor the life and courageous spirit of my mother-in-law, Alda Innocenti Rafanelli. Many decades have passed since I sat with Alda taking notes. Over the years I learned additional details about the family from Aldo and from his elder sister Anna, whose memory remains astounding. While for the most part my story is scrupulously based on these personal accounts, at times narrative momentum required taking liberties regarding the specificity of time and place. Memory is often subjective, but in good faith and with much love for the living generations of the Rafanelli family, I have attempted to tell the true story of their forebearers within a larger historical context.

CONTENTS

PROLOGUE

Summer 1986

Tonight my husband left for his mother's funeral in Florence. I stayed home with our two little boys – who are finally asleep. As I sit in bed listening to magnolia branches scrape against my dark window, stubborn thoughts pursue me. If only we'd granted my mother-in-law's wish of living out her days in her treasured *cinquecento* villa where she'd nurtured her family for fifty years. Closing my eyes, an image of Alda emerges: wise matriarch holding court in her parlor, doling out advice to adoring friends and neighbors. The villa was her village. We took that away from her. Our newborn son briefly ushered in a fourth Rafanelli generation there. He was only three months old when we left. Should we have ignored the crumbling vaults, the leaky terracotta roof and the idea that moving to America held more promise?

Eight years have passed since my mother-in-law moved in with her daughters and we moved to New York with our baby, closer to my family and friends. Since then we've returned to Florence often, but elderly Alda only made one trip to our suburban New York home. She came, brimming with enthusiasm for America, enchanted by our large trees.

I pick up the letter Alda wrote just a few weeks before she died. Searching for signs of rancor, I find none. She thanks me for loving her son and asks me to remind our boys of her from time to time. Her final salutation makes my throat close: *'Che Dio ti benedica.'*

"God bless you too, Alda," I whisper, imagining her gentle voice prodding me from remorse, encouraging me to sleep – *"Vai a letto! Dormi."* Before heeding her advice, I peruse two photographs on my bedside table that span her life: here's the gentle white-haired grandmother that our sons still recall;

and here's an unrecognizable, skinny sixteen-year-old with black hair, sitting next to her uncle Angelo by the sea, wearing a classic early-1900s' bathing suit. Tomorrow I will show the boys this teenage version of their *Nonna*.

As I turn to switch off the light, a large white moth fluttering by catches my eye. Mesmerized by its gossamer wings, I watch it land on the lampshade, as if searching for warmth and safety. A moment later it escapes and flits about my hand, perching on my pinky finger. Breathless, I observe the nocturnal creature slowly open and close its wings, like a hand waving *ciao*. I shiver, suddenly remembering something Alda told me eight years ago, on that final day at the villa: *"If a white moth appears after someone dies, it's the spirit of that person coming to visit."*

"Alda?" I whisper, surprised at myself. The moth takes flight again, dancing above the light, a whirling, incandescent spirit. *Did you really cross the Atlantic to find your final home with us?* Getting out of bed, I open the lowest drawer in my dresser. Under old clothes I find my neglected Italian notebook, a treasure of Alda's memories she generously shared with me when we lived together at the villa. Thinking this winged creature is my muse, I wave the notebook towards the white moth. *Alda, it's time to finally share your story with others.*

THE WHEEL

Florence, 1978

Living in Italy, surrounded by so many layers of history, transformed me into a time traveler. Every time I passed under the arched doorway of my flower shop across from Piazza San Marco, I was called to remembrance. Nearly five hundred years ago my Florentine workspace had been Lorenzo de Medici's sculpture garden – a training ground for Michelangelo and other nascent sculptors. While arranging flowers or tending plants in the greenhouse, I often imagined the young genius sitting here, observing marble figures, quietly sketching their muscular torsos. Because of the location's history, the city refused any commercial signs, which made attracting customers challenging.

One morning, while day-dreaming of centuries past, as I reached up to water a maidenhair fern cascading from its macramé cradle, a somersault inside my womb startled me back to the present. Dropping the watering can, I placed my hand on my bulging front, hoping to feel the occupying force shift again. My fingers followed a poke and a swish. Astonished, I glanced around and smiled. Inside the humid, warm greenhouse, where seeds incubated and saplings yawned, my pregnancy seemed germane.

"*Calma,*" I urged my active fetus. A moment later I sensed the rising nausea that was to have abated at three months. Digging in my pocket for salty crackers, I exited the greenhouse, stuffing one in my mouth. Peering out onto Via Cavour, I heard the metallic clatter of a *bandone* being pulled down, a sign that shops were closing for lunchtime. I grabbed the skeleton key in my office and locked the enormous wooden door.

"*Che bella giornata,*" I said, patting my front; "let's take a walk." I needed to feel better before driving the twenty minutes home to the villa, a feat which required navigating narrow Via Benedetta Fortini in my minuscule *cinquecento* Fiat, often squeezing past cars or backing up so another vehicle could pass. Inevitably I stalled, experiencing that stick-shift grind. A short walk in Florence might clear my head, trick my hormones, or whatever it was that made me throw up several times each day.

Moving briskly past the church and museum of San Marco, I walked down a long, narrow street towards Piazza Santissima Annunziata. There I stood immobilized in front of the *Hospital of the Innocents*, the orphanage designed by Brunelleschi, illustrious architect of Florence's *Duomo*. I'd first seen this foundling hospital four years earlier, as an art history student on my junior year abroad. Then, the graceful *loggia*, with its repetitive arches, had felt like an embrace. Now, having just experienced life kick inside me, I stared with altered interest at the famous swaddled orphans that adorn the façade. Above nine arched columns, Andrea Della Robbia's glazed infants, nestled in roundels anchored in a cerulean sky, reach out, pleading for adoption.

I entered the building to pick up a brochure, reading that a guild of medieval silk merchants, troubled by abandonment and infanticide, built this institute to baptize, feed, clothe and educate unwanted babies. On February 5th, 1445, their first 'innocent' was left on a basin beneath a window. Later the basin was substituted by *la ruota*, a wooden wheel inserted into the wall. One side of this small revolving portal contained a cradle just large enough for an infant to be transported anonymously into the orphanage. Stepping out onto the *loggia*, I found its ghost remnant on a wall behind iron bars, with two fleshy cherubs hovering above it and an inscription below:

'For four centuries this was the Wheel of the Innocents, until
1875, secret refuge from misery and shame for those to whom
charity never closed its door.'

After reading the inscription, I whispered Alda's maiden name, Degli Innocenti, the name she inherited from her father, who grew up inside this orphanage. Pivoting towards the square, I imagined a moonlit night over a hundred years ago and a very young woman clutching a bundle to her chest as she approached the building. A spectral light emanated from the ceramic glaze of Della Robbia's swaddled infants. It's only the moon, the woman told herself. Trembling, she stared at the tips of her shoes to focus on her mission. The seconds it took her to reach the wheel seemed endless. At its flat wooden surface, she pressed inward. As *la ruota* turned, exposing its cradle side, she laid her swaddled infant on the tiny cushion. When he stirred, she avoided his eyes. She had to send him to safety inside those walls. As she turned the wheel again, her infant disappeared forever from her sight. Tinkling bells interrupted her trance. She realized they were ringing to alert the orphanage of a new arrival. Making the sign of the cross, she ran off, far away from Brunelleschi's arched loggia and the luminous Della Robbia babies.

A nun inside the orphanage swooped up the wailing infant from *la ruota*. Like most Florentine foundlings, he was given the surname Degli Innocenti. Perhaps they called the baby Augusto because he arrived on a hot August night. Year after year he was fed and schooled by the institute. When he walked out of there on his own, as a young man, he was determined to rise above his humble origins. He found work outside Italy. When he returned home to Florence as a successful businessman, Augusto met and married a lovely young woman, Giulia Biliotti. He was thrilled to start a family of his own. Yet Augusto's happiness was ephemeral. At the turn of the twentieth century young Giulia died of complications from the birth of their first child. The date of Alda's birth was February 5th, the same day, only four and a half centuries after the orphanage had accepted its first foundling.

And what, then, would become of this motherless baby? Bereft and desperate after Giulia's death, Augusto knew he couldn't take care of an infant daughter alone, especially since his work required extended time outside Italy. Was the cycle of abandonment to continue? His solace and saving grace was that his wife had a loving family, including three siblings, who lived together in Florence. Augusto beseeched his in-laws Letizia, Rafaella and Angelo to raise Alda, promising to visit as often as possible.

Zio Angelo with Alda, circa 1916.

NEW HOME

Florence, 1916

Sixteen-year-old Alda sat on her bed, her hands folded on her lap. Looking around at her emptied room, her eyes fixed on the one remaining object on her bedside table. Years ago she'd removed this photograph from the piano in the living room. She hoped her aunts and uncle wouldn't mind her taking the precious picture. It was the sole image of the woman she never knew yet missed every day. Picking up the Liberty-style silver frame, Alda stared at her mother's sweet, unsuspecting young face, her impossibly tiny waist, and her arms forever stuck in old-fashioned mutton sleeves.

All these years Aunts Letizia and Rafaella and her uncle Angelo rarely spoke of their sister. Only after Alda's repeated questioning did they finally reveal how she'd died. Oh, how they insisted childbirth was the primary cause of death for women! Did they actually think a statistic could make her feel less sorry about the fact that her birth had caused her mother's death?

She shared her news. "*Mamma*, I'm finally going to live with *Babbo*. He promises to stay in Florence from now on, selling Lancia automobiles all over Tuscany." As if expecting the face to smile, she paused a moment before tucking the frame into her satchel. Buffering it with her aunts' lavender sachets released a fragrant memory of all the Septembers they'd made sachets together. Sensing tears surface, Alda flipped her dark braid behind her and walked briskly to her window, peering down on the street. Seeing her father's sporty Lancia parked there reminded her of the personal census she had taken a few days earlier of all the automobiles in Florence. Walking briskly through the city, she'd counted only five, all on one hand. Her father assured her he would make them more than a novelty.

Alda's mother Giulia, circa 1898.

Alda, March 1925.

Turning away from the window, as she left the comfort of her childhood room for the last time, Alda clutched her satchel like a life raft. The familiar corridor suddenly seemed short. At the parlor's edge, she peeked in. Her aunts and uncle sat stiffly on the sofa. How could she cheer them up? To strengthen her own resolve, she quickly revisited the list of benefits she'd made about moving in with her father: 1) After a lifetime of brief visits, I will see him every day; 2) I will manage his household and practice the cooking skills I learned from his friend, the owner of the restaurant Buca Lapi; and, most importantly, 3) I will have the opportunity to practice charity as I assist with the Italian refugee family he will be sheltering until the war ends. She wondered if helping with them was the real reason her father wanted her there.

"Buon giorno, Babbo!" she said, as she entered the parlor smiling. Her father, dressed in a white linen suit, approached and kissed both her cheeks.

"Buon giorno, bambina. Let me get your things."

"What's the hurry? Aren't you staying for lunch, Augusto?" Aunt Letizia interjected, her tone desperate.

"Oh no, grazie," he said, explaining that the refugees would be arriving from Milan the next day. He was anxious to get Alda settled. "My housekeeper has made us something simple. But thank you… for everything."

When Alda said she'd left her valise on her bed, her father seemed relieved for an excuse to be useful. As he exited, Alda looked at her aunts and uncle. Their eyes were fixed on the floor. When her uncle finally looked up, Alda noticed his tears and moved towards him. She kissed his cheeks and held his hands.

"Oh, Zio Angelino, your mother named you so well!" She turned to her aunts. "Please, don't be sad. I'll be close by and will visit often." Her uncle clung to her, releasing her only when Augusto re-entered. Alda embraced each of her mother's siblings.

Out on the street, as her father arranged her belongings in his car, she stole a glance up at the apartment window. Three pale faces peered down. At their feeble waving, Alda opened and closed her gloved hand, waving ciao, before she turned and climbed into the vehicle. As her father drove towards the Arno River, her mind dropped a trail of crumbs, memorizing the way. She struggled to pay attention as he raved on about Vincenzo Lancia, former Fiat test driver, who'd set up his own auto company in 1906. Her father was clearly proud. Alda nodded politely, remembering a few years earlier, on one of his summer visits, when he'd taught her to drive. How free it had felt behind the wheel, traveling over the hills of Settignano!

In no time they arrived at her father's apartment building. After passing through the doorway, they entered an iron-gated lift. The elaborate cage creaked as it rose to the third floor, where a prim housekeeper opened the apartment door. In the foyer, her father introduced Signora Tacconi and asked her to get Alda settled.

She followed the woman down a corridor and entered her new bedroom. As the housekeeper placed the valise on a bench, Alda thanked her, hoping to be left alone to nestle her aunts' lavender sachets in her top drawer. The woman stood with her arms folded as Alda dug out her mother's photograph and placed it on her dresser. Seeing it might sadden her father, but it might also encourage him to talk about her.

Alda asked Signora Tacconi where the refugee family would be staying. She knew that many Italians from the northern border were homeless, orphaned by the war waging there. She knew that her father, like countless Florentines, felt it was his duty to host a broken family until the war ended.

Signora Tacconi ushered Alda to another room down the hall.

"The mother will sleep in the double bed with her eleven-year-old daughter. The single bed is for the little boy," she added. "Prepare yourself, Signorina Alda. They might be quite a sight. You will help me clean and feed them."

Alda nodded, noting the housekeeper's tone of authority. Her father had made a point that Alda was to manage his home, but this woman seemed to have a very different idea. It was understandable. She had arrived a month earlier and had claimed her territory. Alda would wait. Peace was far more important than power.

The next day, despite all the warnings, when the disheveled family arrived from the train station, Alda was horrified as they hesitated at the threshold. How could eyes be so sunken, or flesh so close to the bone? The mother seemed an old woman. The little girl had tender brown eyes, full of wonder – or was it fear? The boy, perhaps four, clung to his mother, his eyes skittish. Their faces and their clothes were soiled and ragged.

Augusto gave his daughter a stern look. "Alda, this is Signora Marchetti and her children, Franca and Paolo."

"*Piacere*," Alda nodded, as the refugees stood frozen in place. The housekeeper rushed from the kitchen, instructing them to enter but to leave their satchels at the door.

"Signora Tacconi is in charge," Alda's father announced, confirming her suspicions.

The housekeeper ushered the sorry family towards the bathroom. As they passed Alda in the corridor, she nearly fainted from the stench of their filth and urine. Mixed with the smell of garlic and parsley sautéing in the kitchen, aromas that ordinarily stimulated her appetite, she felt her stomach turn. In order to remain upright, she kept her distance, while dutifully following the family. Halfway down the corridor, she turned and saw her father already heading off to his study.

"Signorina Alda, stay with the children while I tend to their mother." The housekeeper led the frail woman into the bathroom, then rushed off, returning with a kettle of boiling water.

"Will you take off your clothes or shall I?" Alda heard the housekeeper say from behind the door. When the little boy whimpered, his sister put her arm around him. They slid onto the floor, his head resting on her lap. It was a shock for Alda to see anyone sit on the floor.

"Leave me alone. I'll do it myself," the woman cried from the bathroom. Alda, concerned, opened the door.

"Fine, come in," the housekeeper sighed. The now naked woman gave them both a harsh look. Alda tried not to gawk at the sharp hips and emaciated body as the woman climbed into the tub and sat in the shallow water. The housekeeper asked Alda to fetch more hot water. Glad to escape, she rushed by the children in the corridor.

"*State tranquilli*," Alda echoed; "everything will be fine," but she wondered why she had said that. Their father was dead. Their home had been destroyed by bombs. How could everything be fine?

Returning with the kettle, Alda found the housekeeper carefully combing the woman's hair and applying a smelly concoction to her scalp. Alda carefully poured more hot water into the tub.

"Put that apron on and watch. Next you'll be washing the children's heads and bodies. We must get rid of their lice before allowing them into their room with fresh sheets. I have to burn their clothes. Do not touch their belongings."

Overhearing, the woman looked up and slammed her fist on the tub, disturbed that she was being talked about as if she were invisible. Alda felt for her own braided hair before rolling up her sleeves. While the woman uttered a string of garbled lamentations, Alda noted her accent, one that must belong to people from Italy's far north, where the war had wrought terrible destruction. She recalled *Zio* Angelo's promise, that the fighting would never reach Florence. How could he be so sure?

9

Alda, never at a loss for words, wanted to tell the woman that she and her children would feel much better after a good meal. The woman stared blankly at Alda, who fell silent, afraid to let on that, even though this was her father's home, she too felt a little like a stranger.

Alda in white, circa 1918.

ANOTHER DEPARTURE

Florence, 1918

Florentines filled the railway station, waiting to greet the soldiers returning from war. Alda, rushing across the street arm-in-arm between her aunts, was a vision in her mid-calf white skirt, diaphanous blouse and wide elliptical brimmed hat. Even her elegant, laced suede boots, revealing narrow feet and ankles, were white. She had designed and sewn this all-white ensemble as a sign of resurrection and hope for herself and now for the soldiers, who would need a visual relief from all the impervious black worn by the mourning families of fallen soldiers and Spanish influenza victims.

As more citizens arrived, people handed out little flags to wave. Alda and her aunts stood on the platform observing the welcome banner stretched across the rafters. She'd overhead a report that over six hundred thousand Italian men had perished in this war and another that said over a million had been wounded. Was that possible? Aunt Letizia seemed to understand how anxious her niece was. "Alda, brace yourself," she said; "there will be some grim sights."

The train carrying the returning soldiers blew its whistle in the distance. Alda stood erect, as a brass band began playing the Italian national anthem. With the platform increasingly packed, Rafaella suggested they move to allow more room for the families. Alda was grateful she didn't have a brother who had to face war and relieved that her father and Uncle Angelo had been too old to serve.

They stood under the banner as the train approached. Steam rose as the iron behemoth screeched to a halt. When the doors opened, everyone cheered. A hush came over the crowd as the first tattered men climbed down from the train. Some were missing limbs, struggling on crutches, needing help. Waving little flags seemed almost silly to Alda, as the band played louder and louder, as if to drown out the soldiers' condition with the rousing anthem. The exalted cheers seemed bittersweet. Shock dissolved into relief as young men found and embraced their families. Just as Alda imagined these poor soldiers finally home, eating a warm meal, a group of angry men burst into the crowd. Shouts of their rage sullied the welcoming throngs. She watched as angry, jeering men spewed obscenities and spat in officers' faces.

"*Oddio*!" Alda cried, and her aunts spirited her away from the ugly scene. They rushed out of the station, into the sunlight, catching their breath in front of the church of Santa Maria Novella.

"What was that about?" Alda asked.

"Leftists, no doubt – Italian Bolsheviks – opposed to the war." Letizia shook her head as her sister looked towards the church. "We should go inside and pray."

Alda ignored the suggestion. "Isn't it horrible enough, what they've gone through? Those young men *fought* in the war, they didn't start it."

"Some people use blame to alleviate the senseless things beyond their control," Letizia said.

Taking Alda's arm, Aunt Rafaella changed the subject. "How was the refugee family's departure? Did that ungrateful woman ever smile?"

"Not really, *Zia*. She hated accepting our charity. The children were sweet. I will miss them. The mother suffered a great loss, but for two years she barely looked us in the eye. Despite everything, I really think she looked down on us."

"Well, of course! She's from up north," Letizia laughed.

"I don't understand. Florence is considered northern Italy," Alda said.

"Of course, but it doesn't matter. We're still south of Milan!"

Alda shrugged as Rafaella added, "Well, thanks to you, at least they went back with new clothes, rosy cheeks and flesh on their bones. You should be proud to have helped them return to health, *cara mia*."

"Considering how they looked when they arrived, I'm just happy they survived. But the sad fact remains: the father is gone and they don't have a home to return to. *Babbo* told me that, after the Versailles treaty, their town isn't even considered part of Italy anymore!"

As the three walked silently across the piazza into a narrow side street, Alda realized they were near the home of a classmate who'd been absent from school for weeks. Rushing ahead, she found the dreaded quarantine sign on her friend's door.

"I was afraid of this," Alda said as her aunts caught up. "*Quaranta giorni* – forty days!" She knew she'd have to wait that long before knowing who in her family had contracted the influenza and if they'd survived.

Looking at the sign, her aunt became nervous, thinking that some of the returning soldiers might have been infected.

"Let's take you home," Rafaella insisted.

"Home?" Letizia said. "That begs the question, Alda. When are you leaving your father's place? I don't understand why he's abandoning Florence again and didn't ask us, your family, to take you back? Why are you going to board with your friend Adriana and her parents instead of living with us?"

"*Babbo* would've stayed in Florence forever if he hadn't had a cheating business partner," Alda insisted. "Don't be angry! You took care of me for sixteen years. I'm eighteen now. I'll be fine. Adriana is my dearest friend. I'll see you as always."

"Well, at least your hosts rent a place in the countryside for the summer, where there's less chance of contagion. I pray we don't regret bringing you here today," Rafaella said.

"Oh, *Zia*! I wanted to welcome our soldiers."

As they walked over a narrow cobblestone street, a river of people dressed in black passed by them. As church bells rang in deep, repetitive waves, Letizia paused, clearly shaken.

"How are we supposed to celebrate the end of the war with these death bells tolling all day long? The incessant ringing just causes panic and despair." Alda squeezed her aunt's hand. Entwining their arms again, the trio walked along in silence.

MEETING FLORO

Tuscan Countryside, 1923

Walking in the countryside along a sunny path one late summer morning, Alda grazed her palm over lavender hedgerows to trigger the fragrance of nostalgia. She removed a tiny clipper from her apron pocket and snipped purple sprigs of the *spiga lavanda*, tucking a few into her pocket. She and Adriana would make lavender sacks with old fabric, a ritual she cherished. These past five years living with the Menichelli family, Adriana had become like the younger sister Alda had always longed for. She had no illusions; she was a paying guest; yet they treated her like a family member. She, who had lived in the city all her life, had become especially attached to these countryside summers, living in

Floro, early 1920s.

their rental house, roaming around the landscape, where she was free to read under the shade of olive trees, or harvest vegetables from the garden.

On her way to assist with lunch, grabbing a basket perched on a pole, Alda stopped at the vegetable garden outside the house to cut a bunch of male zucchini blossoms. Seeing them splayed open from the hot sun, she chastised herself for not coming earlier that morning when they would've been closed and easier to fry. She gingerly placed the limp, delicate flowers in her basket, delaying a few minutes more before going inside. Leaning over the edge of the terrace wall, she put down the basket, removed her wide-brimmed straw hat and cupped her face in her hands to feel the sun caress her. While closing her eyes she inhaled the trace of lavender on her palms. A moment later she opened them as she felt and heard the acrobatic flight of thousands of swallows filling the air, swooping and darting to feed on the swarming insects rising from freshly cut fields. Their pointy wings, flashing agile black and white against a cobalt sky, made her dizzy. Alda closed her eyes to focus on the snapping sound of their wings. She smiled, serene, until loose strands from her hair tickled her face, derailing the sensual moment. Suddenly she had a sense that someone was watching her. Bolting upright from her relaxed position, she squinted down onto the field below. She put

Adriana and Alda, circa 1923.

15

her straw hat back on, to lessen the sun's glare. Just as she started scolding herself for her lively imagination, a tall figure emerged from the shadow of an olive tree. The young man gazed up, dipped his cap and bowed. Then he flashed a wide-toothed grin before turning and swaggering off, his shotgun casually slung over his shoulder. Hunters often passed through these fields, but no one had ever been so bold. She watched him saunter away, noting his unusually long legs and slight limp. As he vanished amidst the gnarled olive trees, Alda wondered if she'd imagined the towering apparition.

She darted into the house and shut the door, trying to regain her composure. Adriana and her mother were in the kitchen preparing lunch.

"Here I am!" Alda announced, beginning to prepare the zucchini blossoms. She removed the stamens and the tiny leaves at the base and dipped them into an *impasto* she made, of flour, water and a drizzle of olive oil. After she fried and salted them, Adriana grabbed one.

"Perfection as usual, Alda!"

While everyone else napped after lunch, Alda lay awake in her bed staring up at the ceiling. Her pulse raced all afternoon, with every moment spent wondering if that hunter would re-materialize. She said nothing.

At twilight, Alda sat in the parlor with Adriana and her mother, all three stitching intricate handiwork. As the natural light diminished, la signora got up from her stuffed chair to switch on the overhead light. The trio gazed up, marveling at the dangling bulb, this new illumination they still considered a miracle. Three years earlier, in 1920, electricity had arrived in Florence, but it wasn't until this summer that their landlord, Ugo Rafanelli, had connected power lines to light his countryside estates. Alda, crocheting a cream-colored border to frame a white linen tablecloth, glanced at the two women around her, grateful for the sweet camaraderie that still reminded her of life with her aunts.

Alda started to tell the story of what had happened at the costume party, about the young enamored man who'd tripped as he'd approached Adriana, but their laughter was interrupted by a knock at the front door. Startled, Alda lost a stitch.

"Strange," la signora said, rising, "we're not expecting anyone." She dropped her mending and left the room. The girls glanced at each other from opposite ends of the Victorian sofa. Alda blushed, thinking it might be him.

"I'll just go see..." Adriana said, rushing after her mother. For a few endless moments Alda continued working, before she too abandoned her needlework. Hiding in a shadow of the atrium, she heard a deep voice say:

"*Sono Floro Rafanelli.* I wonder if I might bother you for a glass of water?" The hunter looked down at the matriarch. Alda surmised that this man rose half a meter above everyone else she'd ever known. "I've been out bird hunting all day…" he continued. Drawn by the rich timbre of his voice, Alda moved quietly out of the shadow. The monumental man stood on the threshold, his shotgun still slung over his wide shoulders. His corduroy jacket was the silver-green color found on the flip side of olive leaves.

"You must be related to our landlord, Ugo Rafanelli?" Adriana's mother said.

"*Si,* signora," he nodded, "he is my father."

"Oh… please… enter, enter! I am Signora Menichelli. This is my daughter Adriana and… Come here, dear – this is Alda Degli Innocenti, our boarder," she said, quickly adding, "and dear family friend."

Alda shifted further into the light and nodded, her heart pounding. How she despised the introduction as *boarder*, compounding her lack of belonging with the orphaned association her last name conjured up.

"Pleasure," Floro nodded, eyeing Alda, whose knees felt like *gelatina*. "We are neighbors," he added, addressing the women. "Our villa in Grassina, Il Boschetto, is nearby; it's the long façade on the hill."

"Of course, your *cinquecento* villa was a part of the old Medici Villa Lappeggi estate," Signora Menichelli said. "We've been renting from your father for five summers, ever since 1918, to escape the *Spagnola* epidemic."

"The fear of influenza filled all our country houses," Floro added, shaking his head as if remembering all the dead.

"Oh, forgive me, you said you were thirsty!" Adriana's mother gestured to her: "Please get this young man some water."

Alda followed her friend into the kitchen. Adriana giggled as she filled the pitcher.

"Signor Gulliver is as tall as some of our trees! Did you notice his gargantuan shoulders?"

Alda raised hers, feigning disinterest as she picked up the tray.

"Everything is hyperbole to you," Alda laughed. When they returned, the young man lifted the sweaty glass of water.

"*Molto gentile, grazie.*" He turned and fixed his eyes on Alda. Blood rushed to her face. She wanted to look him straight in the eye, but instead she looked down at his boots. Thanking them, and smiling at Adriana and Alda, the hunter tipped his hat before taking his leave. Alda stared at his formidable figure as he turned. The door seemed to close in slow motion behind him.

The following Sunday, the same confident knock resounded in the house. Alda perked up, trying to suppress a smile as the young hunter again claimed thirst. She noted his tweed hunting jacket and stylish knickers as he exuded gratitude for la signora's hospitality. Just then, Adriana's father stepped up beside her near the front door and introduced himself.

"*Piacere*," the two men said, shaking hands.

"Do you always hunt alone, Signor Rafanelli?" Signor Menichelli asked.

"I sometimes hunt with Mario, my younger brother," he said, "but my family's Sunday nap is sacred. During the week, work starts at four in the morning. My father is Florence's biggest fish importer, but," he rushed to say, "I no longer am around fish. I work in our office, located across from the Medici chapels." It was as if he was assuring Alda that he was worthy of her attention.

When he returned the following Sunday, again requesting water, his eyes never left Alda. This time she returned his gaze. As soon as he left, the family laughed.

"Such tremendous thirst this young hunter has!" Adriana and her mother teased, and her father chimed in:

"Yes, such terrible, terrible thirst!"

"Oh, please," Alda squealed, her hand touching her flushed cheek.

That week she went about her days with growing anxiety. The family was packing, leaving their summer rental soon to move back into the city. She had barely said a word to this man. But then another opportunity presented itself. On their last Sunday, he reappeared at the door. This time, instead of feigning thirst, he held out an offering of birds that dangled from leather strings.

"Today's hunt," he announced, "for your kindness."

"Oh, Signor Rafanelli. *Per un po di acqua!*" Adriana's mother cooed. "We will gladly accept, but only if you stay for dinner."

"I would be honored," he said, and she sent the girls to pluck the birds out on the terrace. When Floro offered to help, Adriana giggled. Alda elbowed her friend, who was too young to be a jealous competitor for this man's attention.

"Follow us," Alda said, grabbing a bowl and handing him one. The three sat around a rustic table under a pergola of grape leaves. As they plucked in silence, a chill filled the early September evening air. Finally Alda mustered the courage to speak. "Be careful removing the fluffy down feathers around their tender heads and necks. We don't want the skin to rip."

Floro grinned, and she smiled as he playfully replied, "Ah, signorina, you are right, thank you."

As mounds of feathers grew on the table, suddenly their visitor recited a tongue-twister: "*Trentatre Trentini entrarano a Trento, tutti e trentatre trotterellando…*" With each breathy 't', downy feathers levitated. The more the trio laughed, the more feathers sailed into the air, tickling their noses and landing in their hair and on their clothing. They tried to calm their gaiety, but after a few quiet moments Floro burst into a second tongue-twister, this one about a goat living on a bench: "*Sopra la panca la capra campa…!*" As he exaggerated the consonants, more feathers took flight.

Alda echoed the next nonsensical phrase: "*Sotto la panca la capra crepa*" – of the goat dying under the bench. Airborne feathers and their laughter formed a cloud in the air until Adriana's mother opened the window, scolding:

"*Bravi bambini!* If we are to eat tonight, you'd better stop your antics." As she closed the window, the admonished three glanced at each other, raising their eyebrows. Their shoulders shook as they suppressed laughter, pursing their lips. When the limp birds were finally bald, Adriana said:

"I'll take them to the kitchen. You two gather feathers." She winked at her friend as she walked away.

Alda and Floro's eyes locked from across the table. Feeling her cheeks ablaze, she rose to collect the loose feathers on the table. As the hunter's helpful hand added more to the pile, she picked up the bowl and moved under the table to collect the remaining scattered feathers. Floro got down on his knees to join her. His proximity made her heart race. They kept their heads down, gathering courage along with the feathers. Floro's hand gently brushed Alda's. Her body tingled. With their task complete, they stared at one another under the table. In that confined space he smelled like the woods. When he inched closer, plucking feathers from her hair and shawl, she felt faint. She removed one from his jacket as he leaned in, as if to kiss her. She panicked and briskly emerged from under the table. As he followed, he hit his head.

"Are you alright?" she cried, her hand over her mouth to stifle a laugh as he unfolded himself, holding his bumped head.

He looked at her with a wide grin. "Cara Signorina Alda… I've never been better."

STARS ALIGN

Rome, Summer 1973

I sat sipping cappuccino at a corner cafe in Rome's Piazza del Popolo. It was here that I'd fallen in love with Italy two years earlier, on my junior year abroad. The tall Egyptian obelisk rising in the piazza's center, stabbing the sky, made me dizzy, but the fountains at its base, with four stone lions spewing sheets of water downward, grounded the upward surge. Across the way my eyes fixed on the massive ancient Aurelian wall and the *Porta del Popolo*, the city's northern gateway. Above the entrance, the cluster of round mountains, crowned with a star, seemed to claim dominion. Carved by Bernini, the heraldic symbol of Pope Alexander, his Chigi family crest, is found throughout Rome.

I was back in Rome, now on vacation, staying two blocks away, at the same Pensione Helene where I'd lived as a student. My mother left early in the morning. I'd been her guide for two weeks, translating menus and showing her all my favorite haunts around the eternal city. I was proud of how much of the place and the language I remembered from my academic year. I had been unlike my classmates, particularly the rebellious clique of students from Oberlin who eschewed their Italian host families as provincial and wanted to escape the orientation in Arezzo to attend a Rolling Stones concert in Milan. Instead, I'd immersed myself in the language and culture, learned hand gestures and was even able to discuss the new Italian divorce law with my host family. I'd relished meeting as many Italians as possible.

This visit had been my mother's first in Europe, a surprise gift from family and friends for her sixtieth birthday. Just three years earlier, she and my father had planned to visit me here for Christmas. That trip was derailed by his cancer. Seeing Rome with me this past week had made my mother smile again, and with her new stylish Roman haircut she looked ten years younger. Although eager to spend time on my own, I now regretted my decision to stay, worrying about her entering her Long Island house alone, without my father.

Soon after his death, my two sisters and I had looked at estates for sale, exploring the idea of pooling our meager resources and living together with my mother, several generations in one home, something absolutely normal in Italy but rare in America. With five opinionated siblings, some already married with children, the communal concept was soon rejected. For a year I lived with my mother in her little home in Great Neck. Once I felt she was okay, I accepted my family's friend Janice's invitation to board on the top floor of her beautiful Stanford White townhouse, located only five blocks away from the Frick Collection where I worked. It had also been the place where she'd offered our family refuge during my father's last month at Sloan Kettering Cancer Center. Although I lived independently, I loved being around this delightful woman and her teenage son. She, an Auntie Mame character, always invited me to her lavish parties.

Now that I was back in Rome on my own for a while, I had no plans. I wanted time to unfold spontaneously, except for one mission – inquiring about a job at Marlborough Gallery. The idea of returning to live in Italy seized me from the moment I stepped off the plane. I knew my mother was stronger now. She'd returned to nursing and was thriving. I could explore options.

"*Signorina, desidera altro?*" the waiter inquired. I shook my head and smiled. Did I need anything else? As he moved away I gazed across the square again, at the immense Roman door. I thought in Italian: *la porta,* and its variation, to carry – *portare.* That door had indeed transported me into a world of both beauty and sorrow. I remembered the day I had travelled with classmates by bus on Via Flaminia, on the other side of this Aurelian wall, headed on a field trip to Matera in southern Italy. I'd opened a letter from my mother and read that my father had been diagnosed with lymphoma and that he would be starting chemotherapy soon. They'd have to cancel their plan to spend Christmas with me. The bus floor had seemed to give way. With my father so sick, I'd thought, how can I be so far away, experiencing Europe, while neither of my parents had ever even been?

I'd found a cheap flight home for Christmas to surprise my parents and was relieved to find my father looking so well. Without really talking about a prognosis, I'd asked his physician friend: "Should I stay or return to Italy for my second semester?" He had suggested I go on with my life. My parents concurred. Reluctant as I'd felt, I spent my second semester learning as much as possible and steeping myself in Italian art, language and culture, feeling guilty about all the moments I forgot about the troubles at home. Then a letter arrived late in the semester. My mother had taken my father to the National Institute of Health for a second opinion. She'd fallen and broken her leg running after my dad's wheelchair on the plane ramp. Her leg broken? A wheelchair? Why was he in a wheelchair? "Things have gone downhill fast," my mother called to say in early May. "There's still time but see if you can take exams early. He's already in Sloan Kettering."

A week later, when I'd entered my father's hospital room and kissed his forehead, he'd pursed his lips. My heart sank. There was my mother, sitting on a chair, her leg in a cast resting on a coffee table. I'd held back tears and given him a gift: rosary beads from the Vatican. My father's expression revealed undisguised displeasure as he dropped the rosary on the sheet covering his thin legs. I knew he'd lost hope and was full of regret about leaving my mother with so little to live on. What good were prayers now? He must have been thinking of the money he'd squandered and the life insurance policy he'd sold to pay the patent attorney for his multiple inventions that had gone nowhere and had left them without savings.

Although he'd spent every professional day in a hospital as a surgeon, my father had only one dying request: that we never leave him alone. So my mother and the five of us children kept a twenty-four-hour vigil, taking turns sleeping nights on a chair.

Months passed as my father hung on. The July night he died, three days short of his sixty-third birthday, it had been my turn to keep watch. My older brother Jerry arrived and noted a change. Perhaps also recognizing the fear in my eyes, he offered to take my place. He assured me he'd call if things got worse. I don't even remember if I thanked him, but I exited that hospital, pushing the revolving door hard to get out into the fresher air as fast as I could, away from all the cachexic cancer bodies that shuffled through those sterile halls, arms attached to IV lines, hanging onto pale hope.

As I'd slept on a king-sized bed next to my mother at our townhouse refuge, at four in the morning she shook me. "We have to go." Gathering our wits and our courage, all five siblings converged around my father's bed. He lay there on his side, with one large hand cupping his weary head. (Since then I never lie in bed with my head in my hand without evoking that image of my father expiring.) No one suggested we talk to him. It didn't occur to us that a comatose person might still hear. We surrounded him for hours, holding hands, weeping in silence.

***

When the waiter handed me the check, I awoke from my sad reverie, paid and headed across the way towards Santa Maria Del Popolo, one of the twin churches that divides Via del Corso. Once inside, I put a coin in a slot to illuminate *The Conversion of St Paul*, Caravaggio's dramatic chiaroscuro painting depicting Paul's sudden blindness, restored sight and conversion to Christianity. Was his divine revelation simply a comet, I wondered? Life transformed in a moment. I left the dark church, stunned by the Roman sun, and walked down Via di Ripetta towards Marlborough Gallery.

"Please hire me," I whispered to the sky, hoping my brief experience at Knoedler Gallery and two years of working at the Frick Collection would help me land a job there. I already imagined working by day and writing during the long lunch break and at night, as I was doing in New York. Life in Italy would be sublime.

At the glass window, I checked my appearance before entering the gallery. A moment later my jaw dropped. Sitting at the front desk was the most beautiful woman from my year-abroad program.

"Oh my God, Karen! What are you doing here?" I cried as she rose sylphlike.

"I work here, *bella*," she explained in her sultry voice, her long fingers shifting a strand of flaxen hair away from her face. "I never left Rome! What are *you* doing here?"

"I've come for your job," I laughed, feeling dwarfed by her six-foot-tall elegance.

"Well, I'm not ready to quit yet," she replied, her smile full of mischief, emphasizing her regal cheekbones.

"Maybe you need an assistant?" I begged.

"That would really be grand, but they're not hiring anyone at the moment. I promise I'll let you know if something comes up. How long are you here for?"

I told her about the weeks I'd just spent showing my mother around, explaining it was to compensate for the trip she'd never had with my father. She remembered my leaving Rome suddenly and was sorry to hear about his death. I uttered a quiet thanks, my throat closing.

"I'm here for one more week, but I have no plans. My only goal was to come here, hoping for an excuse to move back to Rome. I'm staying at my old Pensione Helene."

"Stay with me in Trastevere," she offered, insisting. "I have an extra bedroom, and I'd love the company." She asked about our mutual Roman friend who used to assist his aunt with the American students. "Are you going to Paolo's brother's wedding tomorrow?"

Paolo had been the first native Italian man I'd ever met, part of the welcoming committee that greeted the Temple and Tyler students as we arrived at the Rome airport. Many of us had swooned at the sight of the tall, elegant Roman. He was always around because his aunt was our Italian teacher and the person who arranged our host family sojourn in Arezzo. Paolo had stayed at our house in Long Island the summer my father had died, but there had been no romance. I didn't imagine that changing.

"Paolo mentioned it in a letter a while ago. I'd love to go, but I don't actually have an invitation." I shrugged.

"Well, you know Paolo! He's been working in Sicily this week. Of course he'd want you there. You should call him."

"It's too late now," I said, slapping the back of my right hand on my left palm. "Unless I'm handed an invitation, how could I? I don't know where the church is and I've never even met his brother."

Karen wrote down her phone number on her card, insisting again that I stay with her. For some reason, I was close to tears. I thanked her and promised to be in touch. We exchanged a "Ciao," kissing both cheeks. I wandered out of the gallery, grateful to have found her but disappointed there was no job opening. What had I expected?

In a daze, I wandered on Via del Corso, the central street that forks out from Piazza del Popolo, examining displays of elegant shoes and watching as sleek, fashionable men and women passed by. Yet this bustling, straight-edged avenue felt too chaotic. I longed to walk down Rome's more intimate cobblestone streets that meander like a stream between voluptuous Baroque buildings that seem to sway, in and out, as if breathing. Poised to change direction, I suddenly felt a hand on my shoulder. Startled, ready to defend myself, I looked up to find Paolo's regal face and aquiline nose staring down at me.

"*Ciao, bella!*" he blurted. "I was meaning to call, but I wasn't sure where you were staying! Come to lunch at my mother's."

"Paolo! Ciao! What?" I exclaimed, stunned. A bus stopped, and he swept me on board. I held on, gawking at the lanky figure before me.

"You're coming to the wedding, right?" Paolo said in perfect English.

"You're joking!" I laughed, thinking of my conversation with Karen only five minutes earlier. "It's tomorrow, Paolo! I hadn't heard from you, and I've never met your brother."

"Well, Stefano's right behind you." He moved aside, introducing him.

"*Piacere*," we said in unison.

"This is crazy!" I insisted. "Your mother doesn't need a surprise guest the day before her son's wedding." I looked at Stefano, who seemed amused, holding onto the bus strap.

"Don't you worry," Paolo assured me, asking what other plans I had while in Italy. I confessed I was letting things unfold. "*Perfetto*," he laughed. "Then come with us to Florence the day after the wedding. The newlyweds and I are driving up to my father's home in Fiesole." He explained that his father and stepmother had plenty of room. As if I'd already agreed, he said we'd be attending a soccer game in medieval costume in Florence's Piazza Signoria, followed the next day by a short trip to the Apuana Alps. My mind whirled like a dervish.

"I was just with Karen saying that I hadn't seen you. This is so weird!"

"It's providence," he smiled, arching one eyebrow.

When Paolo, Stefano and I walked through the door of his mother's apartment, she was unfazed, as if expecting me, exuding gratitude for my family's hospitality to her son in New York. Despite the relaxed atmosphere, after lunch I insisted on leaving.

"You have a big day tomorrow."

Rising, his mother said, "Here you are. You must come!" She placed a little envelope in my palm. It was the wedding invitation. My mouth dropped at the wild synchronicity. Exactly what I'd told Karen was happening. I exuded gratitude and couldn't help thinking: if I'd stayed at the gallery just one minute longer, or returned by Via Babuino instead of Il Corso, I never would've run into Paolo. The remainder of my Italian trip was now taking wonderful shape and the convergence of events felt like some strange alignment of stars.

MEETING ALDO

Carrara and Fiesole, 1973

The following morning, I sat in a little Roman church, waiting for the bride, thrilled to attend my first Italian wedding. I spied a man, the spitting image of the actor Danny Kaye, sitting up front in a place reserved for close family members. I figured this must be Paolo's remarried Florentine father, whom Paolo suggested we visit. The bride arrived, beautiful Stefania, her enormous dark eyes shining as she was led up the aisle. Up front, the *simpatico*, adoring Stefano looked on.

At the reception, when Paolo's father Giovanni approached, he insisted, "Ah, you must be the American. I hear you will be coming to stay!" Noting my hesitation, he assured me that his wife Fernanda would be thrilled to have me. After a glass of champagne, I happily accepted.

The next day we drove three hours with the newlyweds from Rome to Fiesole, the elegant hillside town above Florence once occupied by Etruscans. We entered a courtyard with a panoramic view of Florence and Brunelleschi's dominant *Duomo*. A woman who looked like Ava Gardner approached, with two boys in tow. Deep-voiced Fernanda, Paolo's stepmother, with sons Michele and Raffa, gave me a warm embrace. I smiled. Ava Gardner. Danny Kaye. In no time we seemed like old friends.

I counted my blessings the next night as we sat in a *stadio*, the temporary bleachers constructed in Piazza della Signoria in Florence, watching the parade that preceded *calcio in costume*, the wild soccer game in medieval costume. Skinny trumpets announced the coming procession, with medieval standard-bearers wearing colorful tights, their flags soaring high in the air. Bright designs and primary colors unfurled in exact synchrony. Musicians and Florentine dignitaries followed, riding proud on prancing horses.

"Emilio Pucci..." Giovanni gestured towards a poised older man on a festooned white horse. The illustrious designer's entrance was met with rousing applause.

As the procession continued and darkness settled in, I was dazzled by the blazing torches in each of the Signoria's tower windows. My eyes wandered about the square to find the famous sculptures inside the Loggia dei Lanzi. There was the dark bronze figure of Benvenuto Cellini's *Perseus* holding up the snake-filled head of Medusa, and there, Giambologna's *Rape of the Sabines*, the naked woman reaching skyward, desperate to escape.

Before long, soccer players without any visible protection scrambled on the ground for the ball, re-enacting the rule-less medieval game, elbowing, headbutting, punching and choking their opponents, their movement raising terrific clouds of dust. I had to look away from the raucous male fray but was still awed by the setting. Somewhere on this square's pavement was a medallion that commemorated the spot where the Dominican monk Savonarola was burned at the stake, nearly five centuries before. And below this stone pavement, now covered in layers of dirt spread for this game, lay a recently excavated Roman town that pre-dated Florence.

Next morning, Giovanni headed to La Spezia to work on his sailboat. The rest of us, heading to the Apuana Alps for the weekend, would meet up with him for lunch in Carrara on Saturday. We drove a few hours to the seaside before winding up and around the fragrant woods of pine. As we ascended narrow roads, I stared through the windshield at a jagged white mountain and asked: "Is that snow?"

Fernanda chuckled. "No. That's exposed marble; but it does look like snow." As we approached the quarry, I gawked at the sheered-off white, blush-pink and gray cliffs. Fernanda stopped the car and we all got out. As marble crunched underfoot, there was a loud cracking sound. These mountains had been blasted and cut since ancient Roman times. Thick marble slabs, someone's future countertop, were lined up everywhere. The Pantheon in Rome had been adorned with Carrara marble. The stone for Michelangelo's *David* and his *Pieta* belonged to these mountains.

We traveled through little villages nestled in forested terrain and stayed at a charming *pensione*. The next day, Saturday, we waited for Giovanni's arrival at a countryside restaurant in Carrara. A long table was set outside for lunch *al fresco*, next to a garden park where we relaxed on the grass. A blue *Spider* convertible sportscar drove up. Giovanni emerged, as did a tall man in a baseball cap, his friend and partner on the sailboat.

"*Piacere*," Aldo said, taking off his hat. We shook hands. He was many years younger than Giovanni, probably in his thirties.

I ate delicious rabbit for the first time. "A Tuscan specialty," the two Florentines insisted. Dark-eyed Aldo made jokes that I barely heard from the other end of our long table. After lunch, Giovanni and his friend returned to work on the old sailboat; the rest of us drove around the mountains for the day. We planned to meet up again the next evening at Forte dei Marmi, the fashionable seaside resort, at a place famous for serving only *foccaccia*.

Once there, I drooled over the flatbread filling choices: wild porcini mushrooms, caramelized onions, clams, artichokes, and delectable cheese with prosciutto. We even ate *focaccia* filled with tiny wild woodland berries for dessert. I wondered how so many Italians remained so svelte.

The place was packed; clearly the trendy spot in Forte dei Marmi. After dinner Fernanda handed Aldo her keys.

"I hate driving in the dark. Do you mind getting us back to Fiesole?" she pleaded in Italian, asking me to join her as the rest of the family returned in the other car.

"It'd be my pleasure," Aldo said.

Aldo's voice was deep and arresting as he talked about Konrad Lorenz's discovery of goslings imprinting on humans.

"I know his research through my sister Sue, whose degree is in animal behavior," I said, fascinated, as we conversed in Italian. Soon we met up with Giovanni and the family at a *cocomero* stand just outside Florence, feasting on juicy watermelon.

A few days later my dear new friends in Fiesole invited Aldo to dinner. When I offered to make *spaghetti alla carbonara,* the Roman pasta I loved, Fernanda graciously accepted, but Giovanni was clearly in a panic.

"What, you are letting the American make pasta?!" I heard him exclaim in Italian. When Aldo appeared, Giovanni begged his friend, who was famous for making delicious pasta on their sailboat, to make sure I cooked the spaghetti *al dente.* I was nervous as Aldo looked over my shoulder, yet confident of my recipe. I found all the fuss comical.

At the table, the pinnacle of everything Italian, my *carbonara* got a surprised nod from Giovanni and compliments from the three Romans. As we finished the first course, Paolo talked about his visit to my family's house in Long Island, adding that my sisters and I were quite talented at giving neck massages.

"We had a lot of practice on my father, who was a surgeon," I added. "Coming home after operations, he always had a stiff neck, so we took turns."

Fernanda perked up, patting the back of her neck and complaining of arthritis. I laughed, moved behind her chair and dug in.

"*Oii!* Too strong!" she cried.

"Oh, so sorry!" I continued, with less power.

"*Perfetto,*" she said, relaxing. The next minute, Giovanni complained about *his* arthritis. I twittered nervously but moved to massage his neck. Suddenly there was an arthritic epidemic. I traveled around the table, giving almost everyone a short sample. As I passed Aldo's chair to sit down, he sat up, clearly expecting me to continue.

"Okay," I sighed, embarrassed.

Aldo, using his Florentine humor, exacerbated my awkward angst by turning and asking me: "*Sei sposata?*"

"Did he just ask me if I'm married?" I asked Fernanda as everyone except me laughed. I patted Aldo's shoulders and returned to my place. Paolo looked at me with raised eyebrows.

It was a challenge keeping my Italian afloat with this *Dante* crowd. I was well aware that Florence was home to the official Italian language. But somehow, perhaps spurred on by wine or the spirit of the dinner, I recited a joke about an Italian pilot. I suspected it was my bumbled delivery more than the joke that left them in stitches. As Fernanda got up to check on the dessert, she asked aloud if I really had to return to Rome on Friday. Couldn't I stay and drive back with Paolo, Stefano and Stefania?

"I'm fine taking the train," I said, figuring I'd already overstayed my welcome. Just then Aldo piped up from across the table.

"What a coincidence! I have an appointment in Rome on Friday. I'll take you."

"Oh really?" I said and uttered noncommittal thanks. Clearing a plate from the table, I excused myself and cornered Fernanda in the kitchen.

"What's the story with this guy?" I asked. "Should I take up his offer to drive me to Rome?"

"Absolutely. Aldo is a totally honorable, responsible person," she asserted.

I returned to the table and accepted. "Are you sure it's no trouble?"

"Absolutely, no trouble at all!" he smiled.

After dinner we piled into cars to eat more icy watermelon at another *cocomero* stand down in Florence. Aldo rode his motorcycle in front of Fernanda's car. Peering out the front windshield, I was dumbfounded to see him kneeling on his motorcycle seat, extending both arms and then a leg out to the side. He did a few other insane acrobatic tricks before returning to a normal position as if nothing had happened.

I inhaled. "I'm glad I'm not this guy's mother," I said to Fernanda. "I'm a little unsure about this ride on Friday. I thought you said he was totally responsible?"

Fernanda laughed. "Aldo is, I promise… Something's gotten into him. I've never seen him show off like this."

Camilla with Michele and Stefania, Carrara, summer 1973.

Alda, Florence countryside, circa 1925.

THE PICNIC

Florence, 1925

Wild, fragrant bushes of yellow broom and tiny daisies scattered the slope behind Alda. Floro admired his fiancée as she sat at the base of the hill, her dark hair loosely tied. He took out his camera. Adjusting her long dark skirt and white blouse, she pointed her finger at her *fidanzato* who, forever a tease, stuck out his tongue to capture a smile from her. He put his camera around his neck and held out his hand to lift her from the ground. She smiled. They kissed.

All autumn, winter and spring in Florence, Floro had taken Alda to the theater and the opera and out for many countryside jaunts before asking her to marry him. Young Adriana had often tagged along for propriety. Now she was off gathering wildflowers, giving the couple time to be alone.

Alda brushed off her skirt before kneeling on the picnic blanket. Floro reached into a wicker basket for his contribution of *affettati:* slices of *prosciutto, finocchiona* and *salami.*

"From our farm," he said, sitting down, proudly displaying the wax paper layered with meats.

"Naturally," she replied, pulling out fruit and a block of Parmesan cheese. "This is from Parma," she joked, setting a knife with a large round peasant bread on a wooden cutting board. "And this is from me!" she said, displaying *la torta della nonna.*

Floro raised his eyebrows at the *grandmother's cake* covered in white powdered sugar and pine nuts.

"Made by your sainted hands?"

"Of course," Alda laughed. He knew desserts were not her specialty. As

32

Floro lifted a flask of his homemade wine, Alda pulled three glasses out of the picnic basket.

"You do know how spoiled you are, Signor Rafanelli?"

"Of course, signorina," he smiled, bending to kiss her, adding, "Signora Rafanelli soon." She shifted coyly away from him as he stretched his long body, relaxing on his side, propping up his head in his palm.

"Why did you march on Rome for Mussolini?" she asked while arranging the antipasto. "Why did you take such a risk?"

Floro shrugged, admitting that the October 1922 *March on Rome* wasn't really an impressive march until after the King gave Mussolini the job to form a coalition government. He insisted he was among the poorly armed group of merchants, students and old veterans who traveled by train to Orte, outside Rome, and camped out while an emissary was sent to demand that King Victor Emmanuel hand over the government.

"I still don't understand why the King gave up so easily to Mussolini. You wouldn't think a major change like that could happen without a fight."

"I think he was concerned about a civil war so soon after the end of the Great War. He didn't want to risk the chaos," Floro offered. "Once the King agreed to make him prime minister, word was sent to Mussolini in Milan. He wouldn't come to Rome until he received an official telegram. He wanted to pretend the power shift had been a revolution; he ordered a victorious fascist parade *in* Rome after the fact."

Alda sighed. "You could easily have been killed."

Floro frowned, telling her how he'd felt he had to stand with Mussolini, who promised to restore order, respect and prosperity after a war that had left Italy in shambles. "We had become a nation of despair and humiliation. The leftists, because they were against the war, made the mistake of alienating and blaming returning soldiers."

She told him that she'd witnessed a terrible scene at the train station with her aunts – men who'd spat on homecoming officers, shouting obscenities. "It was horrible," she said, taking a sip of wine.

"We were the underdog at Versailles. Mussolini has set us on the path as a proud nation again, befitting our history. He's promised to fix our unemployment, improve public works and build modern roadways."

Making these assertions, Floro stood up, towering over her. He poured himself a glass of wine. "But as I have said before, I mostly fear the rise of Bolshevism, these sleazy factions courting Moscow. If they get their way, Alda, there won't be a middle or upper class left in Italy. If a Russian-style class revolution happens here, people like my father, who worked hard his whole life for his wealth, will lose his property and maybe his life," he said, putting *prosciutto* on a slice of bread and taking a bite.

"But you said your father doesn't appreciate your politics," Alda said.

Floro nearly choked. "Hah! True! He abhors my involvement. His own father died alongside Garibaldi, uniting Italy. He keeps spouting the same complaint: 'From redshirts to blackshirts – what will be different this time?' He doesn't understand that I'm protecting him and his status."

Alda was worried about Floro's fervor. "I have to admit I agree with your father. I'm wary of politics too, afraid what power does to people," she said. "If you had remained at boarding school and hadn't left your studies, I wonder what path you might have taken?"

"Do you think intellectuals are above politics? Look at our ardent poet D'Annunzio! Leaving school has nothing to do with my direction," he said, taking another sip. "It's the sacredness of home that I am protecting. I was thirteen when my father sent me away. I broke my ankle jumping out a window, just to get back home."

"Yes, and you said your mother had to hide you for two weeks from your irate father," she added. "No wonder you limp. Your mother couldn't even call a doctor to set your ankle, she was that afraid of her own husband! And I don't understand why your father also took your brothers out of school at the same time."

"My father is irrational. My older intellectual brother Pietro will never forgive me for ruining his academic life."

Alda, who weighed all points of view, understood his brother's dismay. "You are so spoiled, Floro, like most men! If I could have, I would have studied law, or attended medical school. There's so much to learn! I cannot ever imagine running away from school!" She was still sorry that she'd stopped her studies to become a teacher when she went to live with her father.

Just then Adriana approached, holding out her bouquet of *margherite*. "For the betrothed," she exuded as Alda accepted the flowers.

"O *brava*," Alda blushed. "Come, Adriana, sit by me." Patting the picnic blanket, she lifted the flowers to her nose, even though she knew they held no fragrance. Alda put her arm around her young friend, whose company altered her serious mood, releasing her, at least momentarily, from her nagging concerns about Floro's politics.

THE PATRIARCH

Tuscany, 1925

The morning she was to meet Floro's family, Alda sat at her vanity table, staring into the mirror to greet her soon-to-be identity: "Signora Rafanelli." She repeated the name in various serious and delighted tones, liking the sing-song sound of it. As she combed her long thick hair, she pondered the next few months – the wedding ceremony at the church of San Giuseppe, the cruise with Floro. What jostled her nerves was contemplating the return from romantic Venice to live with Floro's father and mother and his two brothers in their countryside villa in Grassina – people she had not yet met! Throughout the summer and autumn they would remain there and all relocate in the winter to his family home in Florence. How could she leave

Rafanelli family at the villa, 1920s.

Adriana? They were like sisters, confidants. As she raked the comb through her hair she wondered if she would enjoy the same uncomplicated frankness and ease living with a man. While yanking on a snarl, she recalled the proverb:

I nodi vengono al pettine.

She made a silent promise to address any unpleasant issues as they surfaced in her marriage, not allow them to grow into a tangled nest.

At her long vertical window, she opened the shutters, badly in need of repair. *Someone should complain to the landlord,* she thought with a nervous laugh. Today she would meet that man, Ugo Rafanelli, her future father-in-law. Yet the day was bright, the sky azure. Inhaling crisp air, she turned towards her bed and pulled off the sheets and covers and draped them over the window's iron railing, for sunlight and air. Then, performing another daily ritual, she rolled her woolen mattress in half for aeration.

Alda knelt for her morning prayers at the ledge of the antique walnut *prie dieu,* which doubled as a dresser. She beseeched her favorite saint Rita for Floro's family's blessing. When she rose, she heard Adriana calling from downstairs. Floro had arrived. She had promised to be ready. Her heart pounded as she slipped into her cream dress with the drop waist, relieved she didn't have to wear the constricting corsets her mother had to endure. "*Un momento,*" she called down.

Floro, standing by Adriana, looked impatient holding his goggles and brown leather driving cap.

"Oh dear, early again!" Alda teased as she appeared. His large shoulders sank.

"*In bocca al lupo,*" Adriana whispered to her friend. *In the mouth of the wolf* – a wish of good luck as Alda kissed her cheeks. Driving along in Floro's open automobile, holding her hand on her hat, she wondered why she'd bothered to comb her hair. As they rounded the corner in Grassina, Floro pointed to a wide solitary villa set high on the hill, Tuscan yellow, flanked on one side by a procession of dark pointy cypresses. This would soon be her home.

Looking up at the hills, swaths of white obscured the fields, interrupting the green. Grassina was a village of launderers. Under the bleaching sun, white linen sheets and tablecloths hung and swayed in the wind, drying on layered lines held by a parade of posts. This linen belonged mostly to urban dwellers, whose narrow Florentine streets rarely saw sunlight.

Floro's auto sputtered as he ascended the steep hill. Alda felt her stomach lunge. She turned towards the cypress trees reaching for the sky, planted long ago to protect the villa from the harsh *tramontana* wind. Floro would be like that, her tall sentinel, always by her side.

As the car turned into the long driveway, she noticed the tile embedded high on the terrace wall, with the inscription: *Villa Rafanelli*. Floro mentioned that his father had recently changed its name from *Il Boschetto* to *Villa Rafanelli*. She was reassured that her fiancée showed a more humble preference for the traditional name that honored the woods behind the villa, instead of his family, who had only purchased the villa a few years earlier.

Along the high stone wall she also noted a cascade of generous caper plants. Seeing the familiar wild plants flourishing on stony dry cracks filled her with hope.

"*Mamma* uses these capers on fish and liver *crostini*. You should learn a great deal in her kitchen."

Alda smiled. Years earlier she'd learned the liver *crostini* recipe from her father's friend, Signor Lapi, from Buca Lapi. Perhaps she was the only one in Florence, besides the chef of that famous restaurant, who made *crostini di fegato* with juniper berries. Signor Lapi had taught her many other tricks, like how to treat *baccala,* salt cod, and how to extract the gamey bird taste from *folaga*, the coot duck. Even the Vatican, thinking its strong taste a punishment, allowed coot to be consumed on Fridays. Whenever she had served it, she'd amazed guests.

As Floro rounded the driveway, he pointed to adjacent buildings where their two farmers lived. Although she was a city girl, Alda's countryside summers had taught her about *mezzadria*. In this sharecropping arrangement, Floro's father, as the *padrone*, had to provide housing for the farmers and their families, along with animals and tools. Half of the crops would belong to the farmers, the other half to the *padrone*.

High above, Alda noted a line of mud swallow nests under the eaves of the farmers' dwellings and a multitude of sparrows perched on their rooftops. As Floro parked on cobblestones and came around to open her door, she prayed for courage. Getting out, he patted her arm.

When they reached the top of the terrace steps, Floro unlatched a small iron gate. On the long façade of the main villa there was not a single swallows' nest under the eaves. At the end of the enormous terrace was a *loggia* perpendicular to the front door. Spotting three men sitting at a table in the shadow, Alda whispered: "Is that your family?" Floro nodded as the three remained seated, staring. "Perhaps they think we're a mirage," she added, attempting humor. Floro's younger brother Mario finally approached with an extended hand.

"*Piacere*," Mario and Alda said simultaneously, *pleased to meet you*. She realized that this man, eight years younger than Floro, was taller than his older brother but, because he was thin and his shoulders were so narrow, he had less of an imposing presence. The stocky patriarch finally pulled himself up and approached, joined by Floro's older brother Pietro. Alda noticed that the father, although not a small man, reached only to the shoulders of his three soaring sons.

"*Signorina*," Ugo Rafanelli said, looking her in the eye, reminding her he had already met her father, uncle and aunts. His stare of seeming approval, as Alda shook his thick hand, made her feel uncomfortable. Floro introduced his brother Pietro, who extended his hand with long, bony fingers. Before he muttered *piacere*, she heard Pietro correct Floro with the word *fratellastro* – half-brother.

"Please sit," Alda insisted. "I hope we haven't kept you waiting."

"Don't worry, signorina," Mario said. She understood this young man was *buono come il pane*, the Tuscan proverb that likened good people to good bread. "Brave of you, riding in my brother's automobile," Mario added.

"Oh, not at all! Floro is an excellent driver. And I know something about those machines. My father sold the first *Lancia* in Florence. He taught me how to drive years ago."

"Good Lord!" Ugo said. "Whatever for?"

Alda blinked, rendered mute by the remark.

Floro clapped his hand – "So! We should tell *Mamma* we're here."

"Of course!" Ugo said, turning. "*Cara* signorina, if you happen to be hungry, you should know that enormous patience is required here. It seems all we do is wait for meals. And today my wife wants to impress a very important guest!"

"Oh dear!" Alda replied, distressed. "I hope la signora has not gone to too much trouble on my account!"

"Don't worry," Floro assured her. "There's no better cook in all of Tuscany. My mother's meals are *always* worth the wait."

Alda turned towards her fiancée, relieved. In the midst of this strange start,

Floro had defended his mother. *Zia* Letizia had warned: "Pay attention to how your man treats his mother. Men eventually treat their wives the same way."

Once up the round steps and through the thick double door, Alda felt the cool temperature inside the villa and relaxed. A long table was set for lunch, with the backdrop of an imposing hearth. As she caught a glimpse of the manicured woods through a glass door, clanging pots and inviting smells wafting from the kitchen lured them in that direction.

"*Mamma*," Floro announced, holding Alda's hand as they entered. A gargantuan woman stood by the stove. "This is my Alda."

"Signora, what a pleasure!" she said, understanding the origin of Floro's height.

"Ah, *cara*." Her voice was warm and powerful, her smile as infectious as Floro's. She dried her enormous hands on a dishtowel. If this imposing woman had scowled instead of smiled, Alda might have run for the door. Instead, she was enveloped in the woman's warm embrace. Looking up at her kind face, she understood why Floro had jumped out of a window to run away from school, limping home, to be near his mother. Alda had never met a woman over six feet tall. She imagined the children she would have with Floro — sky high! She hoped they would inherit this woman's softness as well as her height.

Holding her hand, his mother said: "Please — call me Elvira."

"Of course, signora. Thank you," Alda sighed.

Floro interjected: "*Mamma*… we'll be acquainted very soon but the wolves out there are restless!"

"Alright, send them in. We're nearly ready," she said, turning to introduce Maria, their maid, who was hidden behind her. They exchanged *buon giorno* and smiled. Suddenly a wiry white hunting dog with brown floppy ears and a lean body came out from under the table. Sizing Alda up, the dog sniffed enthusiastically, poking his nose under her mid-calf skirt. Having never been around dogs, she retreated a step.

"This is Yusk," Floro grinned.

"Yusk, our terror," his mother laughed, shaking her head. "He's been banished under the table: caught stealing food again. We need eyes in the backs of our heads with this devil!"

"Under the table," Floro commanded, but the dog remained immobile at Alda's feet. "He likes you!" he laughed.

"He's a smart dog," Elvira added. "Take him onto the terrace. He's always in the way!"

Watching the dog gaze up at her, Alda believed Yusk understood the conversation was about him. He raised his eyebrows, moving his head back and forth to follow each speaker.

Elvira remarked, "When we take him for a walk in Grassina he struts about, his head up, prancing, never pulling on the leash. Everyone remarks: 'Oh my! What a well-behaved dog'!"

"And that is why," Floro said, "when anyone in our family shows two sides – misbehaving at home but well-mannered in public – *Mamma* always says: 'You're just like Yusk'!"

"Now come," Floro said, pulling the dog's collar. "Enough distractions from getting this meal on the table!"

When the men entered the dining room there was no mistaking who was in charge. Ugo swayed like a bulldog, stepping side to side, focusing on his chair at the head of the table. As he sat down, Ugo turned towards Alda, instructing her to sit next to him.

"Pietro's mother, my first wife, who was Elvira's sister, always served meals on time," he said as Elvira appeared. Ugo's voice rose. "But I must admit, Elvira is the superior cook."

Alda smiled nervously, watching Elvira, who sat and stared at the napkin on her lap. Maria broke up the ensuing silence by carrying in a tray of *prosciutto* and moist figs, an early harvest, and a tray of *crostini di fegato* canapés.

"Our figs are succulent this season!" Ugo insisted. "And our *prosciutto* is perfect. We cure it for a year in a well-ventilated room next to our farmer Giovanni's house. We support two families of farmers here – six in each family!"

He took a slice of bread for himself before passing the basket to Alda. "Our olive grove and vineyard hardly produce enough wine and oil for our family, let alone for our growing farmer families. The grape harvest will be soon – a great celebration for the farmers. And today you will taste our precious *vinsanto.*"

"How wonderful, enjoying the fruits of your own land," Alda said. Ugo recited the list of their fruit trees – apricots, pears, peaches, cherries, persimmon and, of course, grapes. Maria removed the first-course plates and returned with the next.

"*Fettucini al Pomodoro* – one of my favorite pastas!" Alda exclaimed after her first bite. "*Complimenti*, signora. This is the best I've ever tasted!"

"Oh! Thank you, my dear," Elvira came alive and smiled, "but save some appetite for the *arosto misto*."

Ugo's fork dropped, clanging on his plate… "It's *sciocca*, tasteless," Ugo chastised. "Please pass the salt." Elvira passed a silver saltcellar, her red face pinched with anger.

The first course passed with little conversation, but as the table filled with large trays of roasted guinea hen, chicken, duck and roast beef, complemented by sautéed Swiss chard and roasted potatoes, Ugo mentioned that he hoped Alda also liked fish since, as a fish importer, it was an important part of every lunch.

Alda noted that both brothers had rice instead of pasta, and cooked fish and vegetables without sauce. Floro had mentioned something about their ailing stomachs. She couldn't help wondering if it was from all the tension at the table. When Elvira served her fruit tart, Ugo called out: "Maria! *Vinsanto!*"

"Usually this is her best *crostata*," Pietro said after taking a bite, "but the crust is hard today."

"Oh, it seems perfect!" Alda insisted, feeling anger rise.

"Undercooked crusts are difficult to digest. This is just fine, *Mamma*," Mario said, avoiding Pietro's glance.

Alda, happy to find Elvira had two sons as allies, was thankful she would not be in charge of *this* kitchen. Perhaps with her help, she and Elvira would serve meals on time and keep the complaints at bay.

Floro finally rose up, holding the little glass of *vinsanto*. "I propose a toast to the next Signora Rafanelli!" Raising their glasses, they all exclaimed: "*Auguri!*"

Elvira rose and approached Alda's chair, placing both hands on her shoulders. "*Cara*," she said, "you will soon be family!"

"*Grazie*, signora!" she said, forgetting to call her Elvira.

As Floro's mother's hands remained on Alda's shoulders, she wondered if the formidable woman feared that her son's *fidanzata* might run away. Alda wanted to say to her: Don't worry, nothing will stop me from marrying your son. She whispered another proverb as if to assert her certainty: "*Su questo non ci piove.*"

BARGE DANCE

July 1926

After Floro parked his Fiat cabriolet near the Arno, Alda watched him stroll around to open her door. Dressed in his white linen suit, this man she'd married only a month earlier seemed a bright tower against the dark night. Floro smiled and took her hand, leading her towards the river barge. As dance music filled the air, a string of Chinese paper lanterns stretched like a luminous necklace across the deck. Seeing the light reflecting on the river reminded Alda of the Florentine festival *la Rificolona* – that scintillating parade of paper lanterns waved by children high in the air. The children's collective blaze always made the river shimmer, as if alive, filling her with awe.

As her husband walked up the barge plank ahead of her, she grasped his hand, held out behind him. Although Alda was two years older than her husband, she sometimes felt like a child in his presence. As the band played

Floro driving, circa 1926.

the Charleston, he paid the entrance fee, tapping his feet, eager to dance. She adjusted her lavender dress with its low waist hanging perfectly on her hips.

"I never learned this one," she confessed as Floro ushered her onto the dancefloor.

"Just follow me," he grinned. Bending, holding his knees and crossing his hands, his long legs fanned in and out, swaying to the rhythm. She laughed out loud at his antics, shaking her head. He caught her eye and raised one eyebrow and then the other, undulating his eyebrows in synch with the beat of the music and his rubber-like legs. The playful sight of this formidable man in a white suit drew a crowd. People formed a circle around them, laughing and clapping. When the music stopped, he made a sweeping bow and spun Alda around like a top. They embraced.

"*O ragazzo*," she exclaimed, dizzy but suddenly feeling the mature one, "I married a performer."

As the music switched to Irving Berlin's slow *Blue Skies,* she melted into Floro's arms. But only a few moments into the dance, their intimacy was interrupted by loud voices echoing from across the floor. Someone shouted, "Togliatti!! Piece-of-shit-son-of-a-Russian-whore!" The crowd watched as one man pummeled another.

"What's going on?" Alda cried in alarm as Floro stiffened.

"Stay here," he insisted, moving towards the fight, a column separating a sea of people. He reached the groveling men.

"*Imbecilli,*" Floro sneered loudly down at the fighters. "There are respectable women here. Stop spoiling our fun! Take your fight outside." When they ignored him, he reached down, like Gulliver, a giant among Lilliputians, and lifted the two men by the napes of their necks. Extending his arms, he separated them in the air and walked towards the barge plank as they kicked their legs. The crowd cheered, letting him pass. Dangling the pair out over the river, he warned them: "Shall I drop you both in the Arno?" The two stunned men flailed their arms, glaring at the giant.

"Let me down!" one demanded. When they agreed to leave, he dropped both men. The deflated brawlers got up and straightened their shirts. One cocked his head, indicating that they'd move their fight down the street. As they headed down the plank, one man turned and hit the crux of his elbow in the *va fanculo* gesture. He called to Floro: "You'll pay for this."

Alda folded her hands over her chest to calm her heart. This was the first time she'd witnessed Floro's monumental strength.

"He's one of ours from the fascist club," she heard someone remark. "He should've broken that son-of-a-whore's nose!" The crowd clapped for Floro, but he waved them off and grabbed Alda, returning to the dancefloor. As the orchestra resumed with the cheerful American jazz piece *Bye Bye Blackbird*, Alda glanced towards the street, anxious to be sure the offenders were out of sight. As Floro danced, she was too distracted to keep in step. He stopped. The spirit of the night was broken.

"*Andiamo*," he said and ushered her to the bar where he ordered them a bitter *digestivo*. As Floro lit up a cigarette, they sipped their drinks in silence. "We may as well leave," he said, blowing out smoke. She agreed. The newlyweds walked down the plank as the crowd danced on.

They drove in silence along the river before heading up towards *Piazzale Michelangelo*, an expansive square where people stopped for the panoramic view of Florence. She noticed her husband's tension, his hunched shoulders. "Are you alright?" Alda whispered as he turned off the motor.

"*Certo*," he insisted, wrapping his arm around her shoulder. She didn't wait for him to open the door for her this time; she got out and took his hand as they walked towards the view and leaned against the balustrade. Under the moonlight the Arno appeared like an illuminated silver ribbon dividing their Renaissance city. There was Brunelleschi's dome across the river, and the Signoria tower, its turrets ablaze with light.

"How can people from our majestic city full of churches, sacred art and architecture grovel on the ground?" she asked her husband. "And why fight about Togliatti now? Mussolini banned his communist party. He's in exile."

Floro stepped back, giving his wife an impatient stare before he lit a cigarette. "Look at our historic city of commerce and culture before you. Unlike the rest of Italy, Florence has almost never suffered the tyranny of foreign rule. We've always been our own masters." Exhaling smoke that wafted towards the moon, he added: "Togliatti was lucky to be in Moscow when Mussolini disbanded his party; otherwise he'd be in prison now, or worse. He's in bed with the Russians, garnering their support. Don't be fooled, *cara mia*, he's the founder of the Italian communist party and can still cause a lot of trouble while they harbor him there. He continues to have many followers here." He took another long drag. "I cannot fathom how Italy would willingly give up its independence to become a Bolshevik satellite. Togliatti swore we'd be independent, adopt an Italian-style Communism! *Idiota!* The Russians funded his party. If they have their way, they'll make our lives miserable, take away our property. Everything my father worked for…"

Elvira, Ugo and Mario, with Floro driving, circa 1926.

"But didn't you tell me that the government has already appropriated a large portion of your father's property along this very road, Viale Michelangelo, for a community sports facility?" She wanted to counter his argument. She watched his lips purse – a sure sign of his displeasure.

"Well, that's an exception," he insisted, but his voice weakened. "And they exchanged some buildings in the city for that tract of land…"

"I don't know, Floro." She turned, wrapping her shawl over her chilled shoulders and looking into his eyes. "Extremes on either side worry me. And why did you feel obliged to right things on your own back there?"

"I have a God-given advantage," Floro said seriously.

"Things worked out tonight, but please, *amore*, your size and strength may not always be a blessing."

Floro nodded, but his attention turned towards the panorama of his city. She figured his mind was lost in the pursuit of unrealistic ideals. She gave herself some measure of comfort thinking it could be worse. At least he's not one of those fanatical *Futuristi*, who scorn women and families and basically repudiate the past. In their crazy manifesto of modernism, they even suggest abolishing pasta along with every other Italian family tradition. Imagine! *At least Floro values our history, wants to preserve and protect home and family while striving for Italy's prosperous place in the world. How could that be wrong?*

"Let's go home," she pleaded, uncertain, as he took another long drag on his cigarette.

Elvira with Yusk on the terrace, circa 1926.

AN UNEXPECTED VOICE

Grassina, 1926

The morning of the grape harvest, neighboring farmers gathered at the villa with their families, wearing boots and carrying shears. One of the Rafanelli farmers, Giovanni, hitched the oxen to their yokes. As the two white beasts pulled a large wooden cart, helpers fanned out into each row of the vineyard, cutting grape clusters and placing them in wicker baskets. Men and boys worked the *vendemmia* rows while their wives, daughters and neighboring women cooked huge pots of sausages and beans for the traditional lunch out in the field; they were also preparing a more elaborate celebratory dinner for all the harvesters at the end of the long day. After laden baskets were emptied into *bottini* – squat barrels in the oxens' cart – the farmer then led the oxen back to the *cantina*, where several men emptied the grapes into an enormous wooden barrel. Later in the day a few men would take off their shoes, roll up their pants and scurry down a ladder to stomp on the grapes.

Once the harvest was complete, Giovanni emerged from the *cantina* and closed the door, calling out: *"Mangiamo!"* Exhausted and famished after the long day, the helpers sat around tables set on the courtyard below the terrace. Wine from the previous year was poured, liver crostini was passed. Cheers abounded as neighbors raised their glasses, told stories and joked. Laughter and voices merged as they sang sentimental and bawdy songs.

It was expected that *padrone* Ugo or someone from the Rafanelli family would make an appearance. This year it was the newlyweds who appeared at the top of the terrace steps. Alda surveyed the courtyard, thinking she'd never heard such joyful singing or felt such unbridled mirth. As they walked down the steps, Giovanni greeted them, elated, nearly blushing: "Signori!

Thank you for joining us." Sitting with the crowd, they listened and clapped at the endless stories, tongue-twisters and rhyming songs. Once she and Floro had wished the harvesters goodnight and walked across the terrace, Alda turned and closed her eyes, relishing their enjoyment.

Inside, the house was quiet and dark except for a small light in the parlor. "It must be *Mamma*. Let's say goodnight."

They opened the green glass door where they found Elvira dozing, a shirt lying on her lap.

"*Mamma*, you should be in bed!"

"Oh!" she said, startled. "I have to finish mending your father's shirt. Go on. I'll be just a few more minutes."

"*Buona notte*, Elvira," Alda said, smiling. "I can help you tomorrow. I'm pretty good with a needle."

"Oh *cara*... I'm sure you are! But don't worry. Enjoy yourself a while. There will be plenty of time for mending in your life."

The next morning Alda awoke and swept her hand over Floro's side of the bed. He always left at dawn for work. Feeling a void, she wondered how she'd ever slept without the pulse of his warm body next to hers. She stretched under the sheets, relishing the darkness of their bedroom. She laid her head back on her pillow. What euphoric peace she felt, living the warmer seasons at this countryside villa. No sound of horses' hooves on cobblestone, no sound of wheeling vendor carts or honking automobile horns. Despite the ruthless heat of summer, it was cool inside their thick-walled refuge.

As she got out of bed to check the time, a celestial voice filtered into her room. She shook her head. This family, with their operatic obsession, listening to the gramophone till all hours of the night. Yet... all the Rafanelli men had already left for work. Could it be Elvira listening to a recording, so early in the morning? Curious, Alda stepped into her slippers to open the long window. As she pulled the inner wooden panel towards her, sunlight filtered in. Pushing the outer shutter, the mellifluous sound amplified in power. Leaning against the iron railing, she peeked onto the terrace, astonished. Demure Elvira was making theatrical gestures while watering the large lemon trees. Alda assumed the strong voice was coming from a recording. She watched her mother-in-law turn coyly, then dart, as if pursued by an invisible suitor. How amusing! She's mimicking a performance. Alda blinked at the scene unfolding below. Slowly she realized that the sublime voice was not a recording at all. This extraordinary sound was actually coming from Elvira. Thrilled, Alda leaned out for an unobstructed view. As she pushed the other shutter, it clanged against the wall. Elvira looked up and froze, like a monumental child caught in a naughty act. Her long arms fell down by her sides. Alda waved, calling enthusiastically, *"Brava! Bellisima, Elvira! Vai avanti."*

Alda on villa terrace, circa 1931.

She watched her mother-in-law grab the watering can and rush into the house. Alda quickly dressed and ran down the spiral stairs. She didn't bother to hold her long skirt from sweeping the wall in that narrow passageway. After dizzying turns, she opened the little downstairs door, rushed down the corridor, through the dining room and into the kitchen. There she found Elvira, who appeared catatonic, heating milk and roasting bread on the wood stove for Alda's breakfast, like every morning. The only difference was that her mother-in-law didn't meet her eyes or say *buon giorno*. Alda stared.

"What a magnificent voice, Elvira! How can you sing like that?"

A deep blush rose on her mother-in-law's face. "O dear, forgive me for disturbing your sleep."

"What? I disturbed you! I'm so sorry I interrupted you! I've never heard such a powerful voice. What a gift God has given you," Alda insisted, troubled by Elvira's reaction. Her mother-in-law's large chest deflated as toast burned.

"You see!" the tremendous woman sighed in exasperation, taking the toast off the stove; "vanity is a distraction."

"What opera, Elvira?" Alda prodded, ignoring her comment.

"*La Boheme*," she admitted, dropping the charred slices in Yusk's dish and putting two new slices of bread on the little grill, carefully watching them toast now before setting them on the table with her homemade apricot marmalade.

"Please, sit," Elvira insisted.

Alda wouldn't quit. "What part?"

"Oh dear... Musetta — so tragic," Elvira sighed, and her large frame seemed to lighten, as if releasing some dark secret. "Ugo took me to the very first performance of Puccini's *La Boheme* in Turino, in 1898, with Maestro Toscanini. It was the most magnificent day of my life, seeing the unveiling of such a stirring opera." Elvira's eyes brightened as she poured hot milk into Alda's coffee.

"*Stupendo*," Alda said, gently pulling the cup away before the milk overflowed. "Floro took me to the opera. He knows all the lyrics, all the music. I want to learn."

"Well, you'll have your chance, dear. Opera lives in these walls, courses through our veins, you know." Elvira laughed and then whispered, "It carries me through all life's trials. I got carried away this morning. I promise to sing more quietly."

"Oh no no, Elvira! I loved hearing you. You should be sharing your talent with the world – on stage."

"Oh dear," she said with a trace of panic. "That would never be allowed. Ugo places opera performers in the same category as circus people. Having his own wife sing in front of an audience would be unthinkable…"

"Well, if it could be recorded, he might think differently," Alda insisted. "Even if just for your family. Why listen to inferior artists?"

"Inferior, *cara*?" Elvira laughed, her large body shaking with amusement before she suddenly became serious. "Please, no mention of this… Promise?"

Alda nodded reluctantly. Later that night, when she and Floro settled into bed, Alda burst. "Oh Floro, you won't believe what I witnessed this morning – your mother, singing *La Boheme*! Why didn't you tell me about her extraordinary talent?" His body stiffened as she forged ahead. "Such a stupendous voice should be on stage, Floro."

"Alda. My mother is a signora, not a performer. Can you imagine the humiliation?"

"Humiliation? I thought you had great admiration for opera singers!"

"I do," he said, "but they're not my mother. She's very shy."

"Shy? Oh Floro!" Alda said, getting out of bed. "You should have seen her!" Alda got up and waltzed around the floor imitating Elvira's spry darting about the terrace. He watched, impatient, until she climbed back into bed.

"Something miraculous happens to your mother when she sings. She's transformed into a *diva*. The world should not be denied the pleasure of hearing her heavenly voice, which seems far superior to any on your illustrious recordings," she insisted, adding the phrase: "*A lei non legano neanche le scarpe*" -- They are unworthy even to tie her shoes.

"So, suddenly you're the opera expert!" Floro said. "You have no idea what trouble this could cause. Whatever you do, say nothing to my father. He'll blame her late meals on her singing. My mother has enough distractions and trouble without you putting crazy ideas in her head."

Alda sulked. "Now I understand why she asked me to say nothing."

"And yet you divulged her secret!" Floro's voice was tense.

"I wouldn't dream of keeping a secret from you," she cried before an uncomfortable hush settled on their first disagreement. Alda burrowed under the white linen sheets. Dismayed by his dismissive, chastising tone, she turned away, lying on her side, thinking it cruel, perhaps even sinful, to bury such God-given talent, and for what? Appearances? Fighting tears, she prayed under her breath to Santa Rita, the saint who married before becoming a nun. When Floro reached his long arm around her, pulling her towards him, she melted. "Oh *amore*," she whispered, settling her head on his wide chest. Soon he was in a deep slumber, while her eyes remained wide open. While Floro's heaving chest and loud snores drowned out her thoughts, Alda hummed *La Boheme*, attempting to resurrect Elvira's sweet, unheralded voice.

A MEANDERING WAY

Summer 1973

As we drove towards Rome through the scenic Via Cassia from Florence, Aldo asked what I loved about his country. "What's not to love?" Italian was the only way we could communicate, and it poured out: "The beauty, the art, the history, the landscape, the cities, the cuisine, the people…" I explained that I'd grown up in an isolated suburb where people were totally dependent on cars. "I love Italian cities, with zones where no vehicles are allowed, with places just for people. I love the juxtaposition of centuries, with so many layers, like the pagan Pantheon, transformed into a Catholic church. I love that the Roman Forum is flanked by a Renaissance square that Michelangelo designed." I sighed. "Italy was the pinnacle of culture when my country was still wild."

"Hah!" he laughed at my litany. "You Americans dream of old Italy while we Italians dream of young America, land of opportunity, with your wide-open spaces, your forests, your movies, your Elvis and blues, your cowboys and blue jeans!"

I attempted to translate the hackneyed phrase *the grass is always greener…* "You've probably seen too many western movies romanticizing America."

"My older sisters took me to every single Hollywood movie, not just westerns! They were in love with Errol Flynn and Tyrone Power, one always trying to convince the other why her favorite leading actor was more handsome or talented than the other," he smiled. "When I saw *Seven Brides for Seven Brothers*, I dreamed I'd live in America one day, in that log cabin in the woods."

"Geez, what a fantasy," I said, seeing a sign. "Oh! Volterra. I've never been

Camilla with camera, on road to Rome with Aldo, summer 1973.

there! I hear it has Etruscan tombs." As Aldo veered towards the exit, I asked, "Where are you going?"

When he insisted it would be a short visit, I told him about the first time I'd seen the tiny bronze Etruscan figures at the Villa Guilia in Rome. "They must have inspired Giacometti's elongated figures."

"Etruscans remain a mystery," he said, adding that the word *Tuscan* was derived from *Etruscan*. "Since they settled in our hillsides, we like to believe we descended from them."

After an hour of visiting tombs and taking lots of photographs of the craggy hillside, I began to worry about Aldo's meeting in Rome.

"Don't worry," he said. "I've got time."

I knew the autostrada from Florence to Rome took three hours. Instead he was taking a wide geographical zigzag. When I spotted the Mediterranean in the distance, and Aldo pulled up to a parking area near the sea, I sat dumbfounded. "Where are we?"

"Baratti. Elba is out there," he pointed. "You haven't been, right?"

He'd been impressed by all the Italian cities I'd seen as a student, but I shook my head. I got out, holding the Nikon camera on loan from a New York City friend. Aldo pointed towards the beach, telling me how a few years earlier he'd kept his tent under that stand of umbrella pine trees for an entire summer. "I came here weekends after work, on my motorcycle. Left everything right there…"

"That's incredible," I said, taking photographs of the pines against the crystal water.

"*Andiamo*. Let's drive up the hill."

Moments later we were on a narrow road. Entering the stone portal of a walled village, Aldo parked on a paved courtyard in Popolonia. A wall of flat stucco buildings loomed across from us. Reaching the long façade, Aldo stood under a window and called up: "Piero! Elena?"

A woman leaned out, her short blonde hair catching the sun as she looked down and cried in delight. "Aldo! *Che sorpresa… Vieni.*" We walked upstairs. The woman embraced him warmly but gave me a suspicious look. Once inside her apartment, she insisted we stay for lunch. A moment later her jovial husband Piero appeared.

"Aldo! What a surprise!" The two hugged as I wondered what we were doing there. While Elena prepared pasta, Aldo asked Piero to show me his photography, one stunning image after another, some shot for *National Geographic*. I stared at Piero's images of exotic corners around the globe.

"Your job must be the most envied in the world," I gushed, and he smiled, shrugged humbly and lit a cigarette.

Around the table, I listened to the trio reminisce about shared adventures. After lunch I watched Elena take Aldo aside and, glancing at me, ask him something to which he shook his head.

We finally said *ciao* and headed back down the hill, where Aldo noted my longing glance toward the blue Mediterranean. "I love to swim; I always feel at home in the water," I told him. He stopped the car again, just yards from the limpid sea. "It's so inviting," I said dreamily.

"Go ahead," he insisted.

"My bathing suit is packed."

"No problem," he shrugged. Seeing my look, he added, "There's nobody around."

Yeah sure, nobody, I thought, feeling a blush rise. I knew Italians were casual about nudity on the beach, which I found amusing for a Catholic country where divorce had become legal only three years earlier. I told him I reserved skinny-dipping for moonlit nights.

"Anyway, it's late," I said. "Shouldn't we be getting to Rome for your appointment?"

"No rush," he said, driving off. After a while he asked, "Have you been to Gubbio?"

"No, I've never visited Umbria."

"I spent many summers there with my old friend Filippo and his family. Gubbio is a jewel you shouldn't miss."

"Next time," I smiled.

By the time we finally arrived in Rome, it was nearly dark. Around the corner from my friend Karen's apartment in Trastevere, Aldo suggested we get a bite to eat. We stopped at La Tana di Noantri, a trattoria set in the courtyard of a former church. Flanked by the floodlit façade, people dined *al fresco* under white canvas umbrellas. "This looks great," he said, reading the pastas listed on the menu. I reluctantly nodded. A handsome waiter led us to a table.

When we sat down, I finally blurted out, perplexed, "Okay, could you tell me when your meeting is?"

Placing a large linen napkin on his lap, he looked contrite. "There is no meeting. I just wanted to take you to Rome." I felt so gullible. After spending a few awkward moments looking around the restaurant at the faces of adoring couples illuminated by candlelight, Aldo finally interrupted my silence with an apology.

"It's okay," was all I could say. As our waiter approached, Aldo ordered a bottle of Orvieto. I asked for some sparkling water.

"So, when are you coming back to Italia?" he asked once the waiter had poured us a glass of the white wine.

"I have no idea." But he understood I was a desperate Italophile.

"You mentioned you wanted to live here again someday, to write and find work in an art gallery." As we sipped wine, his face brightened. "Why don't you join me and Giovanni on the *Maristella* next summer for its maiden voyage?"

"Hah! You're kidding!" I nearly choked. "Sailing the Mediterranean is a dream of mine."

"Well, that's perfect, then."

Although he'd tricked me, it was a forgivable offense. My instinct told me that Aldo was trustworthy. But thinking about the close quarters on a sailboat, traveling with two men, I was noncommittal. "*Grazie mille*. That's a wonderful, generous offer."

After dinner I thanked him profusely for the day. When I took my bag out of his car, he insisted on carrying it to Karen's apartment. We walked towards a tiny *vicolo*, and I kissed both his cheeks at her door.

The next morning, Karen woke me up. "Your friend is on the phone," she said.

I rolled out of bed. "*Pronto*? Aldo?"

"*Buon giorno*," he said. "You left your camera under the car seat."

"Oh God! I borrowed that from a friend in New York," I sighed in distress.

"Don't worry. Maybe it was meant to be. I can bring it to you tomorrow – and take you to Gubbio!"

"Oh no! That's too much trouble. I'll come get it by train."

"I insist."

More stunned silence followed.

He laughed. "Tomorrow is the weekend, and I'm free. You must see Gubbio before you leave next week." I paused a moment before agreeing.

Sipping her coffee, Karen raised an eyebrow.

"He's a close friend of Paolo's father."

She smiled, showing me the Bialetti espresso machine and the round wheat crackers on the counter for '*prima colazione*' adding "*Ciao ciao, bella*. I have to run off to the gallery."

I served myself *caffè latte*, dipping a sweet cracker, wondering if I'd forgotten that borrowed camera under the seat or if Aldo had hidden it there.

The following day Aldo arrived with the camera. We drove three hours into verdant Umbria, all the while Aldo enthusiastically pointing to hills and fields where he'd hiked and hunted. "*Guarda bello*," he said, and I agreed. We stopped to visit the cathedral in Assisi before we reached Gubbio. As he parked in a lower square, I gazed up at Gubbio's walls, transfixed by the medieval jewel layered upon Mt Ingino, a vision that reminded me of the *National Geographic* images of Lhasa in Tibet. Walking up cobblestone steps, with the precious camera around my neck, we passed under elaborate stone archways.

"Franco Zeffirelli, a friend of Giovanni's, chose this unspoiled medieval city for his *Romeo and Juliet,*" he said.

I gushed, "God. I adored that movie."

Roaming around the quiet streets, we perused shops filled with beautiful ceramics, many painted with images of saints. Aldo explained that the three saints – Sant' Antonio, Sant' Ubaldo and San' Giorgio – are part of Gubbio's *Corso dei Ceri,* an elaborate annual race and festival attended by thousands on May 15th. Pointing up the mountain, he added: "Come on, I'll show you the church of Gubbio's patron saint Ubaldo, where the wooden *ceri* are stored."

I had no idea what he was talking about, but I was curious. We jumped onto a tight, upright funicular, standing face to face as it carried us up the mountain. Under the altar of the mountaintop church I stared at the well-preserved cadaver of Saint Ubaldo, apparently lying in a glass coffin since 1160. Despite being raised Roman Catholic, the display of desiccated bodies and bone relics in Italy's churches always repelled me.

Aldo ushered me over to a side aisle to show me elaborately carved, towering wooden columns that appeared like pagan totems. "These are the three '*ceri*' for the race," he said, explaining that one was for Saint Ubaldo, one for Saint Antonio and one for Saint Giorgio, each one carried by a team. "The teams race while carrying them, from the main central square up to this church."

"That's insane! They must weigh a ton," I said. "Doesn't *cero* mean wax in Italian? But they're made of solid wood?"

"Yes. They weigh much more on the day of the race when each of these three columns is topped with a heavy lead figure of their companion saint," he said, adding; "although the race is usually reserved for Gubbio residents, a few years ago I joined a team carrying Antonio, the saint of farmers and students. It was terrifying! I ran two heats because my substitute didn't appear. I thought I'd die. Some unauthorized person stepped out in front of me and destabilized the *cero*. As it was about to fall, I took the man by the scruff of the neck and threw him out from under. He tumbled down the mountain. Not sure what happened to him. Filippo also raced that day. I found him on the ground, nearly passed out. He also hadn't been substituted."

As he explained the race in more detail and how passionate people were about it, I was fascinated. "We have the San Gennaro festival in New

York where people parade with the saint's figure held up high, but I've never heard of anything as crazy as this." He told me that Gubbio immigrants living in Jessup, Pennsylvania actually replicated the race every year.

That night for dinner I tasted truffles for the first time. They seemed more like a sensual smell hovering in the air than an actual taste. He told me a story of years earlier, in November 1966, a day when he and his friend Massimo, wandering around the Gubbio countryside, discovered a truffle hunter carrying a white truffle the size of a large potato. It was so extraordinary that when they asked the price, the hunter announced he was saving it for the Pope. Eventually they convinced him to sell it to them instead. While they drove back to Florence they planned a party, naming all the friends they'd invite to share the phenomenal truffle. But as they turned on the radio they heard news that the Arno was flooding. When they approached the city they discovered that it was one of the devastating hundred-year floods. As he dropped off Massimo, they discovered that Filippo, Aldo's dear friend and Massimo's brother-in-law, was missing. Through detours, Aldo made it back home, filled with angst. Most communication was down, but days later he learned that Filippo had returned home safe. He'd been caught in the rising river as he'd gone to take his car to higher ground. Swept away in the torrent, nearly drowning, he had held onto the side of a building until someone had heard him shouting. People from the apartment above had lowered sheets and hauled him in through their window to safety. He'd stayed there until the flood had receded. Communication was out, so for days his family didn't know he was alive. That day the Arno River rose above the bridges, measuring twenty-four feet in Piazza Santa Croce, where Cimabue's *Christo* became one of the more famously damaged works of art. At the national library, manuscript treasures were buried in mud.

"Obviously, with that kind of destruction, it was no time to celebrate even the most gigantic truffle imaginable," Aldo said.

That evening after dinner we walked and sat on a bench in the *piazza* in front of the hotel. As he kissed me, he sensed my reserve. We said goodnight and went to our separate rooms. I knew Aldo was far from the stereotypical Italian male I'd encountered. When we said our final goodbyes in Rome, he repeated his invitation to sail the Mediterranean the following summer. Kissing him on the cheeks and saying, "A thousand thanks," I suggested we write.

MEETING ALDA AND FLORA AT THE VILLA

Summer 1974

That year Aldo and I wrote many letters. He continued to suggest the sailing adventure. While I sat at my desk at the Frick Collection during the day or attended writing classes at HB Studios at night, I dreamed of blue Mediterranean waters. Finally, I bought a cheap Icelandic ticket to be part of the *Maristella's* maiden voyage. By early June, Aldo sent an apologetic letter — *The antique wooden boat still needs more work to be seaworthy and won't be ready by July.* Since my ticket was non-refundable, I flew to Rome anyway, with no travel plans. The morning after arriving at my old *pensione*, the owner, Norbert, who had been so kind during my student days after learning of my father's cancer, smiled as he handed me the phone. It was Aldo.

Alda, Flora and Aldo at the villa, summer 1974.

"I'll take you anywhere in Italy to make up for this disappointment."

It would've been the three of us in the *Maristella,* with independent berths and tasks to do while sailing. I wasn't sure of the expectations for this road trip, but after a few moments, trusting him, I tossed away caution. When Aldo arrived the next day, he took me to Lago di Vico, a lovely little lake near Rome. Only one room was available at the lake hotel: a duplex. I looked at him, relieved that he respected my privacy. He stayed upstairs. I was charmed by his knocking on the wall when he came down the duplex stairs. Next day we drove past enormous Lake Bolseno, heading north towards Florence, to visit Fernanda in Fiesole and then assist Giovanni in La Spezia for a few days of dry-dock work on the sailboat. He wanted to assure me that the *Maristella* wasn't a myth.

While driving just south of Florence, he asked, "Would you like to see where I live?"

"Of course," I said. "Who's there?"

"My mother lives with me." I thought it was odd the way he put it. Maybe because he was over thirty, he didn't want to say that *he* lived with his mother. Later I learned that in fact he had inherited the villa from his grandfather, that he'd lived there alone for years, all year round, with no central heating. When his mother decided a year earlier to rent their year-round home on Viale Michelangelo, she opted to live with him.

"My sister Flora is visiting today. She lives near Teatro Communale, in Florence."

"Ah, the sister who's an opera singer."

"Well, yes. It might seem romantic, but it's a ruthless business. Flora has performed as mezzo-soprano with Renata Scotto and many illustrious voices. She's worked with the greatest directors at La Scala, La Fenice and San Carlo. Someday she'd love to sing at your Metropolitan Opera. She inherited her voice from our grandmother Elvira. My mother must have guessed her destiny at birth, because her full name is Elvira Flora."

The thought of a human voice transcending generations nearly made me cry.

As we rounded a corner in the village of Grassina, Aldo pointed to a long, lonesome villa set up on a hill. Through the windshield it looked like a yellow face stretching horizontally, its window eyes peering down on us. As he turned into the driveway flanked by a tall stone wall, I read a plaque: "Villa Rafanelli." Aldo continued on, parking below a terrace.

"*Bellissima*," I said, gazing at the villa's imposing *giallo toscano* façade.

"It was built in 1500," he sighed, "and it demonstrates its age." I noticed uneven surfaces and different yellow paint layers that added interest and color, aging gracefully.

Reaching the top step, I saw two women wearing summer dresses sitting on a bench, looking at us. "My mother and sister," he said. Suddenly I was mortified that I was wearing a mini jean skirt. I winced at the clippity-clop sound my Dr. Scholl's wooden sandals made on the terracotta tile terrace as I approached them. My attire was acceptable for a casual seaside resort, not visiting an elderly matron at home. I picked up my feet, trying to lessen the sound.

They rose, extending a warm *piacere*. I noticed Aldo's mother had a cane, so I insisted she sit. Flora was at least ten years older than Aldo. His mother, I guessed, was in her seventies. Right away I gleaned a fierce, protective love for him.

As we chatted in Italian, two wiry brown and white pointers appeared, wagging their tails.

"This old one is D'oro, a champion, the best-behaved hunting dog in the world, unlike his lazy son Tom here," Aldo said. I petted the dogs, relieved for a distraction.

His mother said she'd heard I was from New York. Flora gushed that she hoped to visit someday for work.

"I'd be delighted to show you the city," I said.

Before going inside, I asked to take their picture. They insisted Aldo join them. In the photo Aldo wears an impatient expression, holding a jacket on his shoulder.

"Excuse us," Aldo finally said. "I'd like to show Camilla around."

I followed him under the shady *loggia* where cats slept entwined, a furry cushion on a chair. Round sandstone steps led to a massive arched double door. Immediately I noticed the difference in temperature once inside: a cool refuge from the hot terrace. A baby grand piano sat by the door and a dining table was situated in front of a large hearth. I glanced at the tall ceiling, at least thirty feet above us, and discovered an arrow planted in a wooden rafter.

"What's that?" I asked.

"My friend Fabrizio, an expert bow maker, shot that up there," Aldo shrugged. "It's too high to retrieve."

"Must've been some party," I laughed.

We walked towards glass doors and peered out onto a wooded garden park. Aldo, unlatching the wooden frame, ushered me outside.

"This is 'the little woods' which gave the villa its original name, Il Boschetto." Evergreen oak trees – *Quercus ilex* – provided welcome shade as we walked down a pebble path flanked by laurel hedges. He brought me to the edge of the woods, where I stood in silence under a regal umbrella pine that rose above all surrounding vegetation.

We returned inside and Aldo headed down a long, narrow corridor lined with small trunks.

"Is someone moving?" I asked, and he laughed.

"No, they're just interminably parked here."

At the end of the long corridor, he unlatched a little arched blue door, and we climbed a narrow, blue-grey, spiral staircase.

"I feel like I'm in an ancient monastery, or a dungeon!"

"It's *pietra serena* – sandstone – original, from 1500."

I was relieved when we reached the second floor. He opened another door to an anteroom, where I slapped the rough surface of a conglomerate country sink.

"What a great little kitchen this would make, with this low rectangular sink and this tiny window set above it," I said, now on tiptoes peering down at the garden park where we'd just walked. From this higher perspective, it reminded me of one of my favorite childhood books, *The Secret Garden*. In the distance, I spied a sophisticated treehouse nestled high in tall branches.

"Who built that?"

"I did, about ten years ago, with the same friend who planted the arrow."

"That's impressive! I'd love to climb up there!"

"The rope's broken and the floor's rotten. It's not safe anymore!"

"Too bad. You built a treehouse in your twenties?" I teased.

"Well, it was a dream since I was a little boy, but there was a war on then, among other things."

"Of course," I paused, wondering about his childhood. "Could it be restored?"

"Well, it's hardly a top priority with all the upkeep here."

We passed through a small room, formerly a dining room. As he unlatched another double arched door, he said, "Also original," and had to bend to pass into the next room.

"These walls are incredibly thick," I said as we entered the larger room.

"This was my parents' bedroom," he said. "The stairs are hard for my mother now, so she stays on the first floor."

Aldo opened the vertical floor-to-ceiling window, and the room filled with light. When he pushed out the exterior shutter, I leaned over the railing, looking down at the gorgeous lemon trees scattered around the terrace. His mother and sister had left their perch on the bench. I pointed to a far-off field.

"Is that your vineyard?"

"Yes," he said, leaning next to me. "Those overgrown vines were here when my grandfather bought this place in the '20s. Alongside them are the scraggly new rows I planted a couple of years ago. Their first harvest is next September," he said. "You should come. We always have a great party for our *vendemmia*! Feeding people is an incentive to help. Especially if my mother is cooking."

"I bet it's fantastic… Who knows!" I smiled. "And there's an olive grove…"

"We make our own wine and olive oil, with the help of my farmer Gigetto."

"You have a farmer working for you?"

"Yeah," he said, pointing beyond the terrace to a small building. "He and his family live there."

"You went to agriculture school and work for a large company, selling grafted vines, right?"

"Yes. I also consult for vineyards in Chianti," Aldo said. "You can't make a living farming a property this size."

"I know. My grandfather was from the last generation of dairy farmers in upstate New York. It's sad."

We moved to the adjacent dark and dusty room where he opened another long window. This time sunlight illuminated a maze of shattered antique furniture. Seeing the pieces strewn haphazardly about and covered in soot-laden cobwebs, I imagined Miss Havisham from *Great Expectations* sitting in the room.

"Why all this broken furniture?" I whispered, afraid to wake some ghost.

"Our villa was occupied during the Second World War. A lot of our furniture was vandalized or stolen. First, German officers and soldiers arrived. Except for stealing our food, they left our possessions alone. But when the Americans occupied, they used this place as their headquarters and carted out all our furniture into the back park. Some neighbors probably stole the best pieces; the rest was damaged by the elements," Aldo said. "After the war, the government sequestered this place as a sanitarium for people with TB, to house the injured and homeless from the war. My mother couldn't get back in here for ten years."

"How could they get away with that?"

"My family only used this villa during the warmer months. The government took over houses that were considered unoccupied, weren't primary residences. But there were plenty of seasonal villas around that were left untouched. My mother believed taking ours was a vendetta for my father's politics. The administration of the village was, and still is, communist. My father was a fascist."

"Oh," I said, wincing.

Aldo continued, "My mother finally got this place back. And then my grandfather left it to me. I should be grateful but it's endless maintenance. I don't need all this space."

I wandered around the room, stopping in front of a badly broken mirror with an elaborate rococo-style gold frame.

"That fell off the wall in 1920, all by itself, the day my uncle Danilo died. When my grandmother Elvira heard it crash, she hadn't heard the news about her son's death yet, but when she heard the sound, she called out: *Oddio mio figlio!*" Somehow she knew. Her son was stationed at a military base in Palermo, due home in just two days. Not sure if it was dysentery or the Spanish flu. My grandfather Ugo had to go to Sicily to retrieve his body. Everyone loved Danilo. He was short in stature compared to the rest of the men in the family, but his strength was legendary." Aldo added, "My grandfather never got over it."

I shook my head. "Damn war…"

Aldo nodded. "Come, let's get out of this room. I want to show you the towers."

He went first up the continued narrow spiral staircase to the third floor. I held my arms across my chest so I wouldn't rub against the dusty stone walls. It seemed a long time since anyone had ventured up there. Aldo served as master cobweb-breaker. As we passed into the tower, I stood marveling at the massive beams converging and soaring upwards towards the center of the room.

"I could imagine Edgar Allen Poe or Victor Hugo writing up here… inspired by this setting," I said, breathless.

"Well," he laughed, "you're welcome to come here and be inspired anytime. Seriously. You said you wanted to live in Italy again and write. This could be the solution. As you see, we have more than ample room."

I swallowed, too nervous to reply.

"I'm serious. All this wasted space is a shame. I've asked so many friends to live here, rent free, just to have these rooms return to life."

I was baffled. "And they didn't take up your offer?"

"Maybe all they saw was the dusty, broken furniture. They say we live too far out in the countryside."

"But it's only fifteen minutes from Florence," I said. "*Sono pazzi!* They're crazy."

"Well, take up the offer…" he smiled.

After a few awkward moments of my dumbfounded silence, he forged ahead.

"The entire second floor is vacant. It's a mess. No one has lived here since the war, but you seem to have imagination. If you came, it would be a good excuse to restore it."

"What a kind offer," I finally said. "I'm speechless."

"Well, don't say anything, just think about it," he said, his expression playful. I walked around to catch my breath, anxious, examining the ground as dry seeds crackled underfoot.

"What's all this?"

"This tower is a granary because it's well ventilated. We dry rye and wheat up here. And in the other tower, on the opposite side, we hang a selection of grapes from the rafters and store little barrels of *vinsanto* there."

"You have a real working farm. Fantastic. Maybe someday you'll visit my mother's old farmhouse in Ulster county, New York, where my aunt still lives, and the dilapidated old dairy barn – when you come to America." I noticed I said *when* and not *if.*

I gravitated towards one of the many little windows throughout the granary. "What a beautiful view of the countryside," I said, but approaching another window overlooking another hill I was surprised. "What are those concrete buildings along that hillside? How could they ruin the perfect Tuscan landscape?"

"Over there they can do whatever they want, while here in our 1500 villa I can't touch a thing. We are *their* Tuscan panorama, our untouchable *cinquecento* villa, while *we* have to look out at that obscenity. They allow construction like that but won't even allow me to widen my driveway for my vine business so my truck can pass. It's politics, which I avoid whenever possible." He was fuming. I'd clearly hit a sore point.

Pivoting towards another view, I discovered the villa's long, expansive red terracotta roof, with sections covered in lichen, some clearly broken. Arched, connected, clay-red tiles paraded towards the other tower.

"I love your red tile roofs. Whenever I land in Italy, I look down from the plane and get so excited seeing them."

Aldo smiled as he opened the little window. At the sound of the antique brass weathervane flag creaking in the wind above the other tower, we looked at one another and said in unison: "*Originale! Cinquecento.*"

Once back on the second floor, on the opposite side of the villa, we descended wide front stairs above the kitchen.

"Were you here when the villa was occupied?"

"We stayed while the German officers occupied. But we were lucky. I remember one German officer, a kind man with a bandaged foot who limped. That's all I remember."

"How old were you?" I asked, curious to do the math.

"Three when the Germans occupied our house, but war was already on when I was born."

"Were you terrified?" I asked as we reached the first floor.

"I vaguely remember being frightened by distant bombs. The last memory was when American soldiers took over this place and slept on mattresses on the floor. I thought it so strange. When they occupied, my family was forced out. We returned to Florence on a donkey cart. While my mothers and sisters walked all the way to the city alongside the cart, I was happily perched on top of our belongings, like some adventurer."

"Was your father in the war?"

"He and my uncles never fought: they were older, their health was compromised; but my father volunteered for some of it. He was captured up north towards the end. That's too sad a story for today."

"I'm sorry. Americans have no clue what it's like to live surrounded by war," I said.

"That reminds me. I want to show you something," he said, guiding me down the corridor to a room where he opened a low shutter. He waited for my reaction.

"What?"

"Take a closer look."

I saw a name scribbled, the address barely legible. "Ohio?"

"Home to one of the American soldiers who stayed here. We never had the courage to clean it off."

"Oh boy. Maybe we should write to him," I said and Aldo shrugged. "You're right. Even if he's alive, he probably doesn't live at that address," I said. "Americans don't stay in the same place generation after generation anymore, not like Italians still do."

As we headed down the corridor again, I was taken by the smell of garlic and olive oil wafting from the kitchen.

"*O mio Dio,* your mother must be cooking something incredible."

He laughed, "I'm sure she'd like us to stay for lunch."

"She didn't expect us, Aldo, and I'm such a mess. I didn't realize I'd be meeting your mother and sister today."

"You're perfect," he said, "but I promised Giovanni we'd meet him this afternoon in La Spezia, so we'd better get going."

"*Ciao, Mamma,*" Aldo said, entering and kissing the translucent skin on her forehead. I noticed lively, kind eyes gazing at him with adoration.

"Stay for *pranzo?*" she said hopefully. Aldo explained that Giovanni was expecting us. "But the sailboat is still on land. What are you going to do, make this poor girl work?"

"Only if she wants to, just a little," he smiled. "We want to drive up the coast too, but I wanted her to see the *Maristella* so she believes it exists," he laughed.

"*Purtroppo,* it does," his mother sighed. "Well, have a wonderful time. *Tanti saluti a Giovanni.*"

"Pleasure to meet you, signora," I said as Flora appeared with a bunch of basil.

"*Ah cara!* You're not staying? You don't know what you are missing!"

I repeated that I would have loved to – perhaps another time. La signora put her hands on my shoulders, but I thought his protective sister Flora looked at me askance as we headed off. I wanted to reassure her.

"Don't worry – I won't steal your brother. We're just friends."

Aldo on villa steps, summer 1974.

VENICE

Summer 1974

The boats in the yard at La Spezia seemed like hulking patients suspended in sick bay, propped high on crutches, longing to return to their water home. Aldo and I approached the old majestic *Maristella*, looking up at the underbelly of the antique vessel, sixty feet of high maintenance. When Giovanni saw us he cheerily called out to me, "*Ciao bella!*"

As we climbed the ladder, Aldo said, "This past winter we fiber-glassed the entire hull. Just in case we ever want to cross the Atlantic."

I already understood he didn't care about owning big things or having big projects; he just wanted to enjoy life. Giovanni met us on deck in shorts, clutching a hammer in his good hand. His chest was bare, and for the first time I saw the stunted arm he had been born with. He smiled with the look of mischief I remembered and embraced me as I asked if Fernanda and the boys ever came.

"They prefer Fiesole," he said. "Fernanda's only been on the *Maristella* a few times. She's jealous of her," he said, patting the mast and offering me a tour. I cleared my throat and looked around. The tall mast, which Italians appropriately call *albero*, or tree, was an awesome brown beauty. Her body shone with sleek swaths of warm, lacquered wood. I could understand falling for this kind of old boat. Walking on a plank, we followed Giovanni below deck. He showed me a minuscule sitting area and my tight quarters for our two-night stay. That afternoon, I learned what seemed to be an endless list of projects to make her seaworthy. The two partners at work, like *Mutt and Jeff*, were hysterical to watch. Aldo, with his long legs, paintbrush in hand, passed gracefully on the narrow planks. Short and stocky Giovanni walked precariously, holding a can of varnish in his one hand. Later that afternoon, as Aldo and I organized the tiny kitchen area for dinner below, we heard Giovanni navigate awkwardly above us. Often a stumble was followed by a loud string of Italian curses: *Accidenti La Miseria! Porco qua, porco la...* After one such crash, Giovanni's foot appeared in the hole, before the rest of him fell in up to his waist. Aldo and I rushed to make certain he was unhurt as he pulled his dangling body back on deck. We all erupted in relieved laughter.

As evening approached and the various daily chores were complete, alluring aromas wafted up from the tiny kitchen. As I set the little table for dinner, Aldo made a pasta with minimal ingredients and equipment.

Sitting in the narrow galley, Giovanni transformed his own awkward balance into an asset, saying, "I am more evolved than my friend Aldo here, who is no doubt from a branch of humans that left the trees more recently."

I laughed. "Ah yes, of course," I said, "that must be why he constructed that treehouse." Giovanni nodded as if I'd proved his point. Aldo set his pasta down on the table.

Taking in the scent, Giovanni said, laughing, "But I forgive my primitive friend, signorina, as his cooking skills are very evolved. He has everything going for him but breasts." As Aldo instinctively crossed his arms over his chest, Giovanni laughed so hard tears pooled in his eyes. His laughter was contagious.

I slept very well those two nights in the narrow berth, undisturbed until voices and hammering echoed about the boatyard soon after dawn. After bidding Giovanni goodbye, we headed towards Volterra.

Aldo said, "I wished he'd kept the old, smaller boat. So what if the *Maristella* is a beauty? Who needs all those fancy complications? At least the small sailboat sailed. We've spent all this time on dry dock, maintaining the damn thing. It's summer now."

"It seems Giovanni is perfectly happy puttering around."

"No question. That's the problem," Aldo sighed. "I'm so sorry. I was certain we'd be out on the water by now. Some complication always arises."

"Don't worry. I just hope you get her out there someday."

As Aldo drove on winding switchback roads, I began to feel carsick and asked him to stop. He sat down next to me on a sloping field, instructing me to look at the horizon. I must have looked pale and pathetic. He wrapped his arm around me. Years later he confessed that that was the moment his heart melted and he "surrendered to destiny."

After Volterra, we drove in the direction of Piero and Elena's, the stop along the coast from the summer before on that long zigzag trip to Rome.

Elena again gave me a suspicious look when we entered their apartment. She stayed home as we, Piero and a group of his friends headed for the ferry to Elba. Once on the island, we all piled into a van. Aldo drove, glancing at me from the rearview mirror. My head turned out the window for glimpses of the crystal-clear *aqua* below. He pulled over so I could photograph shadows of boats reflecting on the limpid sea floor.

"Lucky Napoleon to be exiled here," I said. When we reached a beach, I was already in my bathing suit, excited to jump in. Among the bathers, it was easy to pick me out as the American – I was the only one wearing a one-piece suit. No matter what age or girth, every Italian man wore a skimpy triangle and every woman a bikini. I headed towards the translucent sea and dove in. Swimming underwater with open eyes, I suddenly found myself amidst a large shimmering mass swaying in the dancing current. I stared at the wave of suspended glass needles catching the light. Plankton, I surmised as I stood to catch my breath. When I looked down, I found a multitude of pointy silica sticking to my chest and arms. Although pricking my skin, they didn't sting. I remained calm, emerging, summoning Aldo with a shaky voice.

"Wow. Look at that!" he said, removing a few long silicate triangular needles. I inhaled deeply, trying to keep panic at bay. We began picking off ones embedded like pins in my neck and chest.

"Plankton? Diatoms?" I asked.

"You are probably right. They're beautiful," Aldo said but seemed more distracted by the flesh they were stuck to.

"Okay," I said and thanked him, asking a woman from our group if she wouldn't mind holding a towel around me while I removed my suit. From behind the towel, attempting to screen my nakedness, I tossed my needle-covered suit to Aldo, who intently picked off the remaining prickly creatures, handing my suit back with an amazed look. I scanned for remaining shards while struggling to maintain privacy. I yanked the wet thing on.

"I've never seen anything like this," the local woman said. Piero and Aldo concurred.

We left the beach and walked around the village, where bikinis hung in every shop. I bought my first one, determined to banish fear and self-consciousness. When we returned to Baratti, I wanted to take another swim in my new suit, to clear all remnant angst about what I might discover in the water. Aldo and I bushwhacked down a thick, narrow path flanked by scrubby coastal Mediterranean *macchia* plants. As the crystal-clear cove appeared, I marveled that no one was around. Aldo laughed. He explained how he and his friends would assure privacy and dominion of the cove whenever boats would approach – they'd take off their suits, jump around naked, wave their arms, act crazy. The approaching boats, full of families, always turned and puttered away. I laughed heartily.

Here the sea was deep, pounding against rock formations that looked like dinosaurs emerging from the water. He watched me dive in, swimming among the porous volcanic *tufo* rocks.

"Come on in!" I called, treading water.

"I don't swim," Aldo called back.

"What?" I could barely hear with the pounding water. "But you said you loved snorkeling!" I called.

"I can swim with flippers," he insisted.

At dinner that night he told me that his mother had kept him from the sea until he was a teenager. He never learned to swim. "But that's a sad story for another time," he said. I frowned but didn't press him. The following day we were back on the road, crisscrossing Italy, gravitating towards the country's northeast coast, to the Adriatic Sea, to visit Paolo's brother Stefano and Stefania, the newlyweds from last summer. They invited us to stay overnight in their home in Fano before deciding to go to Venice together for the weekend. It was sweltering hot when we got there so, to cool off, Aldo and I took an endless trek in the Lido's shallow water. I dove in, over and over, like a dolphin, and swam around his legs. He smiled, but he was not at home in the water.

That steamy night I wore my Roman sandals and wrapped a long African cloth around my waist, one that my sister Sue had given me long ago from her years in Nigeria. No talented seamstress, I'd safety-pinned it together. Aldo wore a cool white linen shirt and pants, looking tall and very elegant. When I approached him, he undressed me with his eyes. After dinner with our friends, Aldo and I took a gondola ride. Lying horizontal, my head rested on his chest. The city's Gothic, Byzantine and Moorish façades glowed as we skimmed quietly along the water, listening to the rhythmic call of our gondolier.

Afterwards we met up with Stefano and Stefania in San Marco Square. Orchestras played under the *loggia*, around the *piazza*. Mesmerized by the music, the moon and the blur of gaslight torches captured in shop windows and shining on brass instruments, we waltzed around the illuminated square. Our skin shone wet with the tremendous heat. I felt dizzy, enchanted, riding the crest of a wave, swooning in Aldo's arms, surrendering all caution.

ABSENT FLORO

Florence, 1926

While the family listened to Donizetti's *Lucia di Lammermoor* on the gramophone, the long-legged Rafanelli brothers stretched out on stiff chairs, enraptured by the opera. As the drama intensified, Alda turned towards Elvira, busy mending next to her on the red Empire-style sofa. Then Pietro, holding his long, narrow notebook, sat at the desk with his back to everyone. She noted how he wrote with a flourish, paused at the end of an aria and switched to a different color of ink. What was the significance of this color change? At least Pietro's intensity was directed towards his writing. Floro said his notebook was full of passionate critiques of the papacy, priests, Church hierarchy and the Evils of the Inquisition. It was current politics that disturbed Alda, rumors about the violent *squadristi*. Floro dismissed her as alarmist, insisting that that fascist faction was only a loud and brutal minority of the party.

Ugo rested on his high-backed chair, never losing his posture. With each operatic passage his brow either furrowed or relaxed. Observing the proud patriarch, she imagined him at fourteen, leaving home, unwilling to be subservient to his stepfather. On his own, he labored as a *garzone*, sweeping floors, saving every lira, skipping meals. Paying attention to every aspect of running a successful business and being frugal by nature, in a handful of years he had saved enough to become an equal partner in his stepfather's fish business. Before long he became the most powerful, envied fish wholesaler and importer in all of Florence.

When Alda sighed, thinking about her own father, also a self-made man, only with less luck, Mario looked up at her. She appreciated his kind smile, grateful for how he seemed to pay such attention. And then there was Floro, with his long legs stretched out, in a world of his own, so enraptured by the music that she thought he might levitate.

When Elvira started humming quietly along with an aria, someone shushed her. Stunned, Alda blinked. Who was so rude? No one in her family had ever shushed anyone. Angry at this affront to her mother-in-law, Alda frowned at the blank faces around the room, hoping to admonish whoever it was. She then looked to see how Elvira had taken the rebuke. Her shoulders were sunken, her face flushed and her eyelids at half-mast. Alda now understood. Elvira was a fatalist. Had powerlessness brought her mother-in-law to passive acceptance, thinking everything was predetermined? Alda hoped that if ever faced with anything similar, she would stand up for herself.

Suddenly, as the last act came to a close, as if Floro was already testing her resolve, he opened his eyes, pulled his long legs in and sat up. Clapping his knees, he stood and checked his pocket watch.

"That was sublime! But I'm off."

"Off?" Alda repeated, surprised.

"Yes, dear, a circle meeting," Floro said brusquely, and she heard the anarchist Pietro tsk.

"Oh. The fascist club," Alda said, trying to ignore Pietro.

Floro, annoyed she was questioning him in front of his family, quipped, *"Brava*, Alda," but his haughtiness melted when he saw the desperate look on her face. "Oh, please don't," he whispered, sitting next to her, kissing her cheek. "I won't be late."

She tried smiling as he left the room, but a thickness settled in her throat. Ten minutes later he stood in the corridor as if composing himself before saying goodnight. She smelled polished leather when he entered. He was wearing his black shirt and the tall black boots. She stared at his oily, slicked-back hair. Rather than impressing her, this version of him left her unsettled. He told her not to wait up and disappeared.

For weeks Floro left almost every evening at the same hour, returning exactly at midnight. Alda shuddered when his shiny boots clunked on the bedroom floor. Climbing into bed, he was still effusive, his passion, she hoped, related only to politics. She sensed no alcohol or perfume, which gave her hope that his meetings were actually reserved for political discourse and handing out alms to the needy.

Sensing her restlessness, one morning Elvira asked Alda to forage for wild herbs. "Take your time, dear. Air will do you good."

Alda summoned Yusk from under the table. "Come for a walk?" The dog darted out, wagging his tail. Stepping out to the garden, her shoes crunched on the pebbles and the dried wild oak leaves that carpeted the path. "I will devise a plan to get him back," she promised the panting dog by her side. "You're not the only clever one here." Clutching her straw hat and basket, Alda rushed away from the garden's shadows towards the light, towards the solitary tall umbrella pine that marked the edge of sunny open fields. Patting the massive tree trunk, she was pleased its branches were too tall to manicure into ordered hedges like the gardens loved by so many Florentines. *Why*, she wondered, *are we so determined to tame wildness?*

Under the shade of an olive tree she searched for wild volunteers for the salad. She discovered gentle stalks of *nipitella, terra crepuli, cicerbita* and, further in the fields, succulent purslane. She picked the bounty from the ground and placed it in the wicker basket. Whenever she stopped, so did Yusk. "*Bravo!*" she laughed. "Who says you're a terror?"

Back at the umbrella pine, she leaned on it and slid down to rest cross-legged on moss. The dog's head lay on her lap while a litany of unwelcome thoughts surfaced. Only a little over three months married and Floro had been absent almost every night the past month. During their courtship, he had mentioned that his father had kept him and his brothers under tight scrutiny. They hardly ever went out, he'd complained. His father controlled the purse. Before taking his fiancée out, he'd been given scant allowance, even though he had worked diligently for Ugo. Once he married, Floro received his own salary, controlled his own finances. Through marriage her husband had gained freedom and a higher status, the right to go out without his father's permission. But where did this leave his wife? She knew it was useless to threaten or to rein him in like his father had, but this lack of authority put her in an unacceptable position. She never envisioned spending every evening sitting alone with her in-laws. She was fond of Mario, and of Elvira, but she'd married Floro and assumed they would be together.

As she petted the dog, she wondered if she was doing anything to send him off. Yusk looked up, his furrowed brow mirroring her emotions. "Oh, you'll see!" She scratched under his floppy ears, wishing he could talk. "I'll start going out in the evenings too, visiting Adriana, my aunts and uncle, my father. Why stay here and be predictable? Let Floro wonder for a change."

She wished that political fervor had skipped her husband, as it had both his brothers, and particularly his father Ugo, who had been cured of activism by Danilo's death and his own father dying on the field with Garibaldi. Every so often the patriarch still uttered a sarcastic *Grazie* to his father and Garibaldi for uniting north and south Italy. Ugo's lack of enthusiasm for Floro's involvement with fascism was evident in the language of his dismissive gestures.

Mournful bells lamented down in the valley of Grassina. *How apropos*, she thought, as the ringing continued. Floro had told her that many generations ago the Rafanelli clan had come from Corsica. "We were pirates," he'd announced with pride, adding that later they'd immigrated to Italy and become respectable citizens. Some settled in Pistoia and became the famous Rafanelli bell makers. That was how the Rafanelli heraldic symbol became a bell. *How romantic!* Alda had thought then. She imagined Rafanellis transforming the iron from their cannonballs into sublime, peaceful bells that summoned congregants to Sunday Mass or that announced a birth. She was thrilled to take on the ringing, joyful cadence of a name that aligned itself with the family's historic bell-making occupation. This month, however, with her husband's continued evening absences, she felt more adrift than ever in her lifetime.

"*Ra. Fa. Nell. I*," she sing-songed, her tone bitter and her voice off-key. "Do you hear that name, Yusk?" The dog stirred, suddenly on his feet, wagging his tail as a shadow eclipsed Alda's sun. She looked up.

"Forgive me for disturbing," her towering mother-in-law said. Alda said nothing. "Are you alright, dear?"

"I am," she lied, starting to rise.

"Please stay seated," Elvira insisted as the dog lay back down. "I don't mean you, Yusk!" They both laughed.

"Would you show me where you find your mushrooms?" Alda said, brushing off her skirt.

"Of course," Elvira said as she searched the ground in the wooded park, poking with her cane, lifting leaves along the sun-dappled edges. "Here's one!" her mother-in-law exclaimed, exposing a cluster. "*Russula*, the edible mushroom, quite plentiful here." Alda picked it up since the ground was so far for her tall mother-in-law.

"You'll find solace in these woods." Elvira took the mushroom and threaded her arm through the crux of Alda's elbow. *Solace?* Alda stiffened, wanting to scream. *I'm too young for solace!*

As they picked one mushroom after another, Alda bent, whispering another of her Tuscan proverbs to the dog: "*O bere o affogare*." *Forget that! I'll never settle.*

THE RUSE

Autumn - Winter 1927

Alda was unhappy to leave the villa for the city. As winter approached, she was losing her patience. She furiously rocked the half-moon blade back and forth over a thick wooden block, mincing parsley and garlic for *salsa verde*. She was tired of her mother-in-law advising her *not to worry*, that *young married men were expected to go out at night*. Or *It's a phase that will pass*. Sure, Alda knew things could be worse. Some men gambled, some played cards with friends, some frequented brothels. Floro, she wanted to believe, was merely attending political meetings. Her fists tightened around the wooden head of the half-moon instrument.

Elvira interrupted her black mood, gushing about the talent Alda had in the kitchen, saying how one day it would be all hers.

"Oh no!" Alda insisted. "This is your domain. I'm happy to help, as I did with my aunts, but…" Alda's mood lifted with nostalgia for those days. "We had such fun in the kitchen. They often told me stories associated with food."

"Stories?" Elvira said. "What stories?"

"Well… the first time I made tortellini, they told me how it got its name."

"How it got its name?"

Alda told Elvira the tale of the innkeeper who peered through the keyhole into the bedroom of his beautiful guest Lucrezia Borgia, from the infamous family, hoping to see her naked. Although his timing was right, Lucrezia stood too close to the door for him to see her entire body. Nonetheless, the innkeeper, who doubled as the cook, was enraptured by a teasing glimpse of her navel. He ran off to the kitchen to create *umbilici*-shaped tortellini in her honor.

As Elvira blushed, Alda forgot her troubles and the two broke into laughter at the silly legend. Soon her mother-in-law began humming Bizet's *Carmen*, moving with drama as they worked. Then she raised her wholehearted voice. There were a few joyful minutes before Alda noticed Ugo at the threshold of the kitchen doorway, stopping to listen in silence. She was certain she detected a flicker of reverential admiration before his mood shifted to exasperation. When he entered, Elvira abruptly stopped singing.

"Elvira! It's half past noon. Is the meal ready?"

"Nearly, Ugo! Go to the table!" she exclaimed, spilling boiling water on the floor as she hurriedly drained the pasta, her face bright red from the steam. As Alda watched Ugo turn and vanish, she bit her lip. She wished she could reassure Elvira that her husband's behavior would pass, but she feared his disdain was deeply rooted. It was the reason she felt such urgency to halt Floro's new pattern of dismissing her. She was certain his natural softness and loyalty to family was his true anchor.

By late October, Alda and Elvira had packed their belongings to move back to Florence. The family had been at the villa since late April. Now, like every year, they would return to the city for the colder months. Alda was filled with melancholy as she and Elvira took the corners of white sheets and covered the furniture - a veil of protection until their return the following summer. Alda felt a shrouding of her own spirit. Floro's continued absence at night was altering her perception of the world. She prayed her natural optimism would re-emerge.

As if reading her mind, Elvira said: "*Cara*, we're nearly done. Go visit Adriana before we leave. Seeing your friend will do you good."

The idea brightened Alda's spirits. "Oh Elvira! Are you sure?"

"Of course. If you aren't home by dark, I'll have Floro fetch you."

"Oh no. I want to walk. I'll return before dark."

Alda changed into a lovely brown skirt and a white blouse and rushed down the hill to visit her dear young friend. Longing for her carefree life with Adriana, she knocked at the door of her old host's place.

"Alda!" Adriana embraced her. "What a surprise. I've missed you so."

"I've missed you too," Alda added, glad that Adriana's parents were napping through the late afternoon.

"Come in! I was about to make an espresso." As they entered the kitchen, she smiled at her friend.

"Is everything alright? How is Floro?"

"Oh, I gather *he's* fine," she said, too emphatically. Adriana frowned, quietly looking at the espresso pot until it sizzled with dark coffee.

"Let's sit in the parlor," she said, pouring it into cups on a tray. They walked into the room. Alda sat, clanging her spoon on the cup as she stirred in a few teaspoons of sugar and sipped. Her friend stared at her.

"What's wrong?" Adriana implored. Finally, Alda spilled her heart out about Floro's meetings.

"Is that all, Alda? As long as you're sure he's not out with the fascist squads roaming the streets at night to keep order, beating on socialists and drunkards, forcing them to ingest castor oil. Those *horribile squadristi!*"

Alda sighed. This was not the response she wanted to hear, but she assured Adriana.

"Floro thinks they're some kind of fringe militia. Widows and homeless from the war come to his meetings for help. He distributes money to them," she said. "He doesn't look for an excuse for violence. If anything, Floro breaks up fights." She had witnessed this and was certain, but she was still concerned about what else might be going on.

"Oh, I know how soft-hearted Floro is," Adriana agreed. "Do you get along with his mother?"

"Oh, she's very dear," Alda said. "She has a magnificent voice but only sings when the men are gone. She's like a caged songbird. I just hope that Floro doesn't look to his father as a model for how to treat a wife, that he doesn't abandon the tenderness he inherited from his mother."

"Of course that will prevail! You need patience and time to settle into your new situation," Adriana cautioned.

Alda started, nearly spilling the coffee, blurting out the proverbial phrase of contrasts, "*Chiama e rispondi.*" Even her young friend was trying to console her with platitudes, sounding like her passive mother-in-law. She felt rage rising. "I cannot stand that word 'settle', Adriana," she insisted. "I need to find another way before *he* settles on ignoring me!"

"Of course, of course, Alda," Adriana agreed as the two sat with their hands now folded on their laps. Adriana changed the subject; a nice distraction. She told Alda about parties she'd attended, about her family and school. Alda regretted that she hadn't finished school. Finally she got up and kissed Adriana's cheeks.

"I need to get back," Alda sighed, and they embraced.

It was a long walk home. Had she expected that her friend, years younger and without any experience in marriage, would have the answers to her dilemma? She would have to resolve her problems in some creative way on her own. Huffing up the hill towards the villa, Alda turned as she heard a vehicle behind her. It was Floro, driving in his open auto with his brothers and father. The surprised men stared at her, while Mario made a funny face that made her laugh. Floro frowned but could not stop on the steep hill to pick her up. Alda was pleased by her husband's look of consternation as she waved happily at them. The way she was dressed it was clear she'd been out on a jaunt, not just at the market. Good. She giggled as the auto turned into the driveway. She took her time. Inhaling, she sauntered up the hill, observing a necklace of songbirds perched on laundry lines in the field. When she finally arrived at the courtyard where Floro parked his auto, she saw her husband leaning on it, waiting impatiently for her.

"You were out?" he said as she approached.

"Why yes, dear," Alda said sweetly, wanting to laugh at the obvious, as she climbed the terrace steps, holding her mid-calf skirt while looking straight ahead.

"*Mamma* didn't need your assistance?"

"The idea was your mother's, Floro," she said, turning slightly. "I just lost track of time."

"Well, that's hardly a surprise. It's contagious around here. Let's go in, then," he said as he opened the front door.

"Sorry I'm late, Elvira," Alda said once inside the kitchen.

"Oh dear, don't worry; dinner is *prontissimo*. How is Adriana?"

"Very well, thank you, Elvira." At the mention of Adriana's name, Alda noticed Floro's shoulders relax.

"That was quite a distance to walk, Alda," he said.

"Oh, I so enjoyed it. What a wonderful idea, Elvira. Thank you. I must get out more often. It cleared my head." As Alda and Elvira smiled, Floro left the kitchen in a flustered state. Seeing her husband's reaction, an idea began forming in Alda's mind.

A few days later they returned to Florence for the winter. Alda hoped their move might alter Floro's habits, but it didn't. Through November Alda stood by their bedroom window in the dark, looking out onto the street, timing her husband's arrival at the gate. She gazed at the peeling layers of sycamore trees that lined Viale Michelangelo. A sliver of a waxing moon caught her eye. Every night she kept a vigil. His return was like clockwork. The more the moon grew, the more Alda imagined it smiling with a complicit face. Always at midnight Floro's headlights appeared. She held the small brass alarm clock, counting the minutes it took for him to open the gate, drive through, close the gate, park the car, walk up the path and enter the house.

Early one morning, once Floro had left for work, Alda noted the time and rushed downstairs. She opened the front door and stood momentarily outside. She turned and fiddled with the doorknob, then slithered back inside. Elvira, passing in the hallway, frowned as she watched her breathless daughter-in-law rushing up the stairs.

"Alda?" she called after her.

Without turning, Alda proclaimed: "*Tutto bene,* Elvira." Once back in her bedroom, Alda took off her robe, hung it in the armoire and jumped back into bed before quickly turning to see how long her practice run had taken. Checking the face of the bedside clock, she smiled. Perfect.

"*Chi non risica, non rosica,*" Alda asserted with a laugh as she recited yet another proverb to herself: *nothing ventured, nothing gained*. She was anxious the night of her planned charade. With the family stationed around the parlor in their usual seats, listening to Mozart's *Nozze di Figaro*, she rehearsed the plan in her mind. She bid her in-laws an early goodnight, feigning exhaustion. This was all her idea. If her plan backfired, she would only have herself to blame. Once in her room, Alda opened her armoire door and pulled out the champagne-colored dress that she'd designed during her courtship. She remembered sewing the beads and sequins for the opening night of *Tosca* in Florence. Floro had found it beautiful and eye-catching. Well, that was the point. She hadn't worn it since. She stretched it on the bed. There were still two hours until midnight, so she sat on a little chair re-reading Manzoni's classic tome, *I Promessi Sposi – The Betrothed*. The first time, it had been an academic requirement, but the book meant so much more now that she was married. It was hard to focus; she frequently checked the clock.

With thirty minutes to spare, she rose from the chair, her heart racing. Looking in her vanity mirror, she twisted her hair in a rhinestone-studded comb. She applied powder to her face and lipstick to her trembling lips. She scattered every piece of jewelry that glittered on the table: a lovely Victorian rhinestone choker and a shiny bracelet with matching earrings her aunts had given her, ones that belonged to her mother. If she were still alive, would she have conspired with her? Was this big plan of hers a *stupidagine*?

Exasperated, she got up, struggling to zip the dress she hadn't worn in over a year. She'd gained weight. She put on the rhinestone jewelry. She paced the room, checking: ten minutes to midnight. Slipping on her shoes, she grabbed the matching shawl that covered up the flesh from her partially zipped dress. Gazing at her devotional kneeler, afraid kneeling might split her dress, she stood praying for assistance:

"Cara Santa Rita, aiuto."

She imagined Floro's confusion, seeing the shadow of her figure at the front door. She banked on dousing his trust with a serious measure of suspicion that she had been out somewhere. Alda looked again at the clock: five minutes more. Peering nervously out her bedroom window, her pulse racing, she finally spotted his headlights at the front gate. Grabbing her shawl and stepping out, she tiptoed downstairs, her heart pounding, grateful the house was silent, everyone in bed. From the downstairs window, she watched Floro open the gate. The moment she knew he was climbing back into his vehicle, she held her breath and slithered gingerly out the front door. A chill shivered up her spine as she turned towards the front door, feigning a struggle to open it. "Santa Rita!" She fumbled, breathless with the latch, shaking her wrist, hoping the rhinestones sparkled and caught the light. As she heard the motor rev and the wheels slowly enter the driveway, she whimpered involuntarily. Floro's headlights grazed her dress. "Good," she whispered. The instant of that grazing seemed like an eternity. She prayed he'd discerned just enough movement and glitter reflected from his headlights to wonder, just one moment to perceive the outline of her figure, like a moonlit apparition, dressed for an evening out. Just before his vehicle came to a halt, Alda slid back in, closing the door gently behind her. She raced up to the bedroom. She struggled out of the tight dress, tossing it in the armoire. Yanking the shiny comb, her twisted hair fell around her shoulders. Earrings! Necklace! Bracelet! She put them all back into the jewelry box. Slipping into her nightgown, she sprinted into bed and turned out the light. A minute later she heard the bedroom door open.

"Alda?" Floro whispered, clearing his throat. Breathless in the dark, she realized her face was still full of powder. She could smell the useless lipstick, thick on her lips. "Alda?" he repeated in a low voice. He approached their bed in the dark. Even with her back to the door, she wondered if he could discern her heart clanging wildly in her chest. She closed her eyes.

"Yes, Floro?" she moaned as if he'd disturbed her sleep.

"Were you out somewhere tonight?"

"I've been here all night, dear," she declared groggily, truthfully, turning only slightly, terrified her ruse would backfire. She regained confidence as he sighed, undressed quietly and joined her under the covers without turning on the light. He rolled over, silently looking up at the ceiling, clearly perplexed, while she remained with her back to him, rigid as she feigned slumber. She sensed his mind racing, felt his bewilderment — exactly what she'd hoped for. She waited. After a while he fell asleep, snoring on his back. She smiled, knowing that, as a proud Florentine, he wouldn't allow himself to ask her any more probing questions. She had inserted a sliver of doubt, just enough intrigue for him to wonder, she hoped, to keep him around, making sure his wife stayed home at night.

EXPECTATIONS

Florence, 1928

Elvira and Alda walked down from the villa towards Grassina. Seeing a little boy fishing the Ema, a stream at the base of the hill, Alda leaned over the stone wall, observing a synchronized mass of tiny fish darting and changing direction in the water. *Not one veers off in another direction. How do these little fish all know to turn at the same time?* The sun sparkling in the water made her mind wander to the serene seaside escape she'd had with Floro earlier in the summer. It'd been mesmerizing to be near the endless expanse of Mediterranean blue. And what a luxury, to get away, just the two of them.

Elvira nudged Alda out of her daydreaming, but she remained in a fog of intimacy as they walked towards the village. She followed her mother-in-law into a small *merceria*. This shop had fewer choices than the elegant fabric stores in Florence, but Alda loved its friendliness.

"Signore Rafanelli, how may I help you?" the lanky owner said, nodding at Alda, who deferred to Elvira's choice of materials. Alda turned and gazed out the shop's glass door. The glass became the sea. Before her was the image of Floro lying under the sun outside their canopy. She'd sat reading in the shade but had been too distracted by the view of her formidable husband lying on the sand, his skin visibly darkening. Alda blushed at the sensual memory of Floro dreamily sifting sand through his fingers. She recalled his grin when he turned, knowing, saw his wide mouth and enormous brown eyes.

The ringing cash register woke Alda.

"Let me take that," she insisted as she lifted the heavy package from Elvira. Traversing the street, they entered the corner butcher shop. Little bells attached to the door announced their entry. Elvira bid the butcher Piero *buon giorno,* and he inquired about her family.

"*Tutti bene, grazie,*" Elvira said, and Alda thought – this isn't just a phrase – everything *was* really fine. The tormented time of Floro's detachment was merely an unpleasant memory.

Then Alda saw, in the back of the shop, a carcass of hanging beef. Suddenly she felt dizzy, revolted. Leaning on a glass encasement for support, she looked at the contents inside. Bloody beef. Marbled fat. Gagging, Alda covered her mouth and rushed out the door, the little bells tinkling after her. She collapsed on a bench outside, bewildered. Elvira followed her daughter-in-law.

Towering over her she asked: "*Che cosa e successo,* Alda?"

"I don't know. Suddenly I felt terribly queasy," she said, recomposing herself, a hand over her stomach.

Elvira felt her forehead with her lips. "No fever," she asserted.

"I've been in that shop a hundred times. The sight of raw beef never repulsed me before." Alda turned towards Elvira, expecting sympathy, and instead found her mother-in-law with a radiant smile.

"What's so amusing, Elvira?" she asked, offended.

"*Oh* Alda! *Ci siamo.*" This is it! She clapped in a gesture of elated prayer, looking up to the sky.

"What is *it*?"

She sat down next to Alda on the bench. "You're not ill, *cara mia.* You are *nello stato interessante.*"

"What?" Alda said. "How do you know?"

"It's a sign!" Elvira cried. "Early on. Who knows why, but the sight of red meat revolts many women." Her mother-in-law leaned towards her. "Tell me you're late," she whispered. Alda nodded, and Elvira exclaimed, "*Stai calma!* Don't move!" Stunned, Alda watched her rush back into the shop. She hadn't seen Elvira so spry since that morning she'd discovered her singing on the terrace.

Her mother-in-law returned to her side, holding up a package. "The butcher gave me some extra bones!" she nearly sang. "For a special broth. You have some bones to build."

"You didn't say anything, did you?" Alda asked as they walked home.

"Of course not!" Elvira smiled.

"Good. Let's not *put the cart before the ox.*"

When Floro entered the kitchen an hour later, he found his mother chopping vegetables, unapologetically singing Rossini's *Barbiere di Siviglia* as Alda sat mute at the kitchen table.

"What's going on?" he said. He was used to his mother looking anxious before meals and his helpful wife on her feet, exuding encouragement. Alda stared at Elvira as if warning her. "*Allora?*" Floro insisted. Alda grabbed his hand and led her husband to the back garden for a rare moment of privacy. She could sense Elvira peeking around the corner, watching the glass door as she told her son the news. When they returned to the kitchen, Elvira's eyes were swollen with tears. Floro hugged his mother before placing his hands on her shoulders. "*Mamma*... it's our secret until the doctor confirms everything."

"Certainly!" his mother cried. "Alda! Floro! Just think – a little voice and little pattering feet, filling our home with joy again. You'll see, my darlings, everything will be transformed in this house. Even my husband will be a different man with a baby around."

"*Mamma.*" Floro gave her a warning look. "It's too early."

Elvira insisted: "Oh, Floro. Everything will change."

Once the news was confirmed, the house was indeed filled with elation. Elvira sang only lighthearted arias while preparing appetizing food for Alda and *il bambino*, as she insisted her very first grandchild would be a boy.

One early afternoon, as Clara hung linen sheets to dry on a line near a sliver of sunlight by the back door, Alda and Elvira gathered mushrooms in the wooded garden. When Clara re-entered the villa for another basket of wash, Yusk slithered outside. Before she could catch the wiry dog, he leapt onto a hanging sheet, grabbing it with his paws and pulling it off the line with his teeth. Snarling, his head switched back and forth as if the sheet were a precious bone to fight over.

Hearing the commotion, Elvira yelled, "Yusk!" Turning towards Alda, she said, "Now do you believe he's a terror?" Both laughed at the scene of Clara chasing the dog down the pebble path, with the sheet trailing behind him.

"Maybe we haven't paid our poor dog enough attention these days. All we've thought about this past month is the baby's arrival," Alda said. "I think he senses something is different."

"I'd put nothing past Yusk," Elvira smiled.

As they headed towards the back door, Elvira suddenly stopped next to the hanging sheet, holding onto it. The mushrooms in her apron cascaded to the ground. Alda grabbed her arm.

"Elvira! Are you alright?"

"I know we can count out certain possibilities," she joked, trying to make light of the situation. But Alda was alarmed. Her mother-in-law was as white as the sheet hanging near her.

"Sit down," she insisted, guiding Elvira to a stone bench. Yusk ran over, anxiously licking her ankles, curling up at her feet.

"I'll be fine, Yusk," Elvira said, turning to gaze out into the distant fields across the road, as if reorienting herself. After a while her dizziness passed, and they walked slowly back into the house. But the next day, as she worked over the stove, the same malaise returned. Alda put her lips to Elvira's forehead.

"I think you have a fever. I'll call the doctor."

"I don't understand," Elvira said, collapsing on a chair, her elbow on the kitchen table. "I'm never sick. It's as if my skeleton has given up."

Alda tried unsuccessfully to lift Elvira. "Just stay here," she said, running to call Giovanni for help. He and Alda ushered her to bed. That afternoon Elvira's fever spiked.

Later that evening, while Floro and Ugo stood outside the bedroom, the doctor emerged, looking baffled, admitting he was uncertain.

"Her lungs are clear, but I wonder about the pain in her legs. Feed her some broth. I'll return tomorrow," he suggested. "And, Alda, in your condition you should keep a distance until we're sure what she has isn't contagious."

Alda hadn't considered contagion and was horrified. She thought of the deadly Spanish flu epidemic ten years earlier that had claimed thousands of Florentine lives. Now her thoughts were with her unborn child.

The following day Elvira improved, and the family was reassured. But that evening, rising from the parlor sofa, she collapsed again.

"Mamma!" Mario cried. He and Floro rushed to her. Ugo and Pietro stood watching. Alda followed as the two brothers helped their mother back to bed. As the mysterious illness continued, Alda found herself suddenly in charge of the household, managing the kitchen and seeing to the needs of all four men, ascertaining everything was in order. Even with Clara's help, it was a struggle to make sure that all their clothing was washed and ironed and that meals were ready on time. Soon it would be time to leave the villa and go back to Florence for the winter. While attending to the family and caring for Elvira, who was diagnosed with a non-contagious bone disease, Alda had to pack up the household's personal belongings for the move.

Each day Ugo, Floro, Mario and Pietro arrived at midday, anxious and hungry. As they ate her first course, Alda was grateful that the usual culinary scrutiny was suspended. She looked around at the table full of Rafanelli men silently eating the meals she and Clara had prepared and had no idea if they liked anything. Their silence became worse than criticism. She prayed for Elvira's return to good health.

The day of the grape harvest in September, Alda was too tired and distracted to join the farmers and neighbors in the festivities. She didn't feel like celebrating with Elvira still sick in bed. That evening, with *vendemmia* songs rising from the courtyard, she carried dinner to Elvira on a tray.

Her mother-in-law sighed. "You shouldn't have to serve me, Alda. You should be out there singing and dancing. I've become such a burden — just when I wanted to take care of you."

"Don't worry, Elvira. You'll be better soon." But another month passed, and Elvira still couldn't get out of bed. Every time she tried, she couldn't support herself. The doctor confessed her illness was irreversible. The night before their departure from the villa, Alda felt a sense of dread about returning to Florence. Exhausted, she stopped in the large room with the neglected French antique *carambola* billiard table.

Looking at it in the center of the room she remembered her beginner's luck during her second visit to the villa three years earlier. She recalled the night Mario and Floro had encouraged her to join them for a game. When she'd finally agreed, she'd delighted in their surprise as she continued to score points. "Confess. This isn't your first time, Alda," Floro had said. When she'd won several games, they'd laughed, but her future husband took her stick away and never asked her to play again. Such silly pride these men have. She was longing for more lighthearted times. Alda continued on to Elvira's room. She rushed in when she found her tottering by her bed.

"Elvira!"

"I couldn't lie there any longer," Elvira said. "Melancholy and despair... such terrible sins."

"Come on. Let's look out at this beautiful day," Alda prodded. Dismayed by the sight of her sallow skin and her frail body that seemed to be surrendering to gravity, Alda opened the long window to let in the light. Elvira struggled to move and speak.

"He was as strong as an ox. Poor boy. What did he die for?"

"Who?"

"Danilo. Whenever I look down on those old lemon trees in their antique terracotta vases I'm always reminded of the day my eldest son lifted them."

"Floro told me that story. It seems impossible!"

"I saw it with my own eyes," she said, pausing to explain that the farmers had brought the lemon trees from the *limonaia* and had left them in the wrong place on the terrace. Ugo, on a tirade, had shouted at his lazy sons for not taking care. "It takes at least four men and a cart to lift them!" Ugo wouldn't stop shouting, so Danilo, only eighteen years old then, with superhuman strength, put his arms around an enormous lemon vase and, all by himself, lifted it. Walking around, he demanded: "Is this where you want it, *Babbo?*"

Elvira took a breath before saying that her husband had screamed, "Put that down! Hernias run in our family!" Finally, she said, Danilo put the vase down and stormed off. His face bright red, his father silent. Elvira leaned on the window. "Those two were alike in size and volatile temperament, but Danilo had the kindest heart of us all. Two years later he perished in Sicily, at a military base, just days before he was due home. Ugo had to bring his body back. He never got over it."

"I'm so sorry, Elvira. I cannot imagine losing a child," Alda said. She knew Elvira had also lost a four-year-old daughter.

"No, I couldn't either," Elvira sighed. "I will join them in paradise."

"Oh, Elvira... next summer you'll be standing here at this window, holding your first grandchild."

"Please pray to your favorite Santa Rita for that, my only wish!" Elvira whispered, exhausted. Wrapping her arm around the emaciated woman's waist, Alda put her to bed.

The day they left the villa, before climbing into Floro's car, Alda watched Elvira stare up at the sweeping façade. Seeing her expression, Alda knew what her mother-in-law was thinking. She struggled to hold back her tears.

LIFE AND DEATH COLLIDE

Florence, 1929

The last week of April, with her baby due any moment, Alda felt it was cruel fate that she was bursting with new life while Elvira was wasting away. The mood was glum. Even her art nouveau armoire, with its swirling oak door carvings, seemed to frown. Exhausted from the winter taking care of her bedridden mother-in-law and managing the household, Alda gathered her forces as she entered Elvira's room with a small tray.

"*Cara*," Elvira whispered in reply, "how much time is left?"

Alda shuddered, thinking of the double irony. "Soon," she offered, putting down the tray.

"I must eat."

"*Brava.*" Alda picked up a spoon and fed Elvira macerated fruit. She knew she was near death now. During her long months of suffering, the only reason she'd held on was to see her first grandchild; her only wish was to hold the baby in her arms, even if for only a moment.

That evening, when the doctor arrived after dinner, he called the family out of Elvira's room, shaking his head, saying it was the end.

Alda clasped her hands, pleading. "Just a little while longer. *Per favore.*"

"It's out of our hands," the doctor shrugged.

The next day Ugo walked in to the kitchen and found Alda and Clara preparing a roast.

"Clara," he said, looking stern, "when is your sister coming?"

"Palma is in the mountains with her family, Signor Ugo. She will be here after the baby is born."

"At least that! We cannot jeopardize our little Rafanelli!" Ugo declared, staring at Alda. "My wife is asking for you. Let the kitchen go today. She and your baby should be your priority."

"I checked before coming in here, Ugo. Elvira was asleep."

When Alda returned to the sick room, Floro entered and paused at the pathetic sight of Yusk, by his mother's bed ever since she took ill. The old dog glanced up with sad eyes, without lifting his head.

"*Come stai, Mamma?*"

Her response was barely audible. He propped up pillows behind her back and looked down at his mother's emaciated body, patting and kissing the top of her head, making another excuse to leave the room. As he shut the door Elvira smiled and lifted her bony shoulders.

"He doesn't want you to see his sadness," Alda said, sitting next to Elvira's bed, as she had for long hours every day for months.

As Alda brushed a wisp of hair from her mother-in-law's thin face, Elvira whispered, "*Mia figlia.*"

"*Mamma,*" she answered, kissing her forehead. They had both been bound by loss and the long illness.

That night Floro snored beside Alda, who was too agitated to sleep. Passing her hand over her enormous front, she urged, "Come out, *bambino*, come out! Your *nonna* wants to meet you." Feeling an immediate foreboding about Elvira, Alda lumbered downstairs to check on her. She found Ugo, fast asleep, on a yellow slipper chair. She blinked at the sleeping man who was so rarely quiet. As she approached, Elvira's labored breathing startled her. She had never witnessed death, but she sensed it was imminent.

"Oh no, Elvira," she said, and her mother-in-law opened her slate gray eyes. Her pasty face was devoid of animation. Alda repented having disturbed her with her now unrealistic plea. She fetched a cool cloth to wipe Elvira's forehead and struggled upstairs to wake Floro.

"It's time," she said, shaking her husband.

"What?" Floro woke with a start. "*Il bambino?*"

"No... *Mamma,*" Alda said, not yet giving up on her meeting the baby. "Please go, keep her alive. I must walk around!"

He dressed, staring at his wife with suspicion. "You should be in bed," he insisted.

She looked at him. "No, Floro. If I'm on my feet, the baby might come..."

He sighed. "*Lascia fare*, Aldina. I know what you're thinking. And you call me hard-headed."

When Floro entered his mother's sick room, his father looked dazed. Elvira opened her eyes only slightly. Moments passed. He patted her limp hand. "*Cara Mamma.*"

Alda knocked on Mario's bedroom door. He appeared, his hair disheveled, as Alda paced the hallway.

"Alda?" She raised her hands as if in despair and shook her head.

"I need to keep moving," Alda said, holding her side. She had just felt her first contraction. "You should go to your mother now. It's happening."

"Take my arm," Mario said, noting her discomfort. She held onto the banister with one hand and threaded his arm with the other as they headed downstairs.

Entering Elvira's room, finding Floro and Ugo sitting in silence, Alda went to the little sink to refresh the cloth for her. She whispered, "Don't worry, Elvira," passing the cloth across her forehead, as if anointing her. Suddenly she realized they had to call the priest. At that moment, Pietro entered. *So what if he's an atheist with an aversion to priests. He isn't dying.* She knew Elvira would want the last sacrament, so she implored Mario to run to the rectory.

As Alda paced, hoping for a miracle, another silent half-hour passed before the priest entered and anointed Elvira's forehead with extreme unction.

When Alda had another contraction, she said, "Show yourself, *bambolo!*" still begging her child to be born. When the priest completed the last rites and left the room, offering condolences, Alda stood holding Elvira's hand, while Floro sat on the opposite side, watching. Finally, she heard a long expiration coming from Elvira. Alda shook her head. Tears streamed down her face. How like Elvira it was to go so quietly, to die with her only wish unfulfilled. Floro rested his head on his mother's hand. Mario's hand lay on his brother's shoulder, waiting his turn to say goodbye to his mother. Floro finally got up and looked at his wife. He left the room, calling Clara to attend stunned Alda and to summon the doctor, who would perform two functions: write his mother's death certificate and help birth his wife's baby.

Exhausted and delirious, Alda wondered how she'd found herself suddenly horizontal on a bed. She heard a vague command to push yet felt no pain. Her mind swirled in a dreamy fog in which she tried to breach a wall with no door. She had the sense that her mother was on the other side. Or was it Elvira? She found a soft panel where a window should be. Would she finally meet her mother by suffering the same fate? The thought of her child growing up without a mother made Alda's eyes open wide.

She cried out: "*Niente da fare!*! Not that!" The cycle of life coinciding with death would stop with her right now. Alda heard another plea and felt a tug and a flush as a vital mound of flesh exited her body. An infant wailed.

"*Una bellisima bambina!*" Alda stared. *A girl? Elvira!* The doctor laid the infant by her side as Clara bent towards Alda's ear. "Signora. She is perfect."

"Clara," she struggled, "get my husband."

"Of course."

Four stiff men stood in the room around Elvira's body. Floro turned as Clara entered.

"Is everything…?"

"Fine, Signor Floro." Clara made the sign of the cross, looking at Elvira lying there. "La signora Alda is fine. She has a baby girl."

"Oh Clara, *grazie*. Stay here a moment with my mother." he said.

He skipped steps, rushing up the stairs. Approaching his wife's bed: "*O bella!*" he cried. He kissed her hand, brushing her hair from her damp face.

"Oh Floro! Your mother died convinced I was having a boy. If only she knew I won't be alone in this house full of men."

"She knows." Floro stroked her head as Alda looked towards the window.

"*Benvenuto, bambina!*" Floro carefully touched the baby's head. "I'm your *babbo.*"

There was no time for dissolving. Alda had a funeral to arrange. The next day Ugo, Mario, Floro and Pietro carried Elvira's casket out onto a shiny black carriage. Alda, who insisted on attending, waited at the threshold of the front door. Dressed in opaque black, she moved slowly as Floro came and held her arm. Not yet thirty, at that moment Alda felt like an old woman. The family procession filed behind the carriage, with scores of friends and neighbors following. As the cortege walked to the mass down the street, church bells tolled for Elvira's passing. Afterwards they buried her at the Porte Sante, the cemetery high on the hill flanking the early Christian church of San Miniato al Monte.

After the funeral, as the family entered the house, they dispersed in every direction. When Floro bounded up the stairs, Alda heard him sob for the first time. As if in a trance, she walked about until she found Clara in the sitting room, rocking the bassinet.

"Oh Clara," she said, sapped of force. "Would you bring me some tea?"

"Right away, signora."

As she collapsed on the chair next to the bassinet, Alda realized that this should be a joyful time, but she was overwhelmed. Elvira's long illness and death was the first she'd experienced so intimately. She was bitter, admonishing herself and God for depriving her mother-in-law of her last wish. While her limp hand rested on the bassinet, Alda looked away from her baby daughter.

The swaddled newborn, as if a wise old soul wanting to coax her mother out of deep despair, reached to squeeze her hand. Alda sat straight up, staring at the ceiling, stunned by the astonishing power of her infant's grasp. A knot formed in her throat as her baby held on. How could a mother ignore such conscious determination summoning her back to life? Finally looking at her infant, Alda's tense shoulders released. As months of pent-up tears streamed down her cheeks, Alda felt a great peace wash over her.

EXPANSION

Winter 1930

Clara's sister Palma, who had arrived months earlier to help with the baby, entered the kitchen holding nine-month-old Anna in her arms.

"Signora, are you feeding an army? There must be fifteen pots on the stove!"

Alda laughed, explaining that there was a pot for the Rafanelli brothers' rice, a pot for everyone else's pasta, one for the sauce, another for the boiled meats, one for Anna and the family's vegetables… and two pans waiting, one for the fish and the other to brown the veal cubes for the *fricassea.* "And this big pot is for the leftover bread, bones and vegetables for the cats and old Yusk." She looked down at the poor skeletal dog, whose spirit and appetite had not returned since Elvira's death.

While still wearing black mourning for her mother-in-law, Alda moved about her kitchen with lightness and confidence. She kissed her baby in Palma's arms. "Your food is almost ready, *bambina.*" Baby Anna started mouthing: *Ba ba ba.* "*Babbo*, eh?" Alda smiled. "How about MaMaMa?"

Anna wailed. She'd just nursed her, but it wasn't enough. "*Un momento,*" Alda urged, mashing some carrots for the baby just as Ugo walked through the door. Naturally, she thought, the patriarch always had a great sense of timing.

"Why are you letting my little *nipotina* cry?" he demanded, reaching for the baby; with one arm still banded in black, Ugo lifted his granddaughter as she continued to fuss. "*Mio tesoro!* What in the world is the matter? Are they not feeding you on time? You better get used to it," he insisted, and Anna stopped crying. "You see what a charmer I am," Ugo said. In this household

96

of men, this granddaughter was the princess. As Ugo carried her off, Alda peeked around the corner and watched him stand before a walnut sideboard he'd commissioned from a local craftsman. Raising the baby's hand up to the wooden cornice frieze, he placed her little finger in the gargoyle's gaping mouth, pretending it would bite. "*Aiii,*" he teased, pulling her finger away from the dangerous carved mouth. Baby Anna giggled.

Alda smiled at her daughter's delight and that Elvira had been right. Just as predicted, the baby had transformed Ugo. She only wished Elvira were around to share the joy.

"I know, *amore.* They'll let us starve!" Ugo said to the baby.

"Two more minutes, Annina," Alda called as she slipped back into the kitchen to mash the vegetable and potato *pappa,* letting it cool.

At the front door, Alda heard Floro's familiar, enthusiastic *peep di di peep peep peep* whistle that announced his arrival. She was relieved. The loss of his mother had been so hard on him. Now he'd made a point of transforming the gloom.

"*Buona sera, a tutti,*" he chimed, putting his newspaper on the table.

"*Buona sera,*" Clara, Palma and Alda responded in unison as he kissed his wife's cheek.

"Where's the *bambina?*" he asked, looking at the empty basket. Alda raised her eyebrows, challenging him to guess. "My father is obsessed with that baby!" Floro laughed, sitting down at the table. "Alda... this afternoon we are going to Grassina. No excuses. The butcher slaughtered the pigs this morning."

"Oh Floro, it's too cold to take Anna to the villa..."

"Signora," Palma interjected, "I'll make sure *la bambina* is well swaddled and keep her close to the hearth!"

Floro said, "So, it's settled. We'll all go."

"*Va bene,*" Alda smiled. She relished watching the butchers make sausage links and cure the *salami* and *prosciutto,* all done at the *casa colonica,* the farm building attached to the villa.

"It will be good for you to get out," Floro insisted, rubbing his hands from the cold outside.

Later that afternoon, Floro's car slowed to first gear going up the steep hill towards the villa. Mario sat up front with his brother. In the back seat, between Palma and Alda, baby Anna napped in her basket. As the car turned into the driveway, Alda gazed over the wall down onto the fields. The land appeared bald and stark, the earth a red-brown. Although while living in the city she always yearned for the villa, seeing its dormant landscape filled her with melancholy. The leafless grapevine branches were pruned to thin arcs, splayed above the rows like tamed whips forced into behaving against their wild will. Everything lay fallow, in a hunkered-down state. Even the harvested olive grove was resting, relieved of its fruit.

While Floro parked in the courtyard, she looked up at the villa's wide façade. Taking her baby from the basket, she walked up the steps towards the front door. The terrace was barren without her red geraniums and the display of lemon trees in their enormous antique terracotta vases. Once inside, Alda peered out the glass door to the wooded garden park.

"This is where I foraged for mushrooms with your *nonna*," she told baby Anna.

After Floro built a fire in the hearth, fanning smoke from the damp wood, he stood behind his wife, noting her solemn mood.

"Come on, Alda. The pigs, remember!"

She turned. "Go on. I'll be over soon, Floro."

"You promise?" Mario said as he patted her shoulder.

"Promise," she said and the brothers walked out the door.

December and January were always cold and damp in the villa, but it seemed particularly bone chilling today. She nursed Anna and made sure she was well bundled before handing her to Palma.

First, Alda explored the *cantina* under the terrace to check on the new wine and olive oil. Lifting a round wooden cover, she admired the green olive oil in one of the many terracotta jars around the room. Approaching the old wine kegs, she found the musty air suffocating and rushed outside to breathe. Just then she heard a cleaver pounding, followed by a ruckus of male voices coming from the attached farm building.

Ascending the stone steps, Alda sensed excited energy emanating from the room. Once over the threshold, she was assaulted by the sight of raw pig, black pepper, cloves, garlic and the hefty smell of fresh roasting sausages, some already hanging from the wooden rafters. The figures of Mario, Floro, their farmer Giovanni and the butcher were dark silhouettes against the fire blazing in the room. The room reverberated with their loud voices and laughter. She felt like an interloper, until Floro waved her over to taste a grilled sausage.

"*Senti questo! Squisito!*" Offering her a bite, he ushered her towards the butcher, who tossed another link on the grill.

"Delicious," she admitted, but felt wobbly.

"Come," Floro insisted, motioning to the enormous table full of pig bones picked clean. The pig's heart, liver, lard and the cleaned intestines, used as casing for the *salami*, all sat in a large bowl. The butcher was processing one of the mixes for the sausages, adding lean beef for the Tuscan *salami*. More fat and fennel seeds were on hand for the *finocchiona*, a Florentine specialty. Two other helpers, with their arms extended, hand-mixed the ground meat with the spices, garlic and salt. Another man turned the handle of the meat grinder, churning the raw *salami* mix, while yet another helped slip the mix into its casing. Watching the preparation of the fat *finocchiona salami* had always fascinated Alda, and she'd always loved the smell of fresh roasting sausages, but she shifted her gaze away only to find two pale, thick pig heads lying on an inclined board. Nothing was wasted. The next day the heads would be boiled and wrapped in cloth, for another Florentine specialty. Seeing all this rawness, her head and stomach churned.

"Signora Rafanelli," the butcher nodded as Alda turned away, steadying herself. Raw meat was everywhere. Two posterior pig legs were inclined on another table, soon to be seasoned and dried under rock salt to become *prosciutto*. When she spied the pig's red blood dripping into a bucket and heard the sound of it hitting the tin, her insides revolted, and she rushed out of the room.

Floro followed as she headed down the steep stairs. "What's wrong?" he pleaded, taking her arm once she was outside leaning on the *cantina* wall. "You look so pale; are you alright?"

"Oh yes," she answered.

"Then, what is it?" he asked again. She took his hand and fixed her eyes on her husband. Despite the nausea, she beamed.

"*Caro* Floro," she said, "this one we'll name after you."

GOOD TIMES

September 1936

"Slow down, Flora!" Alda insisted. "You'll break something." When her six-year-old daughter collapsed in laughter, Alda again marveled at the difference between her two girls. Flora Elvira, named to honor both her father and grandmother, was a robust child with dark hair and a giddy lightheartedness that contrasted with her golden-haired sister Anna's more serious, sylphlike presence.

That summer at the villa was a time of playfulness for everyone. Alda loved hearing the unbridled laughter of her girls as they played hide and seek with their father in the back woods. She imagined Floro was particularly lighthearted since, after six years, she was expecting her third child in October.

When Floro's cousin Ilda arrived for her annual visit, his antics and Florentine humor, which revealed a person's Achilles heel, was at a peak. One afternoon Alda also invited her old friend Adriana over. The three women were sitting under the *loggia* in the afternoon, chatting happily, when Floro suddenly appeared.

"*Buona sera, donne!*" he exclaimed, exaggerating a bow while holding one arm stiff. Alda sensed he was up to something; she watched her husband walk in a straight line away from them, bending his knees, keeping one arm straight, opening his hand. She was unable to see that from his sleeve, with each step, he was quietly depositing a trail of hidden gunpowder on the terrace. Alda, keeping one eye on him, again began engaging in conversation with her friends. Floro relaxed on a wicker chair and took a newspaper out of his pocket, casually reading. Moments later, when he was sure the women weren't paying attention, Floro lit his pipe and nonchalantly extended his long arm down with the match still lit. After one failed attempt, he struck another match and it took. As a little yellow and blue flame traveled towards the women, they leapt up screaming. It fizzled out a short distance from their feet, leaving smoke and a metallic odor in its wake. Alda pursed her lips at her husband, whose shoulders shook with laughter as he puffed on his pipe. She couldn't help smiling.

"O *ragazzo! Fai ridere i polli*," she called. Little boy, you make even the chickens laugh.

"He's worse than a hailstorm," Adriana added. After surveying the ground for any remaining danger, the women resettled into another lively conversation.

That night, after saying goodbye to Adriana, Floro's mischief continued. When they went to bed, he and Alda always used the stairway behind the kitchen, avoiding the narrow spiral stairs. Since the railroad-style villa had no corridor on the second floor, when Floro and Alda retired for the evening they had to knock on Ilda's door to pass through her room to get to theirs.

"*Permesso?*" Alda called.

"*Entrate!*" Ilda insisted, already in bed, covering herself with a sheet up to her chin.

Floro lurched towards her: "*Via Via Via, Ilda!* Come on, make room for me! What does it matter that you're my cousin?" Although she suspected he was teasing, as Floro insisted on climbing under her sheets Ilda belted out a full-throated, horrified scream.

"Oh Floro. What's gotten into you?"

"Can't you behave?" Alda sighed, pushing her husband toward their bedroom. As Floro laughed heartily she heard Ugo yelling from downstairs:

"What's going on?"

"Nothing, Ugo," Alda called, glaring at her husband as he turned. "Just trying to get a child to bed!"

The following night when Floro approached Ilda sitting on her bed, she was prepared. Under her covers she'd concealed a long-handled iron pan, which she whipped out, waving it menacingly.

Alda laughed as Floro cowered, pretending to be afraid, exclaiming, "*Aiuto!!*"

Ilda vaulted out of bed with her clothes on, tossing a pillow to Alda.

"Hey!" he cried as both women began pummeling him. A riotous pillow fight ensued, but Alda, abundantly pregnant, was cautious. The flying feathers reminded her of that first intimate evening when she, Adriana and the hunter Floro had plucked the birds together.

The next night Alda insisted they use the spiral stairs that led directly to their bedroom, to avoid bothering his cousin. He complained that there was no light and that the stairway was full of spider nests.

"I've got a candle to lead the way," Alda said.

Floro hesitated before opening the little blue door. She held out the candle and he lit it.

"Alright, madam, after you!" he said, bowing. Chuckling, she held the flame high above her head, singeing dusty webs as she led the way. Floro followed, keeping his head down, making himself as small as possible in a passageway that was not much wider than his shoulders. As Alda opened the door to the second floor and they entered their quarters, she was amazed by Floro's enormous exhale. He coughed, as if hiding his discomfort, and washed his hands at the stone sink below the small window.

"That was an adventure out of Dumas!" Alda joked, her eyes glowing with the candle.

Floro glared. "Never again!"

"I'll keep those stairs pristine. We'll install a light," Alda insisted as they passed the little sitting room to reach their bedroom.

As Alda turned on their bedside lamp, Floro closed the long shutters. A moment later she heard him jump and cry out. *"Gesu di Dio!"*

"Floro! Taking God's name in vain!?"

"God? What kind of a god would make an ugly spider like that?!" he shouted, pointing to the floor. "I knew one would drop on me walking up those stairs."

She walked over to see that indeed the spider *was* enormous. She glanced at her husband, waiting to see what he'd do, but he retreated and sat on the bed, immobile.

"Alright, I'll just shoo it outside," Alda offered, never wanting to hurt any creature.

"Oh no. He's too big. He'll return. You have to kill him," Floro insisted.

"Va bene, caro," she sighed, picking up one of her husband's slippers. She walked to the window, half-heartedly slapping the slipper down on the spider. Suddenly hundreds and hundreds of tiny black specks, baby spiders, fanned out all over the floor. Floro let out an involuntary yelp, lifted his legs and sat cross-legged on the bed. Alda couldn't help laughing.

"That was no he, *amore*! No wonder she was so enormous. That poor pregnant *mamma*, carrying all those babies." She stared at Floro. His face was ashen.

"Oh Floro, don't worry. I'll take care of this." She was suddenly serious, going for the broom. In her state Alda couldn't bear to stomp out the spider babies so, before Floro could protest, she swept them all outside the floor-to-ceiling window. She looked at him, amused. Now she knew his secret. Her monumental man was actually afraid of something.

FROM NEW YORK CITY TO GRASSINA

September 1975

As I stood before Giovanni Bellini's peaceful painting of *St Francis of Assisi* at the Frick Collection, its mystical blue-green light colored my mood. I felt ambivalent about leaving my job at this venerated museum after nearly three years. It had been a privilege to walk around the collection daily, give slide lectures to the public and, on occasion, witness masterpieces being restored on the second floor near my office. But nothing could cloud my excitement about moving back to Italy and having a chance to write, surrounded by a

Camilla in the Fiat 500, September 1975.

landscape similar to this captivating Bellini. Aldo's generous offer to live on the second floor of his villa made my dream of returning possible. I stared at the painting of St Francis, wondering about my decision to live in Aldo's home, wondering about his expectations…

Despite my last-minute questions, a week later I found myself driving with Aldo towards Grassina in his dark blue Peugeot. Puccini's *Turandot* played on the radio.

"Isn't that Pavarotti?"

"*Brava,*" he said, telling me his sister Flora had had lunch with him just before he'd left Italy for America, land of infinite promise. I noted the irony.

"Why would he leave Italy?" I asked.

"Do you have a saying about not being a prophet in your own land?" I nodded, and he said that that was true for Luciano.

As he turned a corner, Aldo pointed to his villa, looming on the hillside. "We're almost home." I quickly turned the radio down.

"Are you absolutely sure your mother is okay with me living on the second floor?" I admonished myself, glancing in the back, filled with my luggage. It was a little late for that question.

"She's delighted," he insisted; "my mother liked you from the first moment she met you."

I doubted this, recalling the mini jean skirt and the noisy clogs I'd worn on that brief visit.

"She decides about people right away. It's actually a weakness of hers," he added. As we drove up the hill flanking his land, I tried to relax.

When Aldo had visited me in New York the year before, he'd reminded me of what a waste it was to have the villa's second floor unoccupied.

When my mother and two sisters met him, despite the fact that he spoke no English, they were charmed. Even my conservative, cautious mother said she trusted him and thought the idea of my living at his villa would be absolutely fine. When Aldo met my friend Hilary, she told him that she'd left Cornell to write poetry and that she and I were attending writing workshops at HB Studios together. After I translated, without skipping a beat he invited Hilary to live and write at the villa too. "There's ample room upstairs," he'd said in Italian, insisting she join me. Extending his kind offer to Hilary made me feel less singled out. I told myself that my friend Aldo was just generous by nature. When she actually decided to join me, I couldn't believe it. My greatest hesitation leaving New York was about missing my family and friends.

Hilary and I excitedly talked about living and writing together. She would arrive a month after me.

As Aldo turned into the villa's long driveway, my throat closed. This wasn't just a casual visit. As we emerged from his car and climbed the wide, precarious steps to the terrace, he pointed to the second floor. "That's your apartment window."

I squinted, looking up. "Am I dreaming?"

"Actually, it was more than a dream," he replied seriously. A little stunned, I ignored his comment and gazed at the beautiful lemon trees, trying to get my bearings. The sound of pots clanging welcomed us as we passed through the big front door. In the kitchen, Aldo's mother was preparing *pranzo*.

"*Cara*..." she said warmly, *dear*, wiping her hands on a dishtowel and embracing me. Smiling, she introduced Vanda, the farmer Gigetto's wife, who was assisting her.

I nodded, hoping my Italian was up to the task of full immersion. Although Aldo had learned a few comical phrases during his New York visit, neither he nor anyone in his family spoke more than a few words of English.

Savonarola chair, second floor
apartment at the villa, 1975.

Pots and pans jammed the stove.

"What smells so heavenly?" I asked.

"*Papardelle al coniglio*," his mother said. My mouth watered at the notion of rabbit stew with the wide flat pasta. "You've had a long journey. Make yourself comfortable. It will be a while."

Aldo looked impatiently at his mother.

"May I help?" I interjected.

"Oh, not today, dear. By the time you settle in and get refreshed, I'll be ready," she said, giving Aldo a stern look.

"*Grazie*," I turned, wrestling my suitcase from Aldo, who in turn wrestled it back.

"*Per favore*," he insisted, and I relented.

As I followed him down the corridor I said that I hoped his mother hadn't gone out of her way to cook something special for me.

"We eat like this every day. She's delighted. It's just the three of us. She used to feed a much bigger family with no problem, only she's never on time."

I told him I would be on my own schedule; they weren't to fuss for me. Along the corridor I noted the same trunks were in the same space they'd occupied the summer before. It was as if he and his mother hadn't settled in after years. At the corridor's end we reached the little blue door to the spiral sandstone staircase. Winding around to the second floor, when Aldo opened the door my mouth dropped. There was the same rustic conglomerate stone sink I remembered, but the rest of the space had been transformed into a sweet little kitchen, with a proper stove, fridge and built-in cabinets. Aldo opened one stocked with glassware, plates and orange juice in wax paper containers.

"What's all this?" I turned, looking at him, stunned to see what he had prepared for my arrival.

"When I visited you in New York I noticed you drank orange juice each morning," he said, throwing in English words, trying to calm me.

"My God! You shouldn't have gone to all this trouble!" I insisted.

"I want you to feel at home," he reverted back to his language. "You need a kitchen, right?"

I nodded, but I'd never expected all these changes. Had I thought I would use the kitchen downstairs? That was his mother's domain. Clearly I hadn't thought through the logistics. We moved into the next room, formerly empty and dust-laden. It was now a pristine dining room with an antique oval table covered with a popsicle-orange and white apple blossom tablecloth. And against the wall, on an antique sideboard's marble top, an enormous burnt-sienna glazed pot sat brimming with tall yellow yarrow and other dried flowers, arranged to welcome me. I felt overwhelmed.

"I finally restored some of the furniture broken during the war. Please, try out this chair," he said, pulling it out for me, sensing I might faint.

"I can't believe what you've done!" I said, sitting, already feeling squeamishly indebted. Had I really expected to find the second floor in the same cobweb-ridden condition as the year before? When he opened the blue-gray arched 'original *cinquecento*' double door, I bent to peer into the next room and gasped. No broken furniture. No Miss Haversham sitting there. This was now a spotless bedroom. I had presumed I would roll up my sleeves to help put the place in order, but Aldo had already transformed these rooms into a beautiful apartment.

As I approached an antique iron bed covered with a thick pink and white blanket, I said, "*Dio mio!* It's perfection; there's nothing left for me to do!" He looked at me, perhaps sensing my fear mixed with my gratitude. I patted the blanket and discovered an electric one underneath it. Aldo noticed my surprise.

"It's very damp and cold here in the winter. This electric blanket is the modern version of *il prete*." When I looked confused, he explained. "Years ago, people warmed and dried their beds with hot coals cradled in a cage. This house still doesn't have central heating, but I thought you seemed strong and willing. I installed a little wood stove, so you should be just fine. I moved here five years ago to live full-time. My mother moved in two years ago. For fifty years this was strictly my family's summer retreat."

"I'm not worried. It never freezes here, right?"

Aldo changed the subject, showing me a large honey-colored armoire standing against the wall for hanging my clothes. As he laid my suitcase on a trunk at the foot of the bed, he motioned towards another door.

"You might want to freshen up before coming down to lunch. Take your time."

Before he walked away, I opened the door and found a small bathroom, complete with shower and bidet. My pulse accelerated.

"Wait a second, Aldo! This wasn't here the last time I was here, was it?"

"It's very tiny."

"You installed this bathroom for me?"

"It was way overdue!" he insisted. "This villa was built hundreds of years before plumbing. The second floor needed urgent updating. Your coming was just a good excuse. Please don't worry!"

I turned, wanting to sit down, and noticed a scissor chair next to the long vertical window.

"That's a Savonarola! The Frick has a few with tassel ropes across them, so no one would sit on them. May I?"

"Absolutely! Unlike the ones in the Frick, this is a reproduction," he laughed.

The stiff wooden chair creaked as I sat gathering my thoughts. "I'll try to find a job right away, to offset some of your expenses," I offered. After a brief pause he pointed to a typewriter sitting on an elegant little desk.

"This is your job," he said. "It's why you came."

How had I missed it? I rose slowly to examine the beautiful little typewriter. "What?" I asked, about to burst out crying. "Aldo!"

"I used to work for Olivetti. It's an electric Praxis. Got a very good price. It wasn't a big deal. You're here to write, aren't you?" he said, but I was too stunned to speak. "You need to settle in a bit. Come down for lunch when you're ready. *Stai tranquilla*. Relax," he rushed, escaping my deluge of thoughts.

I fretted about his efforts, about the expectations he had for me and the ones I had for myself. He'd gone to too much trouble trying to make me feel comfortable. Wasn't there a cliché about a measure of struggle being fodder for writers? I went to the bathroom and washed up. Splashing water on my face, I stared in the mirror. I turned towards my beautiful quarters and the typewriter. "*Calma*." Soon I headed down the swirling stairs for lunch. On the first floor, Aldo's mother's cooking lured me down the corridor. She and Aldo were both already sitting at the table. He got up and held a chair out for me.

"Oh, please!" I insisted, appreciating the gesture but feeling like I was in some chivalrous time warp. "Sorry if I kept you waiting."

"Not at all," his mother said as Vanda appeared with a platter of *antipasti*. After devouring slices of homemade *salami* accompanied by luscious fresh figs from their garden, the next course arrived. "I hope you like rabbit pasta," she asked.

"*O signora, sì!*" I told her I'd first tasted rabbit two summers earlier, the day I'd met Aldo in Carrara.

The large flat *parpardelle* with her rabbit sauce awakened taste buds I never suspected I had. I ate, thinking it was a single-course meal, but soon boiled meats, sautéed porcini mushrooms, white cannellini beans and Swiss chard appeared on the table. Aldo spooned an oily green sauce over the sliced boiled beef, explaining that it was his mother's *salsa verde* made with chopped parsley from the garden, garlic and their olive oil. His mother apologized that the oil was tired – nearly a year old. It still tasted amazing to me.

"You'll see the difference after the olive harvest in November," she said.

"I'm very excited about the grape harvest, the *vendemmia,* this weekend," I said.

Soon the next course of fruit and cheese was brought out, which was followed by *la torta della nonna,* a cake with powdered sugar and almonds.

"You can't possibly eat like this every day?"

"*Certo,*" Aldo grinned. Having struggled all my life with my weight, I wondered how most Italians could be so thin. The meal lasted the whole afternoon. Afterwards his mother suggested I nap.

"Do as you would in your own home."

Lie down after such a huge meal? I never ate like that and rarely napped. I was relieved when Aldo suggested a walk.

Before touring the dark, musty *cantina* below the terrace, I asked him about the enormous wine barrel sitting out in the sun. Encrusted with crystals, I noted its crimson tinge.

"That's from years of wine soaking into its grain. This barrel used to store wine, but it's now obsolete, so I'm going to use the thick chestnut wood to make a large harvest table and two benches."

I thought it wonderful that the barrel would have a new life. As we walked around the corner, he pointed to a small building.

"This door leads to the *limonaia,* where our lemon trees now on the terrace are stored in the winter. The other door is the entrance to our farmer Gigetto's place. He lives here with his family. Come. Let me introduce you."

When Aldo pushed aside strips of glass beads hanging from the threshold, they made clicking sounds. "*Permesso,*" he called in. A small man with lively eyes appeared.

"*Buona sera, signor Aldo e signorina.*"

"*Buona sera,*" Aldo and I responded simultaneously as we entered the dark room. I noted Gigetto's rough hand as he shook mine. He offered us limoncello in tiny glasses. We clinked glasses. "*Salute,*" we said and sipped the lemony alcoholic drink. I shared my enthusiasm for the upcoming grape harvest, my first. He nodded. For him it meant a lot of work and a lot of people. We thanked him and walked outside.

Aldo pointed to his new vines, long perpendicular rows sloping down towards the village. "Gigetto and I planted these a year before your first visit and now they're ready!" He explained that grapevines took three years to mature, adding that this would be their first harvest too.

As we passed a windowless small brick building with little arched openings shaped like half-moon slits, I asked him what it was.

"It's a *fienile*, where we store hay. These crescent openings are for aeration." He added that he and Gigetto also use the floor to store olives, to keep them out of the elements until the entire grove is harvested. "It would be great to press our olives on the same day we haul them in, but it's just the two of us. The harvest takes over a month."

"Really? If I helped, it would go faster."

He looked at me, surprised. "Yes, it would, but that's not why you're here."

"Are you kidding? I love any excuse to be outside. Helping with the harvest could be one small contribution after all you've done for me. And when Hilary comes, if she's willing, your workforce will double. We'll find time to write in between. I am more productive if I have a structured schedule."

"*Favoloso*," Aldo said as we ambled towards the wooded park behind the villa. He referred to it as the *giardino Inglese*, a formal English garden. I noticed it'd gone wild. Beyond the pine and oak trees and laurel bushes, a thick line of cypress trees flanked the road. We sat on a stone bench by the glass doors, breathing in the synergistic scent of the woods around us.

"It's so peaceful," I sighed. "How fortunate we are to be here now. I can't imagine how hard it must've been during the war."

He nodded. I sensed there were scars, even though he was so young then.

Once we re-entered the house, I looked at the framed photographs perched on top of the piano. I stared at a formidable face.

"That's my father, Floro. He died after the war, when I was seven."

"I'm sorry," I said, picking up another picture, of his sister Flora, dressed as Suzuki in *Madame Butterfly*. He told me that she had performed that mezzo soprano role many times to great acclaim.

"And is this smiling, chubby toddler you?"

"No," Aldo said, "that was my brother Ugo. He died of meningitis, not long after this picture was taken."

"Oh my God. No. Your poor mother. I can't imagine."

"It was an impossible time for her, and my sisters. I never knew him. He was born five years before me," Aldo said. "I mentioned last summer there was a sad reason I couldn't swim."

"Yes?"

"When this baby was ten months old my parents took him and my sisters for a seaside vacation. He contracted meningitis there. My mother always blamed that sojourn for his death, so after I was born, she didn't allow me near the sea until I was a teenager."

"It must've been a horrific time," I said.

"Among others, yes," Aldo said.

I patted his arm, feeling overwhelmed. "You know, maybe I will take that little rest after all."

"Good idea," he nodded. "Dinner will be around eight."

At the end of the corridor I headed back up and sat on my bed, staring at the uneven terracotta tiles on the floor, worn down by all the footsteps that had trodden here before me. Despair and pleasure took place in this room. Carbon molecules from the breath of those who'd lived here could still be floating around. How did I come to be a part of this nearly five-century procession?

I walked towards the long window and looked down on the terrace and vineyard beyond. When we'd arrived here at high noon, the sun had felt razor sharp. Now, in the late afternoon, a subdued crepuscular light descended like a gentle shroud. I wanted to belong here, if even for a brief time. I opened my suitcase, hanging jackets, skirts and blouses in the armoire, spreading my belongings, taking possession of the room. Pulling out the top dresser drawer, I found lavender sachets. Lifting them to my nose, I inhaled the heavenly scent. Had Aldo's mother made them for me? I would be forever grateful for what they'd done to make me feel at home.

Tired, I lay down on the antique bed and fell into a deep slumber. When I stirred, it was dark outside. Startled and disoriented, I turned on my bedside lamp, checking my watch, still on American time. I calculated it was eight o'clock, time for dinner. Anxious not to be late, I quickly changed my clothes. I found the light for the spiral staircase. While descending, out of the corner of my eye I spied two dark dangling creatures on the wall and recoiled. As I gaped at the pair of black scorpions, a shiver rose up my spine. Quickly retreating, I closed the little blue door. I didn't know scorpions lived in Italy. *Aren't they desert creatures?* I unlatched the door again, hoping they had miraculously vanished. But there they dangled, menacingly. I swore I heard their appendages rattle. "*Merda,*" I cried. *Okay, relax. It's their territory. Just scoot by. But if they move, they might easily slip under this door, into my kitchen, my dining room and... oh God, into my bedroom.* The thought of finding one nestled under my pillow or in my shoe made me shudder. They were like miniature dragons. "Okay, you can do this!" I pep-talked myself, deciding to slay them. I removed a shoe, debating the angle, then froze as their alert curving tails seemed to warn me that they were poised to strike. Gasping, I resolutely took aim. Rather than hold my shoe steady, I launched it and closed my eyes. Hitting a random part of the wall, my useless shoe fell on the stairs. In my horror and panic, I believed I saw the pair scurry and drop. A bloodcurdling scream escaped from my throat. Shutting the door again quickly, I retreated to my bed, where I sat, crossed-legged. I considered sealing the door with industrial tape and using the main, wide front staircase as my access, even if it was at the opposite end of the long villa. I was disgusted with myself as I prepared to bequeath my shoe to those creatures forever. I knew that at the bottom of the spiral stairs there was another door with direct access to the woods. *This second floor has been vacant for over thirty years. I am the intruder. Who knows what other crawling creatures might already occupy my quarters?*

Suddenly startled out of my reverie, I heard a loud BAM, then another. My face reddened. Aldo... slaying both scorpions and saving my shoe. *Damsel in distress! Damn!* Had his mother heard my pathetic scream? *Way to go, Capitana America.*

"Are you okay?" Aldo, my knight-in-shining-armor, said as he tiptoed into my room. "I'm so sorry. I promise that's the first time I've ever seen scorpions on that wall."

"Oh sure," I guffawed, thanking him for coming to my rescue. He understood I felt foolish and began to say something to level things.

"Don't worry, I'm absolutely terrified of spiders, like my father and my sister Flora," he admitted, adding that if I ever found one near him, I could come to his rescue. I remained silent as he recounted the story of his father taking refuge on this bed after discovering a huge pregnant spider. "My mother saved the situation. She still laughs about all the baby spiders fanning out on the floor."

I didn't laugh. "So, you have a lot of big spiders here?"

Aldo was evasive. "Oh, that was thirty years ago!" I got up and shook my shoe before putting it on. As he led the way down the spiral stairs, I wrapped my arms tightly around myself, avoiding the narrow walls. I finally exhaled as he opened the door. Once back downstairs in the corridor, I was again captivated by the most tantalizing smell wafting from his mother's kitchen. Forgetting fear, my only desire was to taste the food connected to the wafting.

Grape harvest at the villa, 1975.

Vendemmia crew.

Aldo playing around with friends Lisa and Don.

Harvest lunch under the loggia.

GRAPE HARVEST AT THE VILLA

Autumn 1975

I awoke with a start, sensing the sun had risen long ago, that I'd overslept once again. All week I'd been having wild dreams like never before and had slept until noon. I faulted jet lag and the tightly shuttered windows that kept the room completely dark. Aldo's mother decided I must be a person with a clear conscience to sleep so well. Switching on my bedside lamp, I checked my watch and panicked. Today was the *vendemmia*. It was already past nine. Why hadn't I brought an alarm clock with me? Why was I sleeping so many hours? Bolting up, I pushed out one shutter with such force that it hit the façade with a crack. I flinched as light flooded in, relieved that the old shutter hadn't sprung loose from its hinges and decapitated someone below. Hanging over the rail, I looked down on the sunny courtyard. Aldo, having heard the clatter, looked up as he loaded large plastic vats onto his truck with Gigetto.

"*Buon giorno*, signorina." He waved, seeming amused. I returned the wave, assuring him I'd be right down. In my nightgown, my hair spiraling in every direction, I retreated from their view. I combed out the snarls, dressed quickly in jeans and a tee shirt and bolted downstairs. I peeked into the kitchen where Alda was instructing Vanda – and Milena, another helper – to monitor a dozen pots on the stove. While exchanging morning greetings, I eyed the vats of sausages and beans, part of the traditional preparation for the harvest lunch. Aldo had mentioned that thirty or forty people were expected.

"Am so sorry to be late, signora! What can I do to help?" I kept forgetting to call his mother Alda.

"Aldo is expecting you in the fields today, if you don't mind," she winked, already aware I was more at home outside than in the kitchen.

I smiled. She pointed out a tall pot of espresso and warm milk, already prepared for my morning *caffè latte*, with toast and marmalade. I sat dunking toast and sipping at the table as they labored, telling myself soon I would make my own breakfast upstairs.

"*Mille grazie*," a thousand thanks, I said, which weren't nearly enough for the kindness I'd already felt that first week. Excusing myself, as I rushed to open the heavy front door I collided with Aldo, who held out a straw hat for me.

"Oh Aldo! So sorry! When is everyone arriving?"

"Almost everyone is here. Come meet my friends."

A crowd equipped with gloves, shears and baskets gathered near the *cantina*. All eyes looked up, fixed on the American occupying their friend's second floor. As Aldo made introductions, Ernesto, whose copious hair reminded me of a dark young Einstein, flashed me a peace sign. Then Aldo introduced Fabrizio, his arrow-wielding and treehouse-making partner. His elegant wife Vanna reached for my hand and said in perfect English, "Pleased to meet you," the first English I'd heard all week. His oldest friend Filippo (whom Aldo had spent summers with in Gubbio) appeared with his Sicilian wife Rosanda. And there was Simonetta, who also spoke perfect English, with her smiling husband Eugenio. Aldo's hunting companion and neighbor, Pier Luigi, arrived with his tractor and cart to assist with the harvest. After all the introductions, I looked around, hoping my two friends from New York would appear. Honeymooning in Italy, they had promised to join us. As other harvesters arrived, Aldo divided us into sections on the sloping land. He showed me a row where he began cutting Malvasia, white grape clusters, placing them gently in the basket, careful not to bruise the skins. He explained there were four types of grapes in his vineyard, two red and two white, to make Chianti: the principal grape was Sangiovese; the others were Canaiolo, Malvasia and Trebbiano. I followed his lead, snipping with confidence until I found a thick spiderweb, praying there was no baby-carrying *mamma* in the cluster.

"You wash these, right?" I said as he harvested the grapes enmeshed in the web.

"But of course, Camilla," he said with a suspicious smile.

"Okay, what's so amusing?"

"Everyone with a vineyard prays it doesn't rain in the last weeks before the harvest," he said, continuing to snip. "The more sun, the more concentrated the sugars, the better the wine." He explained that rain breaks the grape skins and dilutes the juice. "You don't want water anywhere near the grapes after they're ripe."

"Oh, good to know," I said.

"The fermentation process sterilizes everything."

"Okay, Signor Rafanelli," I said. "This is all new to me." As he tenderly patted my shoulder, a high-pitched voice rose from behind us. Turning, I realized the voice belonged to Aldo's sister Flora, who was waving a handkerchief as she floated, buoyant, down the hill with my friends Don and Lisa. I was thrilled.

"*Eccoci qua!*" Here we are, Flora cheerfully announced.

"*Ciao*, Flora." I kissed both her cheeks, thanking her for bringing my friends.

"*Ciao, bella,*" she said.

"*Ciao, bella!*" my two friends repeated in unison as we all laughed and embraced.

"Have fun, *ragazzi!*" Flora called as she turned towards the villa, swaying on the clumpy plowed soil, unbalanced in her black pumps as she sauntered up the hill for kitchen duty.

"She's a real character," Don laughed.

"A professional opera singer meets two theater people – you should get along famously," I said. "Meanwhile, I'm so glad not to be the only clueless American at this *vendemmia!*"

Aldo waved when he saw my friends and gave them a crash course in grape picking. He then left us to check on the other harvesters. Observing the volunteer crew lift their vats and spill copious clusters into Aldo's blue truck, we got to work. At noon we broke for the traditional lunch of beans and sausages, served on tables set under the *loggia*.

"How's it going?" Lisa asked as we headed up towards the villa.

"Well, I'm still getting settled. Aldo and his mother have gone to great lengths to make me feel welcome. I've yet to write a line."

"It's only been a week," she said, encouragingly. "Don't be so hard on yourself."

While Aldo's friends milled about the terrace, we three Americans examined what was hanging on the layered *loggia* wall – a sculpted face of the poet Dante and a sweet *putto*, a small terracotta angel's head that was overwhelmed by an enormous oxen yoke that hung next to it. This was now a relic from the pre-tractor era of Aldo's grandfather Ugo.

When Milena opened the front door and appeared with a large pot, the crowd looked up. Aldo followed, wearing his wide-brimmed farmer's hat, raising two pitchers and whistling loudly for attention. As everyone cheered, he began pouring last year's wine. Aldo's mother and sister Flora paused on the top step, as if waiting to be announced. Again, cheers and clapping. La signora Alda motioned humbly for silence as Flora bowed with a flourish. As bowls of sausages and white cannellini beans *al sugo* were served, Aldo's mother walked around greeting and joking with her son's old friends. It was clear everyone loved her.

Sitting across from me, Lisa wore a yellow tee shirt with the Broadway musical *Grease* scrawled across her chest. Aldo, in a playful mood, stood next to my friends holding up a large four-liter demijohn full of wine, its glass protected by a covering of willow branches. Don, an actor on cue, put his head back and opened his mouth as Aldo pretended to pour wine directly into his throat. More laughter and glasses were raised. I felt giddy despite only drinking one glass.

Aldo's sister Anna appeared for lunch with her two young sons, Federico and Luca. Anna, a tall, elegant, blonde beauty, born the year before Flora, was physically very different from her younger sister, who was dark, short and full-figured. Anna reached out her graceful hand and smiled, saying how good it was to see me.

"*Piacere mio*," I responded, greeting her two sons, also so different. Federico, the elder brother, with dark hair and impressive posture, was already statuesque for twelve years old. Luca, not even a year younger than his brother, had hair the color of honey like his mother.

After lunch we returned to the fields, feeling lightheaded. Aldo and Gigetto collected our brimming baskets and carried the harvested grapes in the two trucks. Under the terrace, in the dark *cantina*, they unloaded the voluminous fruit into large wooden vats. The grapes would begin to ferment in a few hours. By sunset the harvest was complete; we returned to the villa, exhilarated and exhausted. The long dinner table reached towards a roaring fire in the hearth. The family photographs had been temporarily moved from the piano top, replaced by mouth-watering Tuscan specialties: *crostini di fegato* — liver canapés (from locally slaughtered fowl for the feast) topped with capers (from the villa's wall), and *fettunta* toasted bread scratched with garlic and smothered in their olive oil. A generous platter of *prosciutto* and *salami* (from the villa's pig, I discovered later) was arranged alongside figs picked from a tree below the terrace.

The jokester Ernesto shook his unruly hair. Raising a whole *salami* from a platter, he alluded to its phallic shape. Aldo's mother playfully tapped the back of his head with her cane.

"Behave yourself, *bambino*, there are children here!" She pointed her cane towards her two grandsons.

Mischief man Ernesto cowered, "O *scusi*, signora." Mirthful Flora raised her eyebrows, merrily elbowing Ernesto. Too many glasses of wine were consumed as Aldo passed around the delicious *antipasti*. Once we all sat down, a delectable pasta course was followed by platters of rabbit, chicken and goose, accompanied by roasted potatoes served with rosemary and olive oil and an assortment of vegetables harvested from the property. After we finished the desserts Anna had made, she asked me if I would be interested in teaching her sons English.

"*Certamente*," I agreed. But as the bawdy comments reached a crescendo, Anna bid everyone goodnight and whisked her boys off.

After dinner Aldo and his male friends stood up and sang Alpine choral songs, some naughty and others anti-war. I laughed at the lyrics: *se vuoi vincere la guerra, sia per mare, sia per terra, fai in maniera che i cannoni siano pieni di maccheroni.* I translated for Don and Lisa: "If you want to win the war, by land or by sea, make sure your cannons are filled with macaroni!"

Flora, clearing her throat, stood up. The room grew quiet. She nodded, her sweet mezzo voice gathering force as she sang a part from Verdi's *Il Trovatore*. Everyone was stunned by the power and beauty of her voice. We clamored to our feet when she stopped, roaring with enthusiasm. She smiled graciously, soaking up the attention, before she sat and gestured modestly with her hand to quash the fanfare. Following Flora, Einstein raised a glass to suggest the Americans sing something. Don, Lisa and I looked at each other in a panic. As people cheered in agreement, we stood and sang a pathetic version of *Oh Danny Boy*, forgetting the words. As we slumped back in our seats, I exclaimed in Italian, referring to Flora: "Impossible act to follow," and everyone laughed and concurred.

As the evening waned, Lisa leaned towards me to tell me how brave I was to leave New York and move to Italy. "Brave?" I responded. I'd been thinking just the opposite, that my coming was some naive romantic notion, that I'd abdicated responsibility by leaving and that for now I was depending on Aldo's kindness. I squeezed Lisa's hand. I was feeling uncertain, despite the joyful *allegria* of the day. At the end of the evening, as we said goodbye, I reluctantly released my friends, who said that when our mutual friend arrived in three weeks, our writing together would be grounding.

Eventually all the guest harvesters staggered off. Aldo and Pier Luigi had to shuttle a number of the inebriated home. Alda sighed as she emerged from the kitchen. Resting on her cane, she recited one of the thousand Tuscan proverbs she apparently resurrected for every situation:

"Non e' il bere, e' il ribere." She shook her head. "It's not the drinking, it's the re-drinking." I laughed and thanked her for the incredible day. Sloughing off my compliments, she said, *"Brava,"* as if congratulating me for having had a good time. Bidding me a *"Buona notte"* with her soothing, deep voice, she slowly retreated to her bedroom at the end of the corridor.

While the last embers pulsated in the hearth, I sat on one of the upright logs Aldo left there for that purpose. Relishing a moment of solitude, I listened to the quiet crackling, the only remaining sound in the room. Watching the light fade where fire had danced all night, the room still reverberated with the energy of the day. Reflecting on the spirit, laughter and the singing, I was reminded of childhood holiday parties, dancing with my sister Sue to the *Firebird Suite*, and of occasions my father sang barbershop quartet songs with friends and relatives. A knot formed in my throat. It'd been too long since I'd experienced mirthful singing.

Aldo finally returned from shuttling his last drunken guest and checking on the grapes in the *cantina*.

"Che giornata spettacolare," I exclaimed as he moved an upright log to be closer.

"Meno male. That's a relief. I'm so happy you enjoyed it!" he said. Sitting shoulder-to-shoulder, we watched the glowing embers turn to ash. I knew he wanted our relationship to shift again, but I was afraid of jumping in and being swept away by an intimate relationship that would muddy matters. Feeling perplexed, I soon stood and thanked him for the astonishing day.

I sensed his disappointment "Aren't you exhausted?"

"Not really," he answered, poking the lingering embers with a long iron prod. I confessed that I was and turned down the corridor, my heart in my throat.

"See you tomorrow – A *domani,*" I said, cheerful but confused.

A swollen moon cast an eerie light on the long narrow corridor leading to the little blue door. I floated up the spiral stairs to my apartment, with no fear of scorpions, my head light from all the wine. I was filled with both wonder and confusion. Needing some solitary grounding, I peered out the little kitchen window, down onto the untamed wooded garden. My eyes traveled the white pebble path, an illuminated labyrinth in the moonlight. Pushing out the window, I was charmed by the alluring sweet song of the resident nightingale that lived in the *boschetto*. My impulse was to rush down, quietly open the little door to the woods and listen to the beautiful warbling from under the *ilex* tree. I hesitated. Aldo, hearing my steps, might misconstrue my intentions. I continued listening from the window, traversing the moonlit path with my eyes. My visual journey paused at the treehouse that he and his friend had built. I imagined tall, skinny Aldo, in his early twenties, balancing on a branch with hammer in hand, nailing the last board, creating a little home away from home.

Brave? I thought again of Lisa's comment. It had taken some courage to make this leap, to have moved to a foreign country that I loved, to have tossed caution to the wind to pursue a dream, yet I had been given a safe refuge. I thought of my sister's idol that became mine, Jane Goodall, researching chimpanzee behavior firsthand, her only credentials passion and discipline. She wasn't foraging for food, she had the support of a foundation for her life and research in Gombe. Yet to sit alone all day observing chimps and sleeping often unprotected overnight in the jungles of Tanzania, now that was courage.

As I looked out at the woods, my mind wandered to a fictionalized wild character, in the Italo Calvino story, *The Baron in the Trees*, and I wondered what it would be like to find a home in branches night and day. I surprised myself with a vision of desire and a segue of thoughts: There I was with Aldo, sneaking out, naked, holding hands and climbing up into the treehouse in the precarious dark, our skin shining under a harvest moon. Abandoning fear, accepting risk, sharing intimacy – was that not one way to understanding? Soon, I felt, I would be the one to approach Aldo.

LIGHT AND LOSS

1936-1937

Early September was tinged with melancholy because their season at the villa would soon be over. While preparing lunch on September 8th, Alda stood lost in thought about their rare evening out with the girls that night, something that always brightened her spirits. Pregnant with her third child after a long hiatus, she and Floro were taking their daughters to *La Festa della Rificolona*, a folkloric Florentine festival of light celebrating the birth of the Madonna. The event was four hundred years old, inspired by farmers and their families living in the countryside. Dressed in their best clothes, they carried lanterns as they journeyed to Florence in the dark, the light guiding their way to the Church of Santissima Annunziata. The farmers always arrived with the excuse of worshiping the miraculous image of the Virgin Mary, but the pilgrimage was also an opportunity for them to sell their food and agricultural products, sustaining themselves for the winter. They set up tables next to the church, under the *loggia* of the foundling home, the Hospital of the Innocents.

Alda was shaken from her festival daydream when she heard the sound of her husband's Fiat horn blasting from the bottom of the hill in Grassina. Whenever the men approached the villa for their midday meal, Floro always warned Alda of their arrival by sounding his horn. Much to his chagrin, his wife had inherited his mother's habit of serving meals late.

In a panic, Alda turned away from the window towards the stove. The *minestra* was ready and she'd already sautéed the mushrooms she'd gathered that morning. They smelled delicious, but that wasn't the main course. She wondered aloud to Clara: "*Che se e' detto di mangiare oggi?*" What did we plan to eat today? Opening the pantry door, she discovered the answer. There lay a platter of fresh birds with feathers still intact.

"*O Dio, gli uccelli!*" Alda cried.

Spinning into high gear, Alda urged Clara to start plucking, and rushed into the hallway, calling upstairs. "Palma! Please come down. I need a big blaze in the hearth." Returning to the kitchen, she joined Clara. They plucked furiously, feathers flying. Alda's heart raced as she castigated herself for wasting time *fra ninnoli* e *nannoli*. She was a consummate daydreamer.

After the last bird was plucked, Alda ran outside and quickly gathered fresh sage leaves. Clara was in the kitchen, slicing the special bread from the Florentine *forno* on Via dei Cerchi. Alda quickly skewered the plucked birds between slices of bread and sage and placed them over a pan where she smothered them with olive oil. Clara prepared the side dishes as Alda raced to the raging fire, attaching the bird skewers to the *rosticceria*. When she cranked up the machine, it made an eerie whistling sound as the birds gently turned on the spit over the fire. After the first few rotations, the men entered the front door.

"*Buon giorno!*" Alda exclaimed, standing in attention. Palma stood flanking her, their backs to the hearth, hoping to hide the raw birds.

"Good afternoon!" Floro stared at his wife suspiciously as she declared:

"Give me five minutes and you can come in for the *antipasto*."

The hungry men returned outside to sit under the *loggia*. When they shut the door, Alda turned, terrified the birds would char with the raging fire, but there was no time to wait for the fire to settle. As they rotated on the spit, she checked on the table and called the men and her children for lunch. While Clara served *antipasti* and the soup, Alda glanced nervously at the flames, until she noticed the limp birds' necks were stiff.

"The birds are ready," she announced.

At the table, she watched as Ugo took his first bite. Stiffening with surprise, he stared and said, "This is the most remarkable bird I have ever tasted." Alda nearly fell off her chair at his rare compliment.

"*Grazie*, Ugo," she said. As all the Rafanelli brothers concurred, she nodded, struggling to suppress her laughter as Clara passed by the table, her eyes open wide with amazement.

While Clara served the dessert, Floro rose from the table, returning moments later holding something behind his back. "Ahem." He got their attention by clearing his throat. Everyone turned to see the surprise. Smiling with pride at his daughters, he held a large lantern on a stick, waving it towards the ceiling. When he lowered it, they saw it was a tiny replica of a medieval building, made of cardboard and covered in shiny gold paper, with cut-out windows.

"You made this, *Babbo?*" Anna exclaimed in delight; her father bowed as both girls got out of their chairs.

Flora screeched: "*Favoloso! Per La festa della Rificolona…*"

After sunset the family drove to the festival of the Madonna. Crossing over the Arno at Ponte Santa Trinita, Alda stared at the children playing along the banks. How the activity around the river had changed! As a little girl, she recalled watching the men who sold sand, *i renaioli*. Standing in long boats, they'd dig the river bottom with infinity poles, filling their boats to the rim with pyramid-shape piles of sand that they'd sell for cement. How, she marveled, did they ever keep their boats afloat with all that weight? And where were all the vendors who used to sell baskets brimming with tiny fish caught in the river, bought to be fried? Now it was just a scene of carefree children removing their shoes and yanking up their skirts and pants at the river's edge. How she would've loved to have waded in the Arno, but her uncle and aunts never let her; they worried she'd catch a cold or some illness.

It was dark by the time Floro parked in Piazza San Marco. From there they walked to Piazza Annunziata. Crowds gathered with festive lanterns in hand. The girls cheered seeing the light shining through the medieval windows of their father's lantern. Holding it up high, they joined a procession of undulating light and color that converged on the church of the Madonna. Approaching Piazza Santissima Annunziata, Alda blessed herself, thankful and excited about the coming of her next child. Would it be a boy this time? Turning, her eyes settled on *l'Ospedale degli Innocenti*, the orphanage where her father had grown up. She was startled as she glanced at the foundling hospital façade. The glazed roundels of swaddled della Robbia orphans shimmered with the blaze of the children's lanterns.

***

On October 16th Alda gave birth to her third child, a boy they named Ugo. Floro boasted, "Well, finally we have a male to carry on the Rafanelli name." He teased Anna and Flora as they peered into the newborn baby's bassinet, "You girls thought you were going to take over, eh?"

Six-year-old Flora and seven-year-old Anna scoffed at their father, cooing at their baby brother, both vying to hold him. The entire household was ecstatic.

The following August, when Ugo was a ten-month-old toddler, Floro insisted on taking the family for a little seaside vacation to escape the heat. Alda hesitated to take him away from the villa, but baby Ugo was so robust.

Under the canopy at the beach, the girls kept their brother occupied. Holding his chubby hands, he took a few steps on the uneven blanket, laughing gleefully as he toppled over. They passed glorious days at the seaside until one day baby Ugo suddenly spiked a high fever.

"We have to get him home," Alda insisted. The panic-stricken family poured into the car, rushing back to the villa to summon the doctor.

Both parents watched over the crib while the doctor approached their little one who lay there listless with distant, glassy eyes and a raging fever. After examining the baby and finding his neck stiff, the doctor looked at them gravely, shaking his head.

Alda wondered why the doctor was shaking his head. She hated his grim face. The walls of the room converged. The doctor took her elbow, motioning for Floro to join him, away from the crib, as if baby Ugo might understand what he was about to say.

"Your baby has meningitis. I am so sorry. There is nothing we can do," he sighed.

"What? Meningitis?" Alda cried, looking wild. "How?" She choked as Floro teetered in silence, grabbing the side of the crib.

The doctor said, "No way to know for certain."

Floro told the doctor he was mistaken, and how their baby had just been laughing all the day prior. "He is the healthiest baby in the world!" he said, insisting this illness would pass.

"I'll return in the morning. Give him water. Put a wet cloth on his forehead."

As the doctor left, Floro stood dumbfounded.

"I refuse to accept this," Alda said, gritting her teeth. "I knew we shouldn't have taken him to the seaside."

"Don't say that! There was no way to know!"

"I had an intuition and didn't follow it."

"That's useless thinking, Alda. He was…" Floro said, choking, "He loved the beach. He could have gotten this anywhere."

"But he didn't. He would have been safe here. We have everything here."

"Alright… so it's my fault," Floro said. "It was my idea to go."

"Oh Floro. Maybe we're both to blame. Now we are in God's hands."

The distraught girls knocked at the door. Alda opened it only slightly, telling them to go to their rooms and pray. Fearing contagion, she wouldn't let them in.

Alda prayed for hours by her baby's crib. Floro wandered out the back of the villa for a cigarette and some fresh air. When he returned, he rested his hand on his wife's shoulder.

"Come to bed. You must get some sleep."

"I can't leave him," she said.

Floro, dejected, went to bed.

In the morning, Palma appeared with coffee and toast, which Alda refused. She had spent the night keeping watch, with no sleep. Floro entered, unable to look inside the crib. He sat by his wife, frozen like a statue.

She said to Floro, "Bring me another cool cloth for the baby's burning forehead." He was relieved to help and escape that room. When he returned with the cloth, Alda covered the limp baby's forehead, whispering a lullaby to her unresponsive boy. Floro stared at the ceiling. For the first time in his life he'd lost his voice.

In a little while Floro heaved a sigh and left the room again, pacing out on the terrace while smoking. It was strange to be alone at the villa without his father or brothers, who'd gone to the mountains for *ferragosto*, the August vacation, to escape the oppressive heat and sun. They should have gone with them, but Alda had longed for a little separate time. He understood living every day with his family was hard on her. Yet his father and brothers were breathing healthy mountain air, unaware of what they were facing at home. He returned inside, staring at the wall and his vigilant wife.

The doctor, after examining the unresponsive baby, ushered Floro and Alda out, whispering: "It would be a blessing if God takes him. Your prayers should be for that. If not, he will be... unrecognizable."

Alda choked, clenching her fist as if she would strike the doctor. Floro put his arm around her, trying to lead her out of the room. She pulled away, returning to the crib as Floro staggered out with the doctor, pleading, "There must be something?"

The doctor looked stern. "I know it's devastating, but the poor soul is already gone."

Alda kept a vigil next to Ugo's crib, without saying a word for hours, without eating. Her head was in a vise. *It's a nightmare. This cannot be. I'll wake up.* When she saw that her baby was gone, she thought she would die too.

She sat by the crib, catatonic.

Floro entered. Seeing Alda's head resting on the side of the crib, he knew. He kissed her head. She prayed Elvira would take little Ugo in her arms and sing to him.

All day, Alda wouldn't let them take her baby. Finally, the next morning, she let go. They buried him up at the Porte Sante, next to his grandmother. In the old graveyard, as they stumbled out, Alda saw only the broken stone columns, gravestones signaling the brief, truncated lives of babies. How did other mothers survive such loss?

For the next month, wearing impervious black, Alda went about her daily chores. She got things done more efficiently than usual, focusing only on the tasks ahead of her, without her normal daydreams and usual happy distractions. She prayed on her kneeler every morning and night, beseeching Elvira, her own mother and her favorite saint to care for their little *bambino*.

Floro entered wearing the black band of mourning around his arm, his whistling silenced. The couple spoke very little. They lived for months in a cocoon. Alda refused to listen to the radio or hear any music. She avoided evening family gatherings in the parlor.

Anna and Flora, also distraught about the loss of their little brother, worried about their parents and needed their attention. When extra good behavior didn't work, the girls tried fighting, to distract their parents from their despair. Nothing worked.

Floro began attending fascist meetings more regularly, involving himself more – anything to get out of the house. His sensitive brother Mario was at his wits' end. While the girls' parents were mentally in absentia, he'd taken over their role. After dinner he encouraged the girls to listen to opera on the gramophone and to the concerts of Martini and Rossi on the radio. He read them adventure books.

With his sister-in-law less vigilant, *Zio* Pietro enthralled the girls with terrible tales of the Inquisition and the burning of Giordano Bruno. A born academic, he grilled them on the history of Florence, on Church hierarchy, on the Medici family. He attempted to delight them with his recitation from memory of key parts of Dante's *Divina Commedia* and the sensual poem *Alcyone*, about summertime in Tuscany, from his favorite living poet and WWI hero, Gabriele D'Annunzio. After many months of Floro and Alda doing the bare minimum tasks and acting like automatons staring out into space, Mario entered the kitchen and slammed his fist on the table.

"*Basta!*" he shouted, startling them. "Anna and Flora need piano lessons. They need to laugh. They need music, art and literature, and most of all they need you back in their lives. Enough! I can only do so much as a bachelor." The sound of his fist banging on the table so hard, over and over, got their attention. Alda responded with a deluge of tears.

"*Va bene*, Mario," she sobbed. She turned to Floro, whose face was flushed. From that day on, Alda engaged with her children and everyone around her, trying to be her old optimistic self. Eventually her old self did emerge. She'd sit while the girls had their piano lessons, listening and watching them play and sing. One afternoon Alda remarked to her husband, "Anna has your perfect ear. Have you noticed how she recognizes perfect pitch?"

"Yes, but also like me she has no voice," he said, shrugging his big shoulders.

"But Elvira Flora? We named that girl well! No question! She's really inherited your mother's voice!"

"Yet her piano teacher complains she never sits still; she's always pulling pranks, teasing," Floro complained.

"I wonder where she got that trait. She has another namesake!" Alda broke into a laugh that felt good because it was real. A moment later she felt ashamed, afraid of forgetting.

SONGBIRDS

September 1975

A week after the *vendemmia*, I was in the kitchen with Alda when we heard a loud *peep-pi-di-pee-pee-peep* whistle at the front door. It was Aldo, announcing his arrival, bursting. Followed by his wiry pointer D'oro, he appeared at the kitchen threshold looking handsome and rugged in his suede jacket. His cheeks were flushed from all his walking the land – the part he loved most about hunting. It was something I loved about him. Wherever we traveled through Tuscany and Umbria he knew every tree, bush and edible field green by name. In a food crisis he'd be the one to save the day with his foraging skills, always gathering wild green volunteers to enliven our salads. As he raised his cluster of hunted birds, looking for praise, Aldo's proud but now weary old hunting dog looked up, as if wanting to claim the credit due him. I averted my eyes while Alda clapped and held her hands together in the air.

"*Che meraviglia!*" she cried. Marvelous? I forced myself to glance – oh, poor little dead birds, eyes now opaque white. I couldn't say a word.

As a student abroad in Italy I recalled how shocked I'd first been seeing the markets with scrawny animals hanging upside down, their fur or feathers, necks and heads intact. It was such a visual leap from America's shrunken, plucked, industrial-handled, shining-under-plastic supermarket meats. After my initial revulsion had subsided, I'd learned to respect knowing the animal to be consumed, instead of masking recognition. In my senior year, I would seek out the Italian market in Philadelphia and even did a small painting of hanging sausages and meats. Yet this morning these birds were flying wild and free. How could Aldo take aim and shoot them?

"Lay them on the table," Alda said. She lovingly sorted each bird by name: *fringuello, tordo* – thrush and mourning doves – among other familiar songbirds. *Songbirds? God.* I blinked at the small bodies and wee blank eyes. "They have to be plucked right away," she added, as my heart sank, wondering if she expected me to help. Aldo put a newspaper down on the table and his mother gently began removing feathers. She sensed my hesitation.

"Don't worry. It takes me no time," she insisted.

"My friends will be here for the roast momentarily," Aldo said. "You are welcome to join us if you'd like." I swore I would rebel by not tasting any, but I didn't want to seem ungrateful.

It was an all-male hunters event anyway. "Oh, that's okay, but thanks," I said. Before I turned, Alda had nearly removed all the feathers. Fascination kept me watching as she lovingly constructed the bird skewers. First she spiked a small slice of a baguette.

"I've been getting this bread for bird roasts from the same bakery in Florence for forty years," she said as she added lard, a large sage leaf and a bird, piercing its side. She repeated: bread, lard, sage and bird, over and over until the skewer was packed. Afterwards she set aside olive oil, coarse salt and pepper and created a little brush with a small branch of sage leaves, which she dipped and spread over the birds. Two rows of limp birds lay waiting for the fire. I finally excused myself to go upstairs.

I took yogurt out of my fridge and added nuts and fruit, believing I was set for the night. I even relished the simplicity of my meager no-kill meal after gorging on so many elaborate ones. Maybe I forgot to shut the downstairs door to the spiral stairs, because before long the tantalizing smell of the roast reached my apartment. I vaulted downstairs.

There was Aldo, winding the metal crank for the long rotisserie, now inside the large fireplace. As the birds turned over and over the flaming embers, the moving spit emitted an eerie whistling that sounded like the birds were tweeting. Standing there, I watched wide-eyed with revulsion and fascination as the birds flipped over and over, their heads flopping at every turn. The whistling continued. Minutes later, the birds' necks stiffened.

"They're ready," Aldo announced. The sight, smell and sound were mesmerizing. His friends at the table were thick in discussion about hunting tales – the quintessential guys' night out. They had been so deep in their world that they hadn't even said *buona sera* until I finally said it and they looked up and greeted me. Aldo encouraged me to taste a morsel as he placed the birds on a platter. "Just a taste," he insisted as he cut away a tiny piece of breast.

"Alright," I surrendered, and he fed me like a mother bird. The morsel melted in my mouth; the taste was wild, delicate, a totally astonishing experience. Then he offered a forkful of the roasted bread next to the birds, saturated in olive oil.

"This is the best part of all," he declared.

"Oh my God!" I cried in sensual shame. The exquisite taste converted me into an accomplice. As Alda shuffled by with her cane, before her son served his friends' plates, he set one aside for his mother as she headed quietly towards the parlor. She knew when not to interfere. Before he passed the platter around, Aldo asked if I wanted my own plate. Seeing how precious few birds there were, I graciously declined and offered to take Alda her plate.

"*Buona notte*," I said to the room full of hunters and took Alda's dinner down the corridor. I found her collapsed on her comfortable chair. She asked me to move her hassock so she could raise her feet. I hadn't heard elderly Alda complain, but it was clear she needed to calm her phlebitis, arthritic knee and bulging varicose veins after hours of standing in the kitchen on the hard tile floor.

"I hope you're feeling at home here?" Alda said. It seemed she always thought of others before herself. I sunk into the green Victorian sofa, my hands folded in my lap.

"Of course! I feel so welcome," I said, and her face relaxed. "The roast tonight was... outrageous. Just when I think I've tasted the best morsel in the world, another delicacy you make stuns me," I said, handing her the plate of little birds.

When she thanked me, I took the opportunity to mention that she shouldn't have to feed me, that I'd cook for myself upstairs. I sensed her disappointment.

"Whatever you decide, but I'm happy when you eat with us. Why should you go to the trouble when it's no trouble for me? I have help. You have work to do. What's one more plate?"

"*Grazie*," I said. She asked me to stay, so I watched, fascinated. When she'd finished the precious morsels, a pyramid of little clean bones lay on her plate. She cleaned her hands and sliced a piece of fruit with her knife and fork. Although too modest to rave about her own cooking, at seventy-five her figure attested to the fact that she clearly enjoyed her own food.

"How long have you lived here?"

"Fifty years, on and off," she said. "My father-in-law bought this villa in the '20s as a summer home. It was my mother-in-law's favorite place and it's mine as well," she sighed. "Ugo owned many properties. He owned houses and a great tract of cultivated rural land on Viale Michelangelo, the most prime real estate in Florence, close to the Arno River. His land was appropriated by the government, 'for the common good'. The entire stretch is still public tennis courts and other sports facilities. Fascism loved sport. Florentines love sport. In exchange, Ugo ended up with a few properties in the city, but nothing of comparable value."

"How could they just take your land?" I asked, but then I told her about the eminent domain that had uprooted my own upstate ancestors to build the Ashokan Reservoir for New York City's drinking water.

"*Tutto il mondo è paese*," she said. All the world is the same. "It was perfectly legal," she added. "After my husband died, I had to manage what was left of the patrimony. It was our only income. But with all the taxes and frozen renter fees, the upkeep was often more than what we got for the rent. You imagine me here when the children were growing up, but I spent nearly every day, all day, at the tax attorney's office or at the local government offices, getting extensions, making grievances for the land, shuffling, selling and trading to keep things afloat," she said. "There are only a few properties left, but I'm proud that my children had a good life and that I managed to keep this place for Aldo. I love this villa. I plan to leave it feet first," she declared, looking me in the eye, as if warning me. Feet first. I remembered seeing narrow boarded-up doors on the façades of Gubbio's medieval dwellings, doors constructed adjacent to the main entrances. Aldo had told me they were the 'doors of the dead', opened only when people died at home. Bodies would have been carried out feet first. Being born at home, and dying at home, still seemed so civilized, the optimum way of coming in and going out.

"My daughter Flora is happy living in her little apartment near Il Teatro Communale, but the house on Viale Michelangelo is hers. It's rented now as Hotel Liberty. All my children inherited property. Anna lives with her husband and boys. Her property was part of her dowry when she got married."

"There's still the custom of a dowry in Italy?" I asked, incredulous.

"Nothing official," she said. "Anna is twelve years older than Aldo. That difference is like a generation."

After a moment, I said, "It must have been so difficult, on your own, with three children."

"Well, I always had help," she said, clearly someone who looked on the bright side of things.

Amidst the piles of magazines on the floor and her long cocktail table I noticed rosary beads and little devotional cards with an image of Padre Pio, the bearded mystic monk, with hands bound to cover his stigmata. Aldo had mentioned that his mother had taken a pilgrimage to see the saint in Puglia when he was still alive. I wanted to know more, but I longed for some time to myself upstairs.

"Well, I'll say goodnight, unless there's something you need?"

"Actually, would you mind getting Aldo's shirt on my bed – it needs a button."

Hmmm, I wanted to say, you're still sewing for your son? As I walked towards Alda's bedroom I suddenly remembered the American soldier's scribble on a shutter in the adjacent room. Curious, I turned on a light to check if it was still there. Seeing the soldier's writing again stirred something in me. I touched the name and wondered about all those men, so far from home, probably so afraid. Finally I remembered my errand and returned to Alda with the shirt.

"Someday, would you mind telling me your story and what happened here during the war?"

"Certo, cara," she said, but her voice was hesitant. As she picked up needle and thread without looking up, I felt I'd been too intrusive. She may not be ready to dredge up her war stories, but I suspected that if I was looking to celebrate women who defined courage, I'd found one, sitting quietly in this room.

HILARY'S SOJOURN

Villa Rafanelli, 1975-1976

At my stone sink, I arranged a large urn with autumnal flowers, herbs and branches that I gathered this late October morning for Hilary's arrival. Walking barefoot, something Italians never do, I entered the room we had prepared the past two weeks for Hilary. I put the arrangement on a sideboard and looked around. It was still hard to fathom living in a place that was built only eight years after Columbus stepped onto America's shore. 1492 was the same year that Lorenzo de Medici died. In Florence the Renaissance had already celebrated its glorious peak.

Gigetto, Pier Luigi, Hilary and Aldo, 1975.

As I rushed around, puffing up pillows on her bed, I suddenly heard Aldo's whistle from the terrace, alerting me of their arrival.

"*Ilaria!!*" I called out her Italianized name, leaning out the window.

"Hello dearie!" she waved up. "Can you believe it?"

"No!" I cried. "I'll be right down." I ran downstairs and unlatched the front door, and we embraced under the *loggia*. "How was your trip?"

"Perfect!" she said as we walked into the kitchen.

"Now I see it," Alda said, holding out her hand to Hilary, acknowledging her impressive height and resemblance to Victor McLaglen, who I'd casually mentioned was her grandfather. I'd been astounded. All the Rafanellis were huge fans of the *simpatico* actor, a man I only vaguely recalled. Hollywood fanatic Flora enthused on and on about *The Quiet Man, Gunga Din* and other films he'd starred in. She was especially keen on meeting Hilary. My friend listened patiently as I translated the family's excitement about her arrival. Her smile spread as wide and infectious as her grandfather's. She inhaled the smell coming from the pots, asking about the meal. Aldo's mother had made tortellini with pigeon meat in broth, followed by *cotechino* – a kind of boiled, spiced pork sausage with lentils, mashed potatoes and afterwards, *zabaglione over savoiardi,* a dessert something like custard.

"Good Lord!" Hilary's voice bounced with elation as she saw all the efforts Alda had made on her behalf.

Hilary and I had met at the Frick Collection, where she was the assistant cook. Originally from Seattle, she had left Cornell to write poetry and ended up in New York City using her culinary talents to make a living. Recently she had been the private chef for Diana Vreeland.

I took her upstairs while Aldo got her other bag. Leading my six-foot-tall friend down the corridor, she stooped to enter the little door that led to the spiral staircase. I figured Alda's mother-in-law Elvira and all her sons, with the exception of the shorter Danilo, must have had to do the same.

As we entered the tiny upstairs kitchen, Hilary mirrored my initial glee. Standing there she looked me square in the face.

"Aldo will be up here any minute, so tell me… Anything going on with you two?"

"Well…" I smiled, a little cagey.

"Oh dearie, I knew it!" she exclaimed, slapping her thigh. "You lucky Pisces – with a Taurus – our perfect match. I told you!"

"Oh geez, not the stars again," I laughed. She knew all the astrological influences and optimum mates for us. Although a year apart, Hilary and I were both born on the second day of March.

"Is he living up here?" she asked, getting right to the point. I nodded sheepishly.

"Only since a few days ago."

"And his mother – how's she taking this arrangement?"

"I'm not sure she knows. It's not like we're shouting it out! If she suspects, she's discreet."

"Well… I hope I won't be in your way?"

"Don't be ridiculous," I said, confessing how much I missed my friends and family. And I told her I was hoping that our being together would kick-start a regular disciplined writing schedule.

"Sure. We'll keep each other on task," she promised.

Opening the shutters in her room, I said, "Meanwhile, the olive harvest is approaching. I hope it's okay. I suggested we help Aldo and his farmer Gigetto – a way for us to earn our keep. We can devote late afternoons and early evenings to writing. I think the structure will be good for us. I wrote that play in New York while working full-time!" I confessed to feeling a little lost.

"I'd love to help pick olives," Hilary said, and when Aldo appeared with her luggage she told him the apartment was beyond heaven.

"*Grazie, Ilaria,*" he said, suggesting she freshen up and we come right down. "I'm in shock. My mother said *pranzo* is actually ready!"

At the table, Hilary tasted Alda's sautéed *russula* mushrooms that she and I had gathered that morning in the back woods. The *antipasto*, served on generous slices of garlic toast, could have been a whole meal.

"*Divino*, signora," my friend proclaimed after a two-hour feast. Hilary turned towards me and said, "I need these recipes." When I translated, Alda beamed.

A week later, in early November, Aldo, Gigetto, Hilary and I were spreading out large orange nets under olive trees. Taking our places in the grove, standing on the ground, we used hand rakes to strip olives off the lower branches. Then we climbed into the trees for the unreachable fruits. Meditative hours floated by as we navigated elephantine trunks and branches. As I became more agile in the trees, I thought of WH Hudson's early twentieth-century novel *Green Mansions* and again of my favorite Calvino story, *The Baron in the Trees*. Day after day, hour after hour, for a month we quietly focused on stripping one knotty branch after another. As I listened to the gentle thud of olives raining down onto the net, I thought our harvesting was the closest I'd ever come to being completely present in the moment. The four of us were totally absorbed by our task. At the end of each day, we surrounded the trees and gathered the nets full of scattered olives. As mounds of purple, black and green olives rolled together, we marveled at the rich abundance in motion.

Once they were hauled onto Aldo's truck, he and Gigetto spread them on the floor of the *fieniele*. Soon the entire floor was covered with a mix of green and black olives waiting to be crushed and transformed into green liquid gold.

Walking back to the villa, I asked Aldo why Tuscan olive oil was so treasured. Since the olives in most of Tuscany are harvested by hand and gathered the same day and placed in a dry place, he told me, they are never exposed to the elements or sit around on the soil building acidity. Other regions have trees too tall to harvest manually, so their olives just fall when ripe. Sometimes they're left on the ground for weeks, exposed to rain. They get over-ripe and highly acidic by the time they're collected and processed. "Instead, some of the olives we harvest are still green, under-ripe, but they give our oil bite," he said.

On our last day in the orchard, Hilary gave a cheer and bounded ahead towards the villa. Aldo and I shook Gigetto's hand to congratulate him before we walked slowly home, savoring the last moments of working together outside. Our breath slowed with our pace as we reached the terrace steps. Midway up, Aldo turned towards me with a serious look on his face.

"What is it?"

"I knew you'd come," he said.

"What?"

He pointed up to my window, now our bedroom. "One evening, two years ago, shortly after that first time we met and you were already back in New York, I was walking up these steps and glanced up to that second-floor window. I saw you there, clear as day, looking down at me," he shuddered. "I still don't know what to make of it."

Stunned, I laughed nervously. "Had you been drinking?"

"A glass of wine. Not enough to induce hallucinations."

"Sometimes I visualize people from the past, but I know it's just my imagination. Was it like that, a projection?"

"Not at all. It was involuntary, unexpected and absolutely real," he said.

"Had you ever experienced anything like a vision before?"

"Never before or since," he insisted. "I've always been a complete skeptic about anything like that. Yet there you were. I restored that room feeling confident that you would come because I saw you there. It wasn't just a dream."

A shiver rose up my spine. "God... maybe it was some kind of time warp?" I should have been flattered, but it made me nervous. I'd never been the subject of what seemed like projected desire. What did it mean? I squeezed his hand, dumbfounded.

Later that evening Hilary and I sat around watching Alda roast slices of peasant bread that Aldo picked up every day from the local baker, Valdamaro. Staring at the little square tin grill, we waited impatiently for Aldo's return from the *frantoio* where our harvested olives were being crushed with stone wheels, pressed into oil. We glanced at the clock. I wished he'd asked us to join him! It was nearly ten when we finally heard his triumphant whistle at the front door. We clapped as he entered the kitchen, beaming and holding up a stainless beaker full of new oil.

"*Fantastico*," his mother exclaimed. We stood in reverent silence, our mouths watering as he poured a long dribble of gorgeous green oil onto the prepared toast.

"*Guarda, guarda!* Look at that color," I cried. We savored the pungent green taste that caught in our throats.

"*Mio Dio!* It's really sharp," Hilary said.

Our hosts were delighted by our euphoria. As Alda salted more toast, we devoured slices dripping with the glorious green, newly pressed oil.

"This is the best it gets. Unlike wine that improves with age, the color and sharpness of olive oil diminishes every day," Alda warned. "We store it in dark jars away from the light, in a cool place, to preserve it from going rancid."

That weekend Aldo invited his friend Massimo for dinner upstairs on the second floor. I welcomed hosting rather than always depending on Aldo's mother for all the meals. I prepared a pasta I'd invented, *Spaghetti al Carnivale*, named for being colorful and meatless. I sautéed spinach with garlic and butter and white wine, adding dried red-hot peppers for color and spice, and clams at the last minute, topped with a dribble of the sublime new oil. After taking his first bite, Massimo smiled, insisting the combination was "*la sua morte.*" A direct translation might sound as if the ingredients were a deadly combination, but I knew the phrase was a compliment, a well-suited coupling of taste. I was delighted, since Alda, Aldo and Hilary were the brilliant cooks. By the end of the meal Massimo added another compliment, that I had lost my Roman accent and finally sounded like a Florentine. We laughed that I'd learned the Tuscan-aspirated C.

After the olive harvest, Hilary and I finally began focusing all day on our writing, sharing the Olivetti typewriter. As our cigarette smoke permeated the chilly air, Hilary composed a memorable poem, *The Olive Catch,* and I wrote an essay, *Il boschetto,* about foraging for mushrooms with Alda in the woods. We were moved by this new intimacy with the source of what we were eating. We admired the simple way that Alda prepared every delicious thing, using just three ingredients for most of her recipes. Since we spent so much time relishing Alda's authentic cooking, we decided to celebrate her culinary talents and the joy of our connection to the food we ate by writing a seasonal Tuscan cookbook. Hilary's experience as a cook and chef gave us some credibility. We would record Alda's recipes and write associated poems and short essays that fitted with the seasons, including the grape, olive and mushroom harvests. Other harvests, still to unfold in the coming seasons, would be fodder for additional writing. My mushroom essay would introduce Alda's mushroom risotto and *fettunta* covered with sautéed mushrooms. This idea seemed like the perfect marriage of our interests and experience at the villa. Our tentative title was: *A Sensual, Seasonal Tuscan Cookbook.*

Alda never read a recipe, so we had to watch her every move. All the classic Tuscan *Artusi* cooking and girlhood tips she'd learned from the famous Buca Lapi restaurateur had become second nature to her. While Alda prepared meals, Hilary and I handed her pots and utensils. Watching, we asked questions and took notes. She never offered precise amounts. "Just a little of this and that," she'd say, like most creative cooks. Was her vagueness purposeful, like the cliché of chefs reticent to share secrets?

Most days Aldo was off consulting for Chianti wine producers and selling grapevines grafted with American rootstock. Grafting was necessary because the fatal *phylloxera* louse from America had devastated European vineyards at the end of the nineteenth century. Following that ruination, the only way for European vineyards to survive the American louse was to forever couple their vines with resistant American roots. As an American living with an Italian, I took this solution as a personal metaphor. Rather than thinking that America had been the root of the problem, I focused on the benefits of international coupling and the inevitability of our global dependency on one another to thrive.

When Aldo returned in the evening he found us upstairs, still writing at the oval table. He often started dinner without us. One night we asked about the next harvest we could write about.

"In late December we sow the wheat." When we offered to assist, another chance to be helpful and have hands-on experience to write about, Aldo said, "*Benissimo*." But when he approached Gigetto about the idea, his gentle farmer was uncharacteristically disgruntled.

"I've never seen women sowing wheat, Signor Aldo," he insisted. His resistance perplexed us. He'd been so cheerful and grateful when we'd harvested olives together. Aldo, noting our enthusiasm, ignored Gigetto's plea.

"Farmers have this superstition about women. They think only men should sow seeds," he laughed. "*Non ti preoccupare*, he'll come around."

"Are you sure?" I said, reluctant to offend Gigetto or violate tradition.

"Gigetto claims it's because you're both inexperienced. I called his bluff, saying I would train you." We were impressed that Aldo had opted to break a superstitious, sexist barrier.

When we finally got back out in the field in December, Aldo demonstrated with a sack of wheat kernels hanging across his chest. We observed his long sweep, back and forth, away from his body, scattering the seeds evenly from left to right. The movement was like a dance. Hilary and I soon became proficient. As kernels cascaded consistently across the field, we began feeling cocky, exaggerating the dance, sweeping our long arms and legs. But when Gigetto appeared for inspection, we immediately assumed a serious pose. We contained our glee as his curt nod and slight smile affirmed that we'd done a fine job. At the end of the day, Aldo joined us from where he'd been sowing and stared.

"You two look like *Valkyrie* goddesses."

Our size was decidedly Norse-like. I recalled Giovanni warning Aldo about me: "Have you seen her shoulders?"

One evening in late December, as we finished dinner upstairs, Aldo declared, "Tomorrow would be a wonderful day for the Uffizi."

"Oh really?" I said, having been numerous times. "Is there a special exhibit going on?"

"No. It's what's going on here," he said. "The butcher will be arriving in the morning. You don't want to be around when he slaughters the pig."

"What? You have a pig on the property?" I was astounded, thinking I'd explored every inch of the place.

"Don't feel left out. I've never actually seen the pig either. Gigetto keeps him. Aside from what we feed the dogs and cats, that pig devours all our leftovers. They're very smart, lovely animals. They get attached, like pets." Aldo admitted he was also afraid of getting attached but confessed he could not give up *prosciutto*.

"You really are the quintessential gentleman farmer," I teased.

"It's sweet you want to protect us from the slaughter," Hilary said.

He assured us that the killing was very quick. "The butcher shoots the pig while he's eating, just one shot, in the front of the head, instant death – he never knows. Except that pigs are either ultra-aware or have intuition, as they always suspect something is up when the butcher arrives. They usually let out the most awful squeals as he approaches. They have to be dragged to the trough, kicking and screaming. But when they get to their food, they finally relax and seem to forget all about the lurking danger, when…" We grimaced with a sense of collective culpability, pondering all the bacon and chops we'd consumed in our lifetime. "That's why you don't want to be around, to hear those bloodcurdling squeals."

"Well, we haven't been to Florence in a while," I agreed. I'd been feeling removed from art, ensconced in our world at the villa.

"*Va bene*," Hilary said in her blossoming Italian.

"You'll be happy to know that no part of the pig gets wasted," Aldo added. "Once it's gutted and cleaned, they bring it to the building attached to your side of the villa, where there's a huge hearth. The butcher sets up a table to make different kinds of sausages. They even use the pig's shoulder blade as a spatula to work the ground meat."

"Oh God. We should witness that for the book," Hilary insisted.

"Sure, and you could write a poem about pig parts," I smiled.

"But the museum sounds like a good idea too," she said.

"Okay, we'll skip the slaughter but be here for the preparation."

***

Early the next day, Hilary folded into my little *cinquecento* Fiat. I drove into Florence by way of Via Benedetto Fortini, the narrow road flanked by high stone walls. In the city, I parked near the Uffizi. Once inside, we visited room after gilded room of pre-Renaissance *Madonna col Bambino*. We observed time pass, as flat gold backgrounds in exclusively sacred family scenes vanished and village life emerged with expanding humanistic consciousness. Pre-Renaissance dwellings were stacked awkwardly, like dollhouses on hills; the hilly landscape appeared like arrowheads, intimating the initial attempt at portraying surroundings with perspective. As we journeyed into rooms of the high secular Renaissance, we came upon Botticelli's *Birth of Venus* and *Primavera,* a sensual celebration of neo-platonic love. Mythology abounded. Pagan protagonists pranced in diaphanous gowns, revealing flesh that here in Florence fueled the monk Savonarola's prudish fury, his *Bonfire of the Vanities* and his eventual demise by hanging and fire in Piazza Signoria. In those rooms we traveled a long way from the sacred Madonna and child imagery.

After hours of staring, our eyes began to glaze over. Hilary suggested, "Time for a *cappuccino?*" She was undaunted when I reminded her that Italians never drink *cappuccino* in the middle of the day.

Walking in Piazza Signoria towards Cafe Rivoire, we paused at the embedded bronze medallion on the pavement that commemorates the spot of Savonarola's death. Hilary translated the Roman numerals, dating his death at 1498.

After sipping coffee in that elegant cafe, we decided to return for the pig preparation. Driving back to Grassina, I noisily shifted gears as we reached the bottom of the villa's hill. I held my breath and prayed aloud that we wouldn't slide backwards. As the *500* sputtered, we leaned in towards the hill, as if our movement might help us ascend. Every time I drove the *cinquecento*, it felt like I was a hand and the car was my glove. My Cadillac-driving mother had just asked in a letter: 'Your car isn't as small as a VW bug, is it?' I didn't mention it was about half the size.

Parking in the courtyard, we heard jovial voices coming from the attached farm building. Vaulting up the stairs, we entered an enormous, dark room, overwhelmed by the delectable smell of pig roasting. Aldo, Gigetto and his son stood like silhouettes against the blazing hearth, as the butcher turned sausage links on a grill. The pig had already been divided into multiple parts. Strings of *salami* hung from the rafters. Two *prosciutti* lay on a table, curing under a thick layer of salt. I thought I should find my pad, to sketch the hanging animal parts, as I had in the Italian section of Philadelphia.

Aldo gestured urgently. "Taste this." He gave us a bite of an exquisite sausage. We were breathless.

"My God, why isn't your mother here?" I asked. Aldo said she couldn't navigate the steep stairs anymore, so Hilary and I took her a plate of sausages. We entered the house and found her building a complicated crèche that spread over the entire surface of Flora's antique baby grand piano. Years ago his mother had won a regional contest for her nativity scene. Now she was sculpting a hilly countryside and village with rocks and moss that Aldo had gathered early that morning. We stared at a small round mirror, transformed into a shining lake encircled by moss; tiny dwellings were scattered about her mini village; colorful figures performed daily chores of washing clothes, tending sheep and sawing wood. A sky-blue background was taped on the wall behind the crèche, with a bright north star. We wondered where the three kings were. She explained that she only added them at the end of their journey, on January 6th. We also found the manger empty. "I never place baby Jesus, the Madonna or the animals there before Christmas Eve."

"We brought you something," I said, handing her the plate of sausage.

"Grazie," she said and sat at the table. When she took her first bite she closed her eyes to savor it.

As the winter progressed, Aldo and Gigetto pruned olive trees and grapevines. The only remaining farm task was to make vinsanto. Up in the tower we watched Aldo remove clusters of selected grapes that'd been hanging on the rafters there since the grape harvest. The drying grapes had concentrated so much sugar in three months that they'd shriveled into raisins. After crushing those sweet clusters, the men emptied the precious juice into small barrels.

"The key is patience. This has to ferment for three years before we can taste the vinsanto," Aldo said.

"Well, we have something great to look forward to," I said and looked at Hilary, who sighed. I knew she was getting antsy to move on, that she wouldn't be at the villa much longer, certainly not for the opening of the barrel. Who knew where I would be.

As the holiday approached, Hilary began baking up a storm of American Christmas sweets to share with the Italians: bourbon balls, lemon squares and other treats that required tons of butter. The day before Christmas I watched Alda prepare the traditional tortellini to be tossed into her homemade capon broth. She sat by the cold kitchen window wearing two layers of sweaters to keep warm. Her head down, she focused on the little umbilical-shaped pasta. Light filtered in like a scene from Vermeer. Her arthritic hands were poised in the same intense but serene way as when she did needlework. On the table, a bunch of completed tortellini flanked rows of little, flat, round pasta wafers waiting to be filled and formed into the tortellini shape. I ran to get my camera.

After being distracted by the holiday celebration, Hilary and I hunkered down to write. Winter life was dormant on the farm. We added more recipes and spent every day organizing the book into seasons, losing all sense of time. Too often we allowed the wood in the red enamel stove, our main source of heat upstairs, to nearly burn out. As the air around our table began to feel chilly, I'd jump up, amazed at the hour and the darkness settling in.

"Oh God, we almost let this stove burn out again," I'd say nearly every day at the same time. "Aldo should be back any moment. We need to replenish the wood." Anxiously we stoked the embers, adding wood, and cursing in Italian, which always felt more cathartic. The villa, Aldo warned, without central heating, turned damp and cold if we let the fire die.

By the time Aldo appeared, laden with groceries, the fire was raging again but we felt like naughty children. Gracefully, quietly and efficiently, he would start dinner while we finished our last lines of writing for the day. Our contribution would be setting the table and doing the dishes.

One day Aldo complained, his voice on edge. "This cookbook idea is great, but I thought I'd be sampling more recipes."

"But you know all your mother's recipes!" I said, mortified.

Aldo harvesting olives, autumn 1975.

Gigetto and Camilla, olive harvest, autumn 1975.

Hilary and Camilla, end of olive harvest.

Camilla and Hilary in the wheat field, summer 1976.

THE NOTEBOOK

Winter 1976

Only three months had passed since the end of the olive harvest, but I already felt nostalgia for that simultaneously purposeful and carefree time. Although we hadn't completed our cookbook project, by January Hilary decided it was time to depart. She wanted to improve her Italian and learn other languages. She found an *au pair* position in another part of Florence, with a Milanese family, so she could still visit. Her leaving the villa gave my staying more gravitas. What would become of our book with her living elsewhere, and what would I write next if not that? Would I resurrect *Troika*, the first draft of a long play I'd written while at the Frick?

Camilla in Aldo's vineyard below the villa, winter 1976.

After Hilary left, I spent a good portion of the following day staring at a blank page in the Olivetti typewriter. I suspected our collaboration wouldn't continue. I traipsed downstairs, storming through the corridor, convinced that what I needed was fresh air and a brisk stroll in the back woods to clear my head.

At mid-corridor, a voice called out from the parlor, "Chi c'e?"

"Sono io," I responded, feeling full of conflicting emotions about who the I was who claimed to be present. Peeking in, there was Alda working on her crochet.

"Come in, dear," she said calmly. "Please, sit down."

I entered reluctantly and didn't feel like talking, but she insisted.

"It must be hard with Hilary gone. She was such good company," she said, putting down her work. "Is everything else alright?"

I confessed to staring at a blank page all day and that I was feeling lost. I was sorry our cookbook wasn't finished. "But other than that, everything's fine!"

"You're not homesick?"

"Sure," I said. "I miss my family and friends, but, you know…"

Rather than think about questions regarding writing or Aldo, I thought about how my notion of home had unraveled after my father's death. As if reading my mind, Alda asked about my mother.

"She's remarried now," I sighed, adding that her new husband didn't like her working; he wanted her around, a fact that irked me. "After losing my father, my mother had to work, so she returned to her nursing career. She'd been terrified after all those years staying home, raising five children. But once she began again, it built her confidence. She became a new person, proudly independent. I was sorry she gave that up."

"Brava!" Alda sighed. "Your mother was lucky she had a profession to fall back on. I was born at the wrong time. I never completed my studies to be a teacher. But today so much is possible for women. It would have been good to have depended on myself instead of on my father-in-law's patrimony after my husband died. It was a challenge after all the Rafanelli men were gone. This villa is one of the few properties left."

"It's a treasure. I understand why you held onto it," I said.

"Well. I held onto it for Aldo; it's his now," she said, then changed the subject. "A while ago you asked me if I would tell you about my time here during the war. If now is a good moment, why don't you get your notebook?"

I guessed she was now willing to share painful memories with me because she knew I felt adrift. If Alda was poised to open up to me, I could focus on her story, learn from her life and see where it would take me. I returned clutching my notebook, thanking her, and began scrawling words.

For our mutual March birthday, Hilary returned and gave me a lovely red and white Florentine blank book. On the first page she'd pasted a photo of me with braids, sitting under an olive tree, wearing outdated big glasses and green rubber boots. Amidst a sloping sunny landscape, Gigetto and I are transferring mounds of harvested olives into a sack. She dedicated this as a recipe book. She'd filled in the first few pages with her mother's recipes from their Seattle home. The rest of the book, like my future, was a blank slate.

Alda making tortellini, winter 1976.

SPRINGTIME AND THE RED BRIGADES

May 1976

Spring arrived and the landscape was reborn with a patchwork of color. One late April afternoon Aldo asked me to join him on a motorcycle ride through Chianti. He needed to visit an estate to check on vines he'd sold the prior year, vines recently damaged by hail. Aldo straddled his sleek motorcycle in the courtyard and looked at me with raised eyebrows, waiting for me to climb on. Thinking of his madman antics that first summer we met, I hesitated.

Aldo and Camilla on motorcycle, villa's entrance, with caper plants on wall.

"Only if you promise… no funny business," I insisted. When he nodded, I swung my leg over the saddle and put my arms around his waist. He drove slowly along the driveway, turning onto the road up past the tall cypress trees protecting the villa against the *tramontana* wind. Up and over the hill we puttered alongside olive groves, fruit trees and vineyards, swaths of ground with green shoots of young grain, and large patches of iris - il giglio - the floral symbol of Florence for a thousand years. I was in ecstasy out in the open air observing the hills softly rise and dip, inhaling the intoxicating perfume of fields bursting with flowers. With no windshield and no cars in front of us, their unadulterated scent permeated the air.

I loved the fragrant, lyrical motion that the Tuscan landscape stimulated in my every sense. The juxtaposition of wild meadow and cultivated land created a quilt of light, color and form. Even the rhizomes of the glorious iris were harvested for their scent, for soaps and perfumes. Rotating beauty and delight, every field that wasn't lying fallow grew something edible or useful. No frivolous monoculture lawns on these hills. Aldo pulled over and turned off the motor, pointing to a hillside, a carpet of purple flowers.

"*Che bellezze!*" I cried. As we surveyed the land, I remembered his upcoming birthday. "Any special requests?"

"Sure! A new motorcycle. This Ducati is pretty tired," he joked.

"Do you want the same brand?" I jested, really wishing I could buy him one.

"Actually, I'd prefer a Norton Atlas. English. Old-time classic."

"Darn. You might have to wait until I publish my first book."

"Is that a promise?" he said.

"Promise," I swallowed, thinking of all the pages I'd written and tossed. To earn some money while attempting to write, I had begun translating business brochures from Italian to English.

He restarted the motorcycle, and we rode for a while along the Via Chiantigiana hills, headed in the direction of Greve, the center of Chianti. We stopped at Pampaloni, a countryside store where Aldo ordered a sandwich of *salami* with roast beef, saying it was his grandfather Ugo's invention, his favorite *pannino*. As we continued our blissful motorcycle ride, we were alone on the road. All fear melted away as the wind swept my face and hair. We drove past villas perched high on sunny hills, Tuscan façades the color of apricot and butter. Dizzy with the wind, we finally arrived at the wine producer's estate. Dismounting, I marveled at the elegant driveway flanked by magnificent cypresses. Aldo said it was the English living in Tuscany who'd introduced the use of cypress trees to flank estate entryways.

When we reached the main villa, the few people who milled about frowned at us with suspicion. I was about to comment on how rude they seemed when one man finally recognized Aldo.

"Oh, Signor Rafanelli, welcome," he sighed. "Forgive us. After what happened last week, we scrutinize anyone who comes in here."

"What happened?" I mouthed silently to Aldo as the man led us towards the courtyard.

"I'll tell you later," he said.

The sophisticated wine-making estate was open to the public for tastings – an anomaly here. I somehow expected the Chianti region to be like Napa Valley's vineyards, with tasting rooms, picnic areas and stores selling wine and other agricultural products. This property had all that plus a wonderful countryside *trattoria*. It was a place to return with friends, to eat *al fresco* under a pergola of grapevines.

The owner *Conte* Giovanni approached, a barrel-chested aristocrat with an impish smile under a large mustache. He extended his hand to Aldo before taking mine.

"Signorina," he said, air kissing my hand, which seemed *de rigueur* for the handful of aristocrats I'd encountered.

"Good thing you are here, Rafanelli," the Count turned to Aldo. "Come. I'll show you the damage." We followed him towards a sloping field. "Our *fattore* insists we have to plow up the whole vineyard, but I wanted to check with you first." He motioned to the foreman to join us as we stood before a swath of devastated vines. "These rows and rows of plants were just a year short of producing grapes. You see the damage the damn hail did to your vines? Every hailstone seemed to have marked a plant for destruction," he sighed. "You sold me these vines. Is there anything we can do besides starting from scratch, Rafanelli? My man here is pulling out his hair with this one."

Aldo looked at the foreman, who was nervously dragging on his cigarette. "Oh, no problem. Just cut them back. They'll be fine," Aldo insisted. "Give them some extra fertilizer to give them a boost."

"Really? That's great news," Giovanni sighed, giving his frantic *fattore*, who blew smoke in the air, a stern look. "I hate drama. We've had enough lately," he said as we walked in the direction of his home. "Come in for an espresso, Rafanelli."

Then I heard him ask Aldo, half joking, if he wanted a job as his foreman. As we entered his villa, a woman appeared.

"Espresso for three, please, Valeria," Giovanni said, smiling at me before lighting up a cigarette and offering us one. Striking the match for our cigarettes was a momentary flash of illumination in this dark room. The seventeenth and eighteenth-century paintings and portraits were mostly lost in darkness. *Il padrone* finally opened up a few shutters to let in a column of light. We sat around as Giovanni's son, who was about my age, entered. Aldo started to rise to greet him.

"Don't get up, Rafanelli. Good to see you," he said as they shook hands. "Pardon my appearance: I haven't been sleeping since, well, you know," he said, putting his hand to his head as if it ached. "While this one," he pointed to his father, "sleeps like a baby. *Come se niente fosse.*" The young man, seeing my bewildered face bordering on alarm, said, "Oh, you don't know what happened, signorina? It's no secret! It's been on all the stations, and in the *Nazione.*"

I was embarrassed. I watched *RAI* news on TV with Alda, but I didn't read the paper every day.

"A band of *Brigate Rosse* broke into our offices in Florence last week. They lined us all up against the wall, hands in the air, with our backs to them, while they held pistols to our heads. They yelled epithets about our dirty, wealthy elitist status." He sighed. "And my father here was holding a cigarette in one raised hand. Since it was burning towards his fingers, he asked one of the terrorists, "Mind if I put it out?" Giovanni's son shook his head. "Can you believe this man? We were all thinking we were about to die and my father was completely relaxed, only worried he'd burn his finger."

"Oh *Dio!*" I exclaimed. "And then what?"

"They threatened us, called us bastards and then suddenly took off. But before they left, they exploded a bomb in an empty office. No one got hurt, *grazie a Dio*, but the sound was terrifying and we have to rebuild the ceiling. My nerves have been shattered since."

"We have to do something about these Red Brigades. They are getting out of hand," Giovanni said, lifting his shoulders in a fatalistic gesture that showed that he clearly didn't expect anything to happen. While I marveled at the Count's calm, his son, clearly in awe, slapped his father's back.

"Well, let's hope someone does something!" the son said. "I give you my leave. *Buon giorno.*"

The woman appeared with a tray of espresso. Sipping mine, I peered at Aldo with raised eyebrows. Had he said nothing about this incident to protect me? I felt foolish. I regarded Italy as if it were some sort of *Brigadoon,* a utopian place where all turmoil took place in the past. I swore I would pay more attention.

After they finished talking business, again the Count took my hand up to his lips. "Signorina," he said, with a little bow.

"*Buon giorno e buona fortuna,*" I said, wishing him good day and good luck.

As we drove off, I loosened my grip around Aldo and surveyed the passing landscape. The villas on the hillside suddenly seemed isolated, vulnerable. That carefree sense of abandon had drained from me. My mind filled with a litany of questions. When we returned to the villa that afternoon, I sat upstairs re-reading my notebook of Alda's war stories, from WWI to WWII, searching for clues, wondering about the seeds of conflict that led from one war to the next… and what was it that led to now, to the *Brigate Rosse?*

INVASION

The Villa & Florence, 1939-1940

Alda stood in the kitchen pressing the rim of a thin round glass into a thick layer of semolina that she'd spread on the marble countertop. As perfect round shapes for *gnocchi di semolina* emerged, her mouth watered. She imagined the taste of the golden rounds once baked and covered with butter and *parmigiano* cheese. Just then the front door slammed. Floro entered, without his usual whistling. He was pale and agitated. It was the first day in September of 1939.

"What's happened?" Alda asked, alarmed. Her disgusted husband tossed the newspaper on the table, as if disowning the news. She read the headline: "Germany invades Poland." She inhaled the shock. "Oh God, Floro." Her husband shook his head and left the kitchen.

Two days later the family sat riveted to the radio. Britain, France, Australia and New Zealand had declared war on Germany after its invasion of Poland, claiming they could no longer stand by as they had done when Hitler invaded Czechoslovakia. Floro paced nervously behind the sofa while his brothers and father sat mute. The patriarch broke the silence by clapping slowly.

"*Bravi!*" he applauded, his voice mocking and tense. "What did I tell you, Floro? What do you think your *Duce* will do now?"

Pietro smirked. "Well, *Babbo*, you know war is an inevitable evil – it's part of the natural baseness of our violent human nature." That moment Floro stopped pacing, his eyes wild as he moved towards his brother with a tight fist, ready to strike. Pietro stood up, without flinching, his head held up in defiance. "You see," he jeered. "My brother here proves my point."

156

As Mario jumped between his two towering brothers, Ugo slammed his fist on a table and shouted: "Stop this minute! The government always does what it damn pleases, but there will be no war in this house!"

By mid-September, while America, Italy and other European nations declared neutrality, the Soviet Union also entered Poland, a country torn between two invaders. As autumn, winter and spring passed into 1940, Mussolini, much to Hitler's fury, continued to declare neutrality. Most Italians prayed he would avoid aggression. Alda went about her daily tasks with growing apprehension.

On June 10th, eleven-year-old Anna entered the front door of the villa holding a bunch of sage that she'd picked for her mother. Her sister Flora was practicing piano as Floro barged in and switched on the news. At the same moment, as Pietro walked down the stairs, Alda stood rigid next to her husband. Everyone froze as a solemn voice announced, "Italy joins Germany in declaring war on Britain and invades France." Alda looked aghast at her husband. Pietro remained silent for once, turned and retreated back upstairs. As Alda waited for Floro's response, he sunk onto a chair, cradling his head with both hands.

Looking up in despair, he finally uttered, "*Si rovina, e ci rovinera' tutti.*" He will ruin himself, and he will ruin all of us with him. From that moment on this became Floro's mantra about Mussolini. Alda felt powerless. "Didn't we learn anything from the horrible consequences of the last war? What are we doing?"

That night the family ate in silence as the news sunk in. After the girls were excused to do their homework, Ugo turned towards his fascist son for answers. When Floro just shook his head in silence as his father asked what *Il Duce*'s plan was, Ugo then reminded him that France was not just a neighbor and ally, France was also Ugo Rafanelli & Sons' main fish supplier. Floro got up from the table. He could not sit with his father's insinuation, as if he were part of planning this war. Alda sighed as her husband walked out onto the terrace, but she decided not to go out to comfort him. She was angry too. Any progress *Il Duce* may have made for Italy to become a respected modern nation was now erased, overshadowed by involving Italy in another war. When Alda left the table to check on the girls, she found them doing their homework. Anna looked up.

"*Mamma*, if there's a war, will *Babbo* have to go?"

"Oh darling, he's thirty-seven, too old to serve, and as head of a family I doubt it." She was convincing herself as much as her daughter.

Flora looked up and asked, "And *Zio* Mario e Pietro, *Mamma?*"

"With their stomach ailments, they'll never be drafted. It's fit young men who will make the sacrifice." Hearing Anna sigh, Alda realized that although her daughter didn't really understand the meaning of what was happening, she felt the heaviness around her. Alda's throat constricted. With this war declaration, suddenly France was the enemy. Anna and Flora attended a French school in Florence. They were learning French from French nuns. What would become of the nuns now? And would their school be closed? Alda knew the war would change their personal lives in many ways, large and small, as it would for countless people. "For now, focus on your studies," Alda said to her daughters.

As she slipped back out into the corridor, she remembered the refugee family her father had sheltered from northern Italy, their gaunt mother staring at Alda with proud, resentful eyes. Alda shut her eyes tight to banish the vision. When that family had arrived, the young girl had been about eleven, Anna's age now. The boy, near starving, had been younger than Flora. Although that war had never reached Florence, so many of her friends' brothers had died. What kind of a victory was it if Italy lost over six hundred thousand men as well as territory? With this war, she wondered, would they take in refugees or would they become refugees themselves? Her body shuddered.

She peered into the parlor and bid the men *buona notte* even though she knew it was not a good night at all. Floro was still outside. She decided to leave him alone and returned upstairs to her daughters, already settled in bed. She read a chapter to them from *The Three Musketeers*. Even her favorite authors, Dumas and Hugo, were French. Alda leaned to kiss her daughters' heads.

"*Buona notte, Mamma,*" they whispered as she turned off the light. Then Flora pleaded with her to sing a favorite lullaby.

Tone-deaf Alda sang round after round, almost in a whisper: '*Stella stellina, la notte s'avvicina, la fiamma traballa, la mucca nella stalla, la mucca col vitello, la pecora e l'agnello, la chioccia col il pulcino, ogni ma con suo bambino…*' She closed her eyes on the last round, picturing the flame dancing and all the little animals snuggling in with their offspring. Her two girls had fallen asleep. Pursing her lips, Alda took a long breath and tiptoed out of their room. Once in her own bedroom, she stared up at the cracked ceiling, tears streaming. It wasn't just the French. *The English have, for centuries, spent their summers in our Tuscan hills. Their sojourns have influenced our landscape, our long driveways lined* with cypresses and our gardens to be more natural. Florentines, unlike the rest of Italy, eat steaks rare. Our famous Bistecca Fiorentina comes from the English having lived among us here in Florence. Now they are declared our enemy?

Floro quietly entered the room to say he was going to a fascist meeting that night, hoping to learn something. Alda just shook her head. He returned much later, surprised and disillusioned by his fellow fascists' enthusiasm for war. When he crawled into bed next to his only solace, Alda turned, pulling him towards her. He laid his head on her chest.

After a long silence, Floro whispered, "I'm so ashamed. If you could have seen them gloating, cheering, Alda. Maybe Pietro is right. War is inevitable and man is a lowly creature."

"Not every man, Floro," she said, holding him tight, kissing his head.

THE MADONNA'S MIRACLE

1940

Mussolini's brash voice thundered across the radio, demanding that Italians unite against the enemies, France and Britain. Alda's eyes avoided Floro's; she knew he had no ability to reverse *Il Duce's* path. In the months that followed, young Italian men would leave to occupy British East Africa and to invade Egypt. As part of their patriotic duty, men and women were asked to donate their wedding rings to help the war effort and combat the economic recession. Alda refused to give hers up. She didn't care if Mussolini's wife had donated her own ring. Floro gave money instead.

Dismayed with the all-encompassing rhetoric of war, one afternoon Alda headed towards the *Chiesa di Santissima Annunziata,* the same church where foreigners, farmers and Florentines flocked in September for the *Festa della Rificolona* to honor the Madonna's birth. Entering the celebrated Piazza Annunziata, she glanced only briefly at the church's adjacent building, the *Ospedale degli Innocenti.* Today she was on a personal mission and wanted nothing to do with any orphaned thoughts about her father's beginnings or her mother's end. Today, Alda was determined to pray for life.

Dressed in her best Sunday clothes, Alda moved purposefully towards the side altar of the church and knelt in front of the painting of the *Madonna of Miracles.* This Madonna was declared a miraculous painting in the 14th century after Fra Bartolomeo had told his story. A known artist, he had created a beatific face for the angel of this Annunciation scene. Anxious that he could never meet the challenge to surpass the angel's beauty in his

160

depiction of Mary, Fra Bartolomeo had fallen into a deep sleep. When he awoke, he was astonished to find a magnificent face already painted for the Madonna. Afterwards the painting was declared a miracle.

Alda stared at that face, unveiled only for the Madonna's few feast days during the year. There were gold necklaces, earrings, a crown and precious jewels laced around the virgin's neck, attached by devotees who'd had miracles granted. *At least these treasures will not be melted down to fuel the war*, Alda thought. She prayed, asking that the war be over quickly, that it take few victims. Then she settled in, entering a deep, prayerful state that revealed the real reason she had come. Clasping her hands and close to tears, Alda apologized to the virgin, who she knew must be very occupied. There were so many countries entering the war, so many mothers from around the world, no doubt beseeching her to keep their sons safe. Alda quieted down, thanking the Madonna for her two daughters, and begged forgiveness for this selfish request. She reminded her how she'd suffered the sudden loss of her darling baby boy.

Then Alda whispered, "I must attend to the present and the future." She began her plea, saying she was afraid that at forty her time was running out. Lifting her hands reverently, she prayed: "Oh Santa Annunziata, please grant me another son." After closing her eyes, she decided to bargain: "If you answer my prayers, when the time comes I will gladly give him back to you, as a priest, if he is willing." Rising from the kneeler, Alda humbly bowed her head. She was confident her supplication had been heard. She offered thanks to the maker of miracles. "*Grazie, Santissima Annunziata*," she said, promising that her son would be a good, peaceful boy. Alda made the sign of the cross before exiting the church.

In October, as every year, the Rafanelli family and their farmers prepared for the grape harvest. The *vendemmia* was no easy task with all the young Grassina men already off to war. Every able person left behind pitched in, even *padrone* Ugo and his three sons. While the farmers and their families tended to the harvest, Flora and Anna assisted their mother in the kitchen, making the harvest meal. This year there was no exuberant celebration for the new wine. When people sang after the harvest was over, their quiet voices exposed their heavy hearts.

After all the exhausted workers wished each other goodnight, Alda grasped Floro's hand, ushering him up onto the terrace. In the silence, they heard their own steps passing over the terracotta tiles. Floro was chronically tense now that Italy had entered the war. Alda squeezed his hand, pulling him towards the stone bench.

"Sit a minute," she pleaded softly.

"I'd rather go inside," he answered curtly, pulling away.

"Please," she coaxed, urging him onto the bench. She looked up at the sky, clear and vast with the round moon. He stared straight ahead. She watched Floro's jaw move as he ground his teeth. There was no way to calm his spirit. He refused to meet her gaze, but she took his hand again.

"*Caro*, we are all worried about what will happen, but I want to tell you something that is personally hopeful."

"Hope? What could that possibly be?" he frowned.

"Darling, you know how dormant nature appears in the winter and how spring always comes with the miracle of renewal, the miracle of life?"

"Is this a riddle?" he asked, impatient. "Just tell me."

"You know I'm forty, Floro, but perhaps you don't realize how barren and beyond hope I've felt. And yet..." she choked.

"What are you saying?" He turned and looked at her, distressed. She was quiet, but smiled slightly, suddenly feeling shame.

"I know," she said. "This war, this insane world. How can we bring a baby into it? But I have to confess, I prayed at the church of Santa Annunziata for this. I even had the audacity to ask for a boy. And my prayer..." She lifted her husband's hand to her heart, as if protecting them both.

"Alda... how could you?" he whispered.

"How could I not?"

He wrapped an arm around her.

"Is this true? You are certain?" he said.

"Oh yes, Floro, absolutely."

His eyes were suddenly brimming with tears. "When?" he asked.

"Early May."

"Dear God!" Floro exclaimed, rising, then lifting Alda from the bench, carrying her in his arms.

"Careful! You'll hurt your back! *Sei pazzo*," she cried.

"I'm not crazy," he replied, carrying her under the *loggia*, up the front steps and through the threshold of the double-arched door. Once inside, he put her down, then let out a shrill whistle announcing the good news.

"Shhhh," Alda laughed. "You'll stir the whole household!"

"Good!" Floro cried, pulling her towards him and burying his face in her neck.

A NEW LIFE AMIDST WAR

1941-1942

Before Anna's twelfth birthday in April, 1941, Alda prepared to give birth any day. That same month, Yugoslavia surrendered to the Germans and the Italians. When Greece also surrendered, Alda asked Floro if he thought the war might be over.

"I doubt it," he sighed.

The war persisted. Business lagged, inflation rose, money was tight. Along elegant Viale Michelangelo, residents were asked to donate iron entrance gates to the war effort. Alda refused to watch them dismantled, knowing the iron would be transformed into weapons. She wished they'd be transformed into bells instead, bells announcing peace.

On May 3rd, 1941, the day before Alda delivered her baby, a triumphal parade was held in Athens, celebrating the Italian occupation of Greece. As the family gathered around the radio in Florence, *Il Duce*'s brash voice claimed the Mediterranean Sea as *"Mare Nostrum,"* just as the Roman Empire had referred to it. *Our Sea*. Mussolini's hubris was designed to challenge the British and French, whose colonies dominated the area. Exasperated and fed up with his arrogant posturing, and with the thought that her unborn child might be hearing that voice, Alda rose from her chair. Struggling to move her cumbersome body, she bid her family goodnight. She, along with everyone in Italy, wondered how long the war would remain outside the mainland.

"Take my arm, Alda," Floro said, helping her into bed. Before dawn, as she entered into labor, he called the doctor and rushed to get Palma. Sitting at the kitchen table, he kept adding teaspoons of precious sugar to his coffee, stirring and clanging his cup, waiting for the doctor, who appeared just in time to deliver a baby boy. Palma entered the kitchen to share the news.

"*Un bel maschio*, Signor Floro!"

"Really? Already? A boy! My God, it's a miracle." He jumped up. Spilling his coffee, he rushed up to their bedroom. He kissed Alda's hand and stared at their son. "*Un Rafanellino*, Alda. This one we name after you. You are truly blessed," he said.

"*Benissimo*! One for each of us seems fair." So, they named the infant Aldo. She gazed adoringly at her son as the girls appeared at the threshold.

"*Mamma*, are you alright?"

Insisting she was fine, she showed them their new brother, saying, "Keep a little distance."

When Mario entered and observed the newborn, he remarked, "*Brutto in culla, bello in piazza.*" As Alda glared at her brother-in-law, Floro slapped the back of his head.

"You should talk! *Ugly in the cradle, handsome in the square*! If you could've seen yourself as a baby, little brother of mine! Only you didn't improve with age," he laughed as Mario scoffed and examined the infant more carefully.

"What's this tiny hole in the upper side of his ear?"

"What hole?" Alda said, finding that her son indeed had a minuscule indentation.

"Anything else, inspector?" Alda said then to Mario, raising her hand in a teasing, *watch out* gesture.

"*Basta*," Floro insisted, affectionately booting his brother out of the room.

The family, enamored with the new baby, looked forward to the summer in Grassina. At the end of June 1941, Germany invaded the Soviet Union; Italy followed with a declaration of war on the Soviet Union. When Anna and Flora came home from their last day of school, they showed their mother how they'd been taught to march like *fascisti*. Alda, sickened, told them to stop immediately. As they ran upstairs, Alda thought about the French nuns, who'd been sent home right after Italy had declared war on France. The transition was too seamless. Italian nuns simply replaced them.

The day before they left for the villa, a neighbor knocked on their door. "Carla, come in." As the woman entered the kitchen, Alda handed her a tin full of used coffee grounds.

"*Grazie*, Alda," she said.

"It's nothing. Stay safe this summer. See you sometime late September."
Alda sighed as she watched her leave. Although she took nothing for granted,
with Ugo's contacts at the market her family was unaffected by the shortages
of sugar, coffee and other staples. The land around the villa provided them
with an abundance, with its fruit trees, and a large vegetable garden that
Giovanni, their dedicated farmer, tended. Their hens laid eggs. They had
chickens, pigeons, turkeys, pigs and ducks.

Ever since the Spanish influenza, Alda had thought of the countryside as
a refuge. War felt like another contagion. Despite constant apprehension, as
more countries entered the war, the family passed a quiet summer at the
villa before autumn inevitably arrived. Dread descended as Alda prepared her
family to return to Florence.

On December 7th, the Japanese attacked Pearl Harbor.

Alda held her chest. "O Dio! Now what?"

"Now the Americans have no choice but to enter the war, which will
make Churchill very happy, but Italy is in deep trouble," Floro said.

A day later, Alda asked Anna and Flora to watch their baby brother
upstairs as the adults gathered to listen to the radio. They looked at each
other in grim silence as they heard that America and Britain had declared
war on Japan.

Three days later, after tucking the children up in bed, again the family sat
glued to the radio and learned that Italy and Germany had declared war on
America. That same day America responded, declaring war on Italy.

"This is madness," Alda whispered.

***

The following summer when they returned to the villa, Alda observed
her husband with increasing angst. He'd gained weight and smoked three
packs of cigarettes a day. His entire comportment had changed. He seemed
shorter than his once towering self. One night, as the children slept upstairs,
Floro entered the parlor where Alda sat on the sofa and collapsed next to
his wife.

"This time next summer, foreign troops will be swarming in Italy," he said,
taking a big drag on his cigarette.

She sighed. "Is there no way to stop this madness, Floro?"

"Alda! Why do you always ask me this?" he responded curtly. She bit her lip.

"We should get away, while we can, to the seaside for a week or so. We need a distraction." When he slapped his knees, Alda looked at them and remembered that barge dance, so long ago. His legs were lanky then and his knees swiveled back and forth to the Charleston. How she longed for that time of elation before things fell apart. How had they allowed this conflict to happen?

"It may be our last chance to get away with the children for a very long time. We should spend *Ferragosto* away from this oppressive heat, find a seaside breeze."

Alda paused, putting down one of the woolen undershirts she was knitting for Italian soldiers, hoping, in some small way, to protect them from the inevitable winter. She peered at her husband, incredulous, still crippled by the memory and loss of baby Ugo. She finally said, "Aldo is still too young. Perhaps next summer."

Floro shook his head. "Alda. Next summer our beaches may be full of foreign soldiers."

"Floro," she stiffened. "We have everything we need right here. Let's hope the war is over by next summer. Why don't you and the girls take a week? I'll be fine here with Aldo." She sensed her husband understood and knew better than to defy her intuition. She'd seen him observe their skinny toddler, Aldo, probably recalling how robust baby Ugo had seemed. *Nothing can be taken for granted. Life changes in an instant.*

"You don't mind that I take the girls?"

"Not at all. You love the sun and the sea air."

Days later, holding her toddler under a bright blue sky, Alda waved from the terrace. The fifteen-month-old lifted his hand, moving his fingers up and down, mimicking his mother's clasping *ciao* gesture. The girls, gleeful to go but sad to leave their brother and mother behind, called up from below, that they would return soon. Floro tipped his straw hat, smiling for the first time in a long while, as the girls piled into his automobile. After they drove off, Alda turned towards the terrace. She took in a deep breath and stood her little son on the lip of one of the enormous terracotta lemon vases there. Stretching on his tiptoes, Aldo wanted to grab a little white blossom. She blocked the lemon plant's green spikes and directed his nose towards one tiny, potent flower.

"Aldino, isn't that the sweetest fragrance?"

He smiled as she let him down, holding his hand as he waddled on the terrace in his leather booties. She helped him up the three round steps, one at a time. As they passed under the arched door into the villa, Alda picked up her boy and recited poetry that Lorenzo dei Medici had written nearly five hundred years earlier on the occasion of *La Bella* Simonetta Vespucci's untimely death:

"Quant' è bella giovinezza che sen' fugge tuttavia. Chi vuol essere lieto sia, di doman non c'è certezza." How beautiful is youth and how fleeting. Be merry, for there is no certainty of tomorrow.

GRASSINA REFUGE

1943-1944

The family knew the mainland of Italy would be invaded soon. After Italy and Germany lost the North African campaign to the Allied forces in '43, the Rafanellis decided to take refuge in Grassina for a year. It was too dangerous to remain on Viale Rosselli, their city home so close to the train station. "They'll bomb the rails," Floro insisted. Necessities were more difficult to find, even for the fortunate, and the lira lost value. Ugo abhorred debt. He sold properties, even for a pittance, to get some cash. At least around the villa there was land to grow vegetables and keep livestock, enough to get them through the year.

They'd wait until the end of June, after the girls finished school. Since they would miss a year, Alda found a couple of Greek and Latin professors in Grassina to tutor them, to keep up with their studies. Preparing for their move, Alda placed her husband's leather valise next to now two-year-old Aldo, napping on her bed. He looked so tranquil asleep. She was sad. He clung to her every waking hour, sensing the tension of the war, even if it was still far away.

Removing Floro's clothes from the armoire, she spied his black shirt and examined the left sleeve. Alda's fingers grazed the fascist party insignia, the raised bundled twigs and the *fasci* column axe, the ancient Roman symbol of authority, power and unity from which the fascist party got its name. Hubris and hollow promises. Her needle and her hands had mended this badge's fraying edges. She should have refused to repair it, just let it unravel like the symbol and the party it represented. She dropped the shirt on the bed, sighing. Could real balance ever be restored to Italy after this war? She looked at her son and thought about *Il Duce*. Mussolini's father had been an ardent socialist. He'd named his son Benito after the Mexican revolutionary, Benito Juarez. Had his father hoped that giving him that name would influence his destiny? It had, for a while, but he'd turned away from socialism after being fired from the socialist newspaper *Avanti*. When he'd advocated involvement in the war after 1914, Mussolini had been expelled altogether from the socialist party. Perhaps Mussolini's father would have approved of his son's support for the union's eight-hour workday. And returning to his roots, he'd even established health and old-age insurance for the first time in Italy. *But nobody cares about that now*, she thought. Extreme nationalism and his unholy alliance with Hitler were to blame for this insanity. Her mind conjured up the newsreel footage of Hitler's pre-war visit to Florence in '38, long before anyone knew what the arrogant pair was capable of. She recalled the image of Hitler and Mussolini, in an open car, saluting the euphoric throngs as their motorcade drove through Florentine streets and squares. She knew Floro had been among the cheering crowd. As the motorcade drove up the *viale* to Piazzale Michelangelo, they'd passed Rafanelli homes and Ugo's confiscated land. Standing on the square above Florence, *Il Duce* had turned towards the panoramic view, his fez bouncing with excitement, his square jaw fixed, looking at our city as if all her treasures belonged to him. Alda looked down at her little son as he woke from his nap. She picked him up and squeezed him. "Good thing you are named after your mother, who values peace above all." Then she told him: "Never, ever, get involved in politics."

When they finally arrived that summer for their year-long stay at the villa, Flora and Anna ran towards the *fienile* and the other outbuildings, eager to find the farmer's children to play with.

"Everything seems strangely peaceful here," Alda said to Floro while carrying Aldo up onto the terrace. Standing on the stone bench she pointed out to him the olive groves and vineyard below. In the early morning light, the verdant green and silver sage on the hillside across the way was a calming elixir. Floro peered down, pondering their position. Like the Etruscans, the Tuscans, whenever possible, lived perched on a hilltop, embraced by sunlight. But the real reason was that the hillsides afforded protection, a better perspective for spying advancing enemies.

Entering the front door, the villa smelled musty after being closed for months. Palma and Alda stormed through, opening shutters, letting sun stream into the dank place, removing the white sheets that covered all the furniture.

Alda called out, *"Al buio si sta bene solo dopo morti."* We are happy in darkness only after we die.

Their farmer Giovanni appeared at the front door with some scrawny chickens.

"Permesso," he called from the threshold, holding up his offering. "You had a safe journey, signori?"

"Yes, Giovanni!" they said, thanking him. "Is everyone in your family well?" Alda asked.

"Better than the souls who passed through here in the last six months, signora — hungry, displaced families in need. I gave them food. I hope it was alright."

"Of course, Giovanni," Alda said.

The farmer looked at little Aldo. *"Eh, piccolo.* You've grown so tall!"

"Rafanelli blood," Alda laughed. She should have said Banchelli blood, as the credit for the family's height came from Elvira's family.

That first week of July, with no soldiers in sight, the family relaxed into some approximation of normalcy. Even sullen Ugo's spirits lifted. One morning he announced a new salad he'd invented, which he called *segato*. Alda raised her eyebrows as her father-in-law meticulously sliced celery and onions and cut up flat anchovies, dressing the salad with a little salt, pepper, their own olive oil and vinegar. Alda tasted it.

"Favoloso, Ugo," she admitted.

After dinner, Mario, who was the family member most passionate about music, played a recording of *The New World Symphony* to share with Anna and Flora. In those sublime moments in the parlor, Alda closed her eyes and pretended the peace they all longed for had already come.

Alda had found a husband and wife, professors of Greek and Latin, to tutor the girls through the year. With every attempt to create some semblance of normalcy, the war was always on their mind. In July the Americans and British invaded Sicily. Every day they listened to the radio after the children went to bed. Having been victorious in North Africa and now confident of their victory in Sicily, Roosevelt and Churchill called on all Italians to reject Mussolini and Hitler and to "live for Italy and civilization." They knew the war would soon reach the mainland and their city. They could no longer be sure of their safety.

A few days later, Floro walked through the front door at the same time that Alda entered from the back, holding Aldo's hand and carrying a basket of zucchini blossoms. When she saw her husband's face, she knew something terrible had happened. Placing the basket on the dining room table, Alda ushered her boy into the parlor where Anna and Flora were reading.

"Watch your brother for a while," she insisted. She shut the door and approached Floro. "What is it?"

"Rome was bombed this morning – Allied troops, for three hours, in broad daylight. If they bombed Rome like that, with all its antiquities, they won't hold back from Florence."

That night the adults learned that only military targets were destroyed in Rome. But relief turned to horror when they switched to the Italian radio station, where there was a conflicting story. Thousands of civilians had been killed during the bombing, a voice said, and the grand Roman *Basilica di San Lorenzo outside the Walls* was leveled. Who were they to believe? The voice of Pope Pius XII came on then, speaking live to a stunned crowd amidst the cathedral's rubble. Alda, fighting back tears, knew that even the Pope was powerless to end the war. Staring furiously at the radio, as if blaming the messenger, Floro turned it off.

The next evening he said, "Walk with me in the garden." He took Alda's hand as they passed over the dry pebble path. Dust caught in her throat. Her chest felt heavy. Yet seeing the evening's waning light filter between branches of their *boschetto* lifted her spirits. A strange, spectral breeze toyed with the leaves. She sensed Elvira's presence. When they reached the stone ledge by the tall umbrella pine, she and Floro sat down on the bench.

"Mussolini and Hitler met yesterday, but the meeting backfired. Hitler demanded the command of the war be turned over to the Germans," Floro said, his face rigid. "*Il Duce* intended to convince Hitler to release us from the war, but he was powerless."

"Powerless?" Alda said quietly. "Everyone is so powerless! How can you still defend him?"

"You know I don't," he insisted. "He has betrayed reason. Italy will be crushed again. All promise and hope gone." He folded his hands as if in surrender, then lit another cigarette. He took a deep drag and let out the smoke as she waited. "Many deny they were ever fascists, to save their skins. You know I can't pretend, Alda. We may lose the war, but I have to take responsibility. I can't lose my dignity and lie about my past."

"Dignity or pride, Floro? I can't help thinking that pride got us into this mess. A good man should also have the humility to admit when grave mistakes have been made. You were disillusioned even before he declared war. That isn't pretending. He doesn't deserve your loyalty. Look what he's done. Most opportunistic fascists jumped ship only after they knew we couldn't win."

"Alda, I won't," he said, peering at the ground, taking another drag on his cigarette.

"Then let's move forward despite your stubbornness!" she insisted.

"The war may come here to the villa… certainly to Florence."

"And so?"

"We must hide our supplies of food, oil, grain, wine and every personal item you care about. We need to have a plan," he said, his head down, "in case something happens…"

"What, Floro? Nothing is going to happen." Alda slapped her hand on her knee.

"That's my spirited wife," he laughed bitterly, looking directly in her eyes. "Alda, you are the center, the strong column here that keeps us all together. Just keep yourself safe. Promise."

Safe, she nodded, thinking of the irony of his words, thinking of the fractured fascist symbol her husband once idolized, a column of bundled reeds, all hope for Italy now dashed. She was indignant. "Ah, so now you expect the women and mothers to hold Italy together?"

As they walked on the path, Floro urged, "Long before Aldo is a young man, make sure he stays out of politics."

Why was he saying this now? Alda exploded. "*Caro mio*, you tell him yourself when he's old enough to understand!"

A sense of helpless silence grew between them until a sublime voice lured them into the house. It was Flora, practicing Gounod's *Ave Maria* for a solo choral piece. They approached the threshold of the glass doors, buoyed by the sublime clarity of their daughter's rising voice. Alda turned towards the woods again and, before shutting the doors, gazed at the wild oak tree, sending a prayer to Elvira.

IL DUCE RESIGNS AND GERMANS OCCUPY

1943-1944

In late July '43 King Vittorio Emmanuel accepted Mussolini's resignation, appointing Marshal Pietro Badoglio as Prime Minister and Chief of State. The announcement ended with the Italian Royal Anthem rather than the usual fascist youth anthem, *Giovinezze*. Was fascism really over after twenty years? Italians longed for peace but were badly disappointed when war continued. Perhaps Badoglio was fearful of retaliation from the Germans, who by then were occupying their cities. The next day martial law was declared with a strict curfew. Floro tried to hide the news from his wife and children, but the papers reported fascists being killed in cold blood by partisans seeking revenge. Although Italians were told it was a crime to congregate, people demonstrated in their main squares, shouting, "We're not just against fascism: we want peace!" Meanwhile, Italy was teeming with angry Germans who sensed the tide was turning against them.

One morning, as Alda, Palma and Giovanni hid food rations and precious family heirlooms behind wooden planks in the *cantina*, Floro ventured down the hill to buy the newspaper. Returning home, his eyes were caught by the sunlight glistening on glass shards cemented above the old wall bordering their property. He knew that without this protective wall, every apricot, pear and cherry tree would have been denuded. At least his family still had the fruits of their land to resist hunger, especially with food supplies increasingly scarce. The country road was so quiet that he could hear his own footsteps. Over and over he kicked a small stone uphill, watching it slide backwards.

A metaphor for life, he thought bitterly. Then suddenly, as he neared the entrance to the villa, he sensed something wrong. Realizing someone was lurking behind a bush, he kicked the stone again, feigning nonchalance, as three men suddenly appeared in the middle of the road. Two carried large sticks and blocked his way. One man snarled, *"Maladetto fascista."* Damn fascist. Floro sprang into action, immediately landing a punch squarely on the face of the first man who lunged towards him. The man toppled by the side of the road, his stick flying away from him. Grabbing the other stick from the second man, Floro threw it over the wall, took the man's arm and swung him around, tossing him by the wall. Witnessing Floro's astonishing agility and strength, the third man was already halfway down the hill. Floro turned towards him, took out his pistol and fired two shots in the air. The other two on the ground remained stunned, staring up at the imposing man. Floro picked up his fallen newspaper and dusted it off, taking a good look at them. He sauntered back up his driveway at his normal stride.

Hearing the shots from the terrace, Alda rushed towards her husband as he appeared on the courtyard. Giovanni stood by.

"What?" Alda cried.

"Three men ambushed me. Don't worry. I scared them off."

"I knew this would happen," she said. "Maybe we should return to the city." Floro's size and strength made him feel invincible, but she had always worried it would get him into serious trouble.

He dismissed her. "Don't be silly. I took care of them. They won't be back."

Farmer Giovanni, who'd known Floro since he was a young man, shook his head.

"Maybe Giovanni could pick up the paper in the morning?" she suggested, and Floro glared at her.

"So, you want me to be a prisoner in my own home, in my own town?"

She turned. It was useless to try to restrain his movement. How long would the war drag on? On September 8th, 1943, after lighting a candle for peace at the church down in Grassina, she opened the door to the square and found people gathering, celebrating.

"What is it?" she asked an old woman dressed in black.

"Signora! *La Pace.* Armistice! Badoglio surrendered to the Allies."

"*Grazie a Dio!*" Alda exclaimed.

Unfortunately, this declaration did not suddenly change everything. The war waged on, as Germans occupied their cities. Days later Nazi forces took complete control of Rome. They freed Mussolini, while the King and Badoglio fled the city, joining their new allies in the south.

"Fantastic," Floro said sarcastically as the family sat around the table. "Now Italy is without a central government!"

"But that's the best solution of all!" his anarchist brother Pietro insisted. This time Floro remained still and silent.

Italy, menaced by continued occupation, was now suffering a full-blown civil war with chaos and violence breaking out between *fascisti* and *partigiani*. Families found refuge in their homes, hoping for safety. Mussolini's amplified voice came over the radio from a makeshift satellite government up north on Lake Garda. *Il Duce* appealed to Italians to unite and join the new Italian Social Republic, which was really a German puppet state. Alda turned towards Floro.

"He's finished," he insisted, his face tense.

Days passed, with Italy's future uncertain. Still the grapes had to be harvested in October. With so many young men gone, everyone pitched in again. The big green leaves and the generous clusters of grapes comforted Alda, as plants pursued their seasonal production despite human folly. Soon olives would be harvested, the wheat sown, somehow.

As their first winter at the villa approached, Floro stoked the stoves and the hearth with wood to remove the damp chill. Palma filled the *prete* – a little cage that safely contained hot embers of wooden charcoal. Twenty minutes before the family went off to sleep, she placed one at the foot of each bed between the sheets. The heat dried out the dampness, warming the beds. Almost every day Ugo returned with fresh fish left over from the market. Through his connections, he continued to provide almost everything they needed to survive. Months passed waiting for resolution.

One late spring night in 1944 three-year-old Aldo opened the door to his parents' bedroom and crawled into their bed, telling them he hated thunder as he hid under their sheets. Alda and Floro were already awake, sitting up in bed, having heard a sound they both knew wasn't thunder.

"Our liberators," Floro whispered, grabbing her arm.

The next day Mario and Floro rode their bikes down to the newspaper stand in Grassina. There they discovered that the Allies had destroyed the rails, trying to cripple the Germans' movement, and that a nearby hospital had also been hit, killing over two hundred people.

Mario looked at Floro, who kept silent, reading intently until he glanced around and saw a young man stealing his bicycle. As he sped off, Floro ran and overtook him. Grabbing the thief by his shoulders, he threw him to the ground. Without a word, Floro peddled back to Mario, who stood in awe of his older brother's strength and agility.

A few days later, while their father was upstairs napping, Flora and Anna sat under the *loggia* watching Aldo play with marbles. Suddenly there was a strange rumbling. The two sisters rushed to the edge of the terrace to see dust clouds rising from Grassina. Anna ran inside to get her mother from the kitchen. The roaring sounded closer as Alda, the girls and Aldo watched a line of military vehicles climb their hill.

"Go inside," Alda insisted. All the horrific stories she'd heard about German retaliation surfaced in her mind. Floro appeared on the terrace, hastily tucking in his shirt. Suddenly vehicles filled the lower courtyard. Alda stood as tall as possible, taking a deep breath. Three officers emerged wearing tight-fitting leather jackets, jodhpurs and tall boots. Since Italy had signed the armistice with the Allied troops, she assumed these men would perceive them as the enemy. She prayed as she watched soldiers pour out of trucks. One officer gave the soldiers a command, and a few ran towards the outbuildings and fields. As Floro and Alda stood still, one older officer with a bandaged foot limped up the steps and held out his hand, as the others followed.

"Signori," he said, "Capitano Wilhelm Schmidt."

"Floro Rafanelli, and my wife Alda," he said. Alda was relieved by the kind look in the officer's eyes as he bowed.

He added in odd but understandable Italian, "I hope you aren't harboring prisoners of war or *partigiani* here? Our soldiers circle your villa looking right now. They are impatient, so you should tell us immediately."

"Oh no! No partisans here!" Alda insisted.

When Floro ushered the officers inside, they found Palma standing next to Aldo, her hands on his shoulders, while the girls sat on the piano bench, looking up at them.

"These are your children and…" the captain asked about Palma.

"Palma works for us," Floro said, adding that two farmer families lived on the property. "And soon my father and two brothers will be returning from the city."

"We will need to occupy a few rooms here," Schmidt said, his tone apologetic but his Italian understandable. Floro looked dismayed, but Alda softened, relieved all they wanted was lodging.

"Fine," she said.

"Our soldiers can stay in the outbuildings. Dry floors meant for wheat are much better than muddy fields," he sighed. "We have some rations, but we will need to supplement. And another imposition, signora – my fellow officers and I would appreciate eating at your table."

Sensing Floro's body tense, she grabbed her husband's hand. "*Certamente*," she said. Talking with the officer, she didn't realize that Aldo had slipped down the corridor.

"*Grazie*, signora. We have for such a long time been away from our families," Officer Schmidt added.

"Yes. Of course, Captain."

Suddenly Aldo appeared, pointing the new wooden rifle his father had made him for his third birthday. The officers were stunned for a moment.

"Ta da!" Aldo exclaimed, circling them.

"Aldo!" his mother cried. "What are you doing? Put that down immediately!" A younger officer laughed, breaking the tension.

Aldo glanced at his father, who frowned at him. Weren't these men real soldiers? Tears pooled in his eyes, but he refused to blink. Floro gently took his wooden rifle away. Aldo buried his head in his mother's skirt, peering out only when his tears had dried.

"I'm so sorry," Alda insisted, looking at the officer. "It's only a toy."

"Oh, dear signora, if only they were *all* toys," Captain Schmidt said. "My sons are older than your boy. They won't be happy with me, but when I get home no guns will be allowed in my home." Alda, amazed by the man's frankness, looked at the other officers, who clearly understood no Italian. She figured he would not have dared make such an admission if they did.

The younger officer pointed to the piano, asking who played. Even though he spoke German, Alda understood.

"Both our daughters," Alda said proudly, "but my youngest daughter's real instrument is her voice."

"Perhaps she will sing for us!" Schmidt smiled and turned to look at the girls before translating to his fellow officers.

Seeing the look of desperation in Flora's eyes, Alda quickly added, "Oh, but she's so shy!" and changed the subject, offering the officers glasses of water.

As they finished drinking, they asked for a tour.

"Please follow me," Alda said, leading the men up the main stairs. On the second floor, one checked under beds for partisan spies.

Aldo on terrace, circa summer 1944.

"Your villa is deceiving from the distance," Officer Schmidt remarked; "I expected it to be much larger. It's so long and imposing on the hillside."

"Although we have many rooms, it's very narrow. One has to walk from room to room with no corridor up here." The captain was Alda's height. It was a relief to look someone squarely in the eyes, besides Ugo, who usually avoided a direct gaze with her. Although she had seen his affection for Anna and his other grandchildren, he still dismissed her, as he had Elvira.

The two other officers seemed impatient as she led them up to the towers on the third floor. But Captain Schmidt, slapping the wall as he ascended the narrow *cinquecento* spiral stairs, remarked, "*Molto bello*. Centuries old!" When Alda opened the tower door, he stopped, looking up at the dark wooden rafters merging towards the center of the high ceiling. "This is a granary, signora! Do you have some flour to share with us?"

"It's wartime, Captain. We have just enough for the family," she insisted, pointing quickly out a tiny window. "And the other tower across the way is used to dry special grapes for our *vinsanto*. You shall have a taste after dinner."

One officer sneezed, complaining about the dust, and turned back downstairs. The other, after looking around the granary and seeing nothing suspicious, followed. Schmidt remained, peering out a window.

"How very peaceful it is here," he remarked. He seemed in no rush to retreat.

"Those are wild poppies in the distant field," Alda pointed. "See those beautiful red splashes against the green landscape." But as she spoke, he turned away, his face suddenly pale. "Are you all right, Captain?"

"It was just that red in the field," his voice cracked. "I've seen too much blood, signora. I don't know if I will ever know real peace again."

"I can't imagine," she sighed, feeling blessed that everyone in her family had been safe so far, that no one had witnessed death. "Come over to this window. It's all green – a more tranquil view," she gestured across the way. "Our landscape is perfectly framed through these tiny windows. On rare afternoons I come here for quiet. It's magical up in these old towers."

The officer with the bandaged foot smiled gratefully. "*Grazie*, signora."

EXODUS

1944

"We'll serve *pappa al pomodoro*," Alda said, so Palma cut large chunks of dried peasant bread and removed tomato jars from the shelves. As she lifted an enormous pot for the Tuscan tomato and bread soup, Alda thought of the miracle of the loaves and fishes, wondering if she could actually have enough to feed her family and the German officers. She hoped Ugo would bring home abundant amounts of small fish from Viareggio, *la primavera del mare*, which she could fry and have ready in a few minutes. She dreaded seeing Ugo's reaction to the occupiers. While overseeing other lunch preparations, she was relieved her in-laws were later than usual.

Hearing the car horn that announced the Rafanelli men's arrival at the bottom of the hill, Alda wiped her hands on a kitchen cloth. Rushing onto the terrace, she found her vigilant husband there. She was sorry he'd been feeling sick and had stayed home but was glad he was with her. When Ugo, Pietro and Mario emerged from their auto, they looked around, stunned by all the military vehicles jammed together in the courtyard. They turned to find German soldiers wandering about their property.

"Is everyone alright?" Mario asked urgently as Floro walked towards them.

"So far no problem," Floro said cautiously as Officer Schmidt emerged from the *cantina*. "This is one of the four officers staying here," he added, with a warning; "he speaks Italian."

With his bandaged foot, Schmidt limped towards them, extending his hand to Ugo. "Excuse the intrusion, sir, but your position is perfect on the hillside. You understand… war."

Looking at Ugo, Alda sensed his disgust, imagined his litany of thoughts:

his father dying on the field with Garibaldi to unite Italy; his son Danilo's senseless dying at the military base in Palermo the day before he was due home; the government confiscating his precious land on Viale Michelangelo; the Germans occupying his city – and now his home.

Suddenly the pause was interrupted by a commotion from inside the *cantina*. The soldiers who'd been tapping the walls appeared at the door and called out triumphantly. Alda realized they'd found the food hidden behind the wooden panels. She rushed down to flank Ugo, afraid he might say or do something rash and put the family in danger.

As the looters appeared in the courtyard, they raised flasks of olive oil and wine, bags of flour, sugar and other precious staples, including the *prosciutto* made last winter. Alda cast her father-in-law a cautionary look.

"We still have what's most precious," she whispered.

As the German soldiers celebrated their discovery, Ugo climbed the steps, seething. Near the edge of the terrace he heard laughter and splashing and marched towards the commotion. Peering over the garden ledge, he found two soldiers bathing in their *vasca*, the small oval fountain that pooled with rain collected from the roof – water that traveled below the terrace to the cistern and eventually overflowed there. Ugo glared down as one laughing soldier playfully pushed the other. Alda, more compassionate by nature, understood it as a rare moment of relief from war. As the oblivious soldiers continued their raucousness, Alda and Ugo heard a crack. After a moment of silence, one solider cursed and held up a broken bronze spout. He shrugged. Laughter followed.

Alda pulled irate Ugo by the arm into the villa.

"What fish did you bring today?" she asked as he glared at her.

In the kitchen, the patriarch noticed the enormous pots on the stove.

"What's all that for?" he asked.

Alda explained that the soldiers would be sleeping out in the *fienile*, but that the officers would be staying inside. "They requested to eat with us."

She observed Ugo's cheeks move as he ground his teeth. "I see. Perhaps they'll share our *prosciutto* with us," he scowled as he left the kitchen.

Later, as the family sat around the table with the officers, Schmidt took his first spoonful and paused. Smiling at Alda he exclaimed, "*Squissito, signora!*" with delighted enthusiasm, as if he comprehended her cooking was rarely appreciated. An involuntary blush rose as Alda thanked him. The other officers added curt praise in German. After the meal was finished, they excused themselves. In their wake, Floro, Pietro, Ugo and Mario looked at Alda curiously. She shrugged.

With the villa occupied for weeks, Alda rose to the challenge of feeding her family and the officers. Mornings, she walked confidently out in the woods with her children, but kept them close to her, gathering as many wild herbs and salad greens as the land offered, passing groups of young soldiers lying in the shade. As they passed, the soldiers sat up and greeted them in the only Italian they knew, removing their hats as if they were polite guests. Alda felt her family was fortunate, until one evening at dinner when a serious argument erupted among the officers. As a discussion heated up, Floro glanced nervously at Alda. The children were frightened by the tone and harsh language that none of them understood. Alda got up from the table, insisting the children go upstairs. As they retreated, she patted their shoulders, hiding her fear. On her way to the kitchen she gave Ugo a look, beseeching him to remain calm. She returned to the table with a tray full of little glasses, pouring the officers a treat of homemade *vinsanto*. She hoped the special offering would interrupt their argument. For a moment it did, but it was only the eye of the storm. Ugo finally motioned to his family to leave the table. Schmidt's expression made Alda think her family was in danger. Gathering in the parlor, to drown out the shouting and to calm their nerves, Mario turned on a recording of the sublime tenor Beniamino Gigli. When the shouting escalated, Alda reached for her knitting needle. Suddenly a gunshot rang out. The startled family froze in terror. As the voice of the tenor sang on, Floro rushed to turn it off. They stared in silence. If an officer had been shot, if there was a dead body in their dining room, they understood that the Germans would not allow any witnesses. The family would be the scapegoats. It would be the end. They waited, barely breathing.

Impatient with the tension, Floro was the first to emerge from the parlor, moving cautiously towards the dining room. All three officers stood there, chastened. No one was hurt. Schmidt shook his head, apologizing. Another officer pointed to the bullet lodged in the rafters. The officers chuckled and shrugged. The family exhaled. Alda, realizing the children must have heard the shot, ran upstairs. All three were sitting on one bed together, staring, wide-eyed. After that incident, Alda prayed the occupiers would leave.

The next day Schmidt approached Alda while she and Anna picked lemons on the terrace.

"The Americans and English are advancing," he said, taking her aside. "We are leaving, signora." He urged her to take the children and return to Florence immediately. "I have heard terrible stories of the troops advancing ahead of the Americans and British. Your girls, women… in danger. *Portare via le bambine*," he insisted in a hushed voice so Anna didn't overhear. Her head was spinning at the irony of this enemy concerned about her family's safety. She nodded.

With that warning, the family prepared for their immediate return to Florence. The following morning, as the Germans departed, Schmidt stood by the terrace steps. He shook Mario, Floro and Ugo's hands, then kissed Alda's hand.

"*Grazie*, signora. Don't worry: the war *presto finito.*"

"*Essere bravo, bambino!*" the officer said to tender Aldo who was staring at him. Schmidt tipped his cap and limped down the steps towards his auto.

As the jammed military vehicles revved their motors, Alda watched Schmidt struggle in. The last sight of him was that white, bandaged foot.

AMERICANS OCCUPY AND FLORO DEPARTS

1944

They heard that the offending troops had been shipped back to North Africa.

"It should be safe to stay here at the villa, Alda, but I have to leave, check on the Po fish nursery," Floro said following the German exodus.

Alda pleaded, "Can't it wait?" She reminded him of how blessed they'd been so far. The war was nearly over. He couldn't risk everything to go north, still a dangerous fascist stronghold, thick with partisan retaliation.

"Alda," he continued, "war or no war, we have our livelihood. I have to go if our business is to survive."

"Why do I think you're compelled for other reasons, Floro?"

She had observed his restlessness and understood that, despite his disillusionment with fascism, having been a part of its inception, he felt morbidly drawn to be part of its end. She asked him to sit down, hoping she could level with him.

"Floro," she urged, "only two kilometers away neighbors are turning viciously on one another. We have our little oasis here at the villa but, out there, there's a civil war. We've been lucky, but the Americans and Brits are coming this way. We must return to Florence."

"I won't be gone long, just a little over a week."

"How dare you tempt fate?" she said. She wanted to scream *testardo* at his big, hard head, but she knew that once Floro had made up his mind, there was no use arguing.

The next morning, he stood by the door with his satchel. "I'll see you soon," he assured his children.

"Why are you going, *Babbo*?" Anna pleaded.

"Visiting suppliers."

"Please don't!" Flora said.

As he unlatched the door, Alda turned, so her children didn't see her fury. Flora clutched at her father while Anna gently held onto his arm. Floro patted his daughters' heads and then lifted his little son, who looked confused. Releasing Aldo, Floro said, "Don't worry." He kissed his wife, closing the heavy door behind him. Alda refused to follow him.

On April 25th, Anna turned fifteen. The girls were busy studying their Greek and Latin. The only joy was listening to Flora sing, her voice always reminding Alda of her mother-in-law, who she hoped was watching over them. Weeks and weeks passed and still not a word from Floro. Alda was full of anxiety but she had to be strong for the children, her in-laws and herself.

Floro was still missing on June 5th, when the radio announced that the Allies had entered Rome and liberated the city. Although the villa was seven miles from the outskirts of Florence, they knew Germans were still swarming there. Two more months passed with no news from Floro. On the night of August 4th, Alda, alone in bed, woke to the sound of distant explosions, sounds that in peaceful times might have been drums or fireworks for the festival of Florence's patron saint, San Giovanni.

Alda got out of bed to open the long window, pushing the shutters out. She was distracted for a moment by the beauty of the stars and the dark night. Perhaps it had been her imagination? A second later the blasting sound repeated, followed by a distant flash of light that obliterated the stars.

"Florence," she whispered, trembling. Perhaps it was the retreating Germans. "Oh Floro!" she called out to the dark.

She turned and saw her little Aldo standing in his white sleeping gown. Closing the window, she held her three-year-old trembling son. During these five months without his father, he often wandered into her room complaining of bad dreams. They climbed into bed.

"What's that noise, *Mamma*?"

"I don't know, Aldino. Try to sleep now." As he curled up next to her, shaking, her heart was heavy. She whispered the lullaby, *Stella Stelline*, until he gradually fell asleep.

At dawn the next morning, Ugo and Mario left to discover what had happened and make sure that Pietro, who had left the villa to live in an apartment in the city, was safe. They needed to check on how their tenants fared and if their houses along Viale Michelangelo were still standing. They drove half an hour on the narrow back roads. Seeing the homes that Ugo had built were intact, they were relieved. Then as they parked in their driveway on Viale Michelangelo, they found the garage leveled. They got out of the car.

"*Guarda, Babbo,* there's a huge bomb crater in the back field." Ugo was silent as he surveyed the damage. With a bomb having struck so close, no serious damage to any houses seemed like a miracle.

Back in the car, they drove a mile only to discover a blockade. Italian soldiers approached, shouting, "Turn around; the roads are mined." Mario backed up and drove around the square to reach Pietro's apartment building. After ten minutes of tense driving, they finally arrived. Mario ran into the apartment building and returned minutes later with Pietro, who looked disheveled.

As he climbed in, he reassured them, "No explosions near here." They wound around narrow streets towards the river and found more roads blocked. Mario pulled over and parked off the road.

"*Babbo,* please stay behind with the car," he said.

"Of course," Ugo agreed. One of their cars had already been confiscated. He wanted to make sure no one would take the only remaining one.

As the brothers approached the river, Pietro commented on the eerie, deafening silence. Reaching the river's walled banks, they gazed downstream and saw that only one bridge was left crossing the Arno, the Ponte Vecchio.

"*Mio Dio,*" Mario said.

"They only spared the old bridge," Pietro sighed.

They walked in its direction but couldn't pass. Shattered buildings surrounding the Ponte Vecchio blocked access.

"The Germans must've set off explosives to stall the Allies," Mario said as they looked around trying to recall the elegant Renaissance structures that were now a jagged mass of debris on the ground. Dazed and disoriented by the wreckage and the strange openness in their city, the brothers stared.

As they moved around, raising mortar and dust with every step, their throats closed. No soul to be seen, they assumed everyone was in shelters. Pietro muttered disbelief. He had just been at the apothecary on this corner the other day.

They finally found an old man. "Yes, it was the Germans, retreating," he mumbled. "I can't find my wife. We tried to get into Palazzo Pitti. Thousands of people are sheltered there."

Mario put a hand on the man's shoulder. "You'll find her."

They struggled on. Mario pointed towards the elegant Signoria tower, the central Florentine government building, still visible. He sighed: "Thank heaven, it wasn't destroyed."

"But look over at the Uffizi… The Vasari corridor – it's gone!" Pietro exclaimed. The distraught brothers headed back to find their father.

"Ponte alle Grazie. Ponte Santa Trinità… Gone!" Mario told his father.

"But they spared Ponte Vecchio," Pietro said.

Sighing, Ugo insisted, "We'd better get back to Grassina."

Mario took a circuitous route to avoid the main roads. With all the detours, it took them over an hour to drive the seven miles home.

As they drove to the villa, farmer Giovanni was there looking out the window of the supply room that shared a wall with the main house. Washing his hands at the sink, he surveyed the landscape. He wondered how, with everything that the Germans had confiscated, they or their beasts could survive if the war didn't end soon. Beneath the floor where he stood, two cows were in their stalls, hungrily chewing hay he'd finally just fed them. As he turned off the water, he opened the window and heard a curious cranking sound in the distance. As he looked down the valley at Grassina, down beyond the little stream, across the hill, his jaw dropped. He spied an enormous tank, maneuvering, raising its gun towards the villa, in his direction. In a flash, he thought, *This is my last sight of this world.* His throat clutched and he froze with fear as the tank fired. Suddenly there was a tremendous clamor as something blasted through the wall where he stood. Knocked to the floor, stunned, Giovanni lifted his head slightly and saw sky through a gaping hole where the now pulverized sink had just been. Shocked, he was too terrified to look down at his legs, certain they must have been blown off and that he would die at any moment. Yet… incredibly, he felt no pain. Cautious, terrified, his hands ventured below his knees. To his utter amazement, his legs were intact. He inhaled deeply and slowly got up. When he turned around, he gasped. There was an identical round hole on the opposite side of the room, opening a view to the woods behind the villa. Checking himself again, he made the sign of the cross. Certainly this was a miracle! His pants were dusty and torn, but he'd escaped with only a few bloody scrapes.

Panic rose with the possibility of a second blast. Not wanting to push his luck, he rushed from the room and stumbled down the stairs: "O, signore! *Grazie! Grazie*," he cried. Out on the courtyard he saw that the blast had destroyed part of the building's first floor, so he ran towards the rubble to check on the cows. One lay dead on the ground; the other was wild-eyed with fear but seemed unhurt. Hearing the poor surviving creature's pathetic lament, Giovanni wanted to cry. But there was no time – he had to run and warn the signora.

"I'll be back," he promised the cow, gently patting her flank before rushing out. Wobbling up the terrace steps, he ran into Signora Alda, anguish written on her face.

"Giovanni?" she cried, seeing the gaping hole.

"Oh, signora... I was... at the sink... A tank fired!" he stammered. "Between my legs!"

Her hand reached her mouth. "Are you alright?"

He nodded, telling her the story. "One of our cows is dead."

"Oh God," she sighed, hastily sitting him down on the stone bench. Alda looked down the valley, frantically searching for the culprit. A line of jeeps followed the creaking tank as it crept up their hill, lifting dust in volumes.

Palma appeared on the terrace, holding Aldo's hand. Anna and Flora followed.

"*Mamma?*" they cried.

"Palma, please, get Giovanni some water," Alda said. "And you three, go sit in the garden park, just outside the door, until we come get you," she demanded. Anna and Flora took Aldo's hand as Palma returned with a glass of water. Standing by the edge of the terrace, Alda was relieved the tank was too large to enter their driveway. It parked along the cypress trees as a convoy of military jeeps turned into their drive and jammed their courtyard. *Oh, blessed Lord... where is my husband now?* Alda thought.

A tall American officer emerged from one of the jeeps wearing khaki pants that matched his shirt. When he approached Alda on the stairs, he took off his cap. She noted wisps of thinning brown hair. He had no knowledge of her language, but ventured a tentative: "*Bona sera*," and uttered a chain of unintelligible words of which she only understood one: *sorry*. How apologetic these occupiers are! Like the Germans, they were probably attracted to their villa with a good vantage point.

The officer entered as a few soldiers checked the house to make sure no Germans were harbored there. Palma gathered the children inside by the hearth.

"Chocolate," one soldier offered to Aldo, who reached for the bar before his mother could say no.

The girls, seeing their mother's exasperation, shook their heads. "No, grazie."

Some official kept uttering, "Headquarters."

Alda shrugged. "No English," she said. More soldiers entered, clearly on a mission. Alda and her children and Palma watched helplessly as the Americans carried their furniture out of the house, into the back woods.

"Cosa fate?" Alda asked, breathless. They ignored her. Their beautiful antique walnut chairs and side tables were now outside on the pebble path. She rushed to the officer to complain. He called one of his soldiers.

"Hey, Torchia – tell the lady not to worry. We're here to liberate. We won't be long. But for now, we need the space for temporary headquarters."

There was that word again. Alda listened carefully to the young soldier's translation, his Sicilian–American dialect difficult to comprehend. She understood a few words here and there. As soldiers approached the old piano by the door, she rushed over, making a wall with her body, knowing if they moved the precious piano outside, it would be ruined.

"Signor Torchia, this instrument stays!" Alda insisted.

As they tried to move her aside, she repeatedly blocked their way. The officer relented.

"Okay, okay! Leave it. But tell her she'd better play for us, or it's going out while she's asleep."

As they stripped her home, Alda stood guard by the piano. She was losing control. The soldiers arranged their own supplies, passing her as if she were invisible, setting up desks and makeshift furniture.

When Anna and Flora complained about the furniture in the woods, Alda whispered, "They are just things. Things. Don't worry. We stay right here until your grandfather and uncles come home, and we decide what to do."

Torchia approached. "Signora, materassi?"

Alda told him and the children to follow her up the wide front stairs and pointed to two spare mattresses under the beds. They hauled them downstairs, through the corridor and back rooms. She wondered again... Where is Floro? Has someone given him a mattress to sleep on?

When she opened the door to the parlor, it was already transformed into a dormitory. Aldo, tugging on his mother's hand, was stunned to find men lying on mattresses strewn about.

"What are they doing on the floor?" he asked. Although the Americans seemed good-natured, their presence made him skittish.

"They need a place to rest," Alda said, squeezing his hand. Palma entered, asking for guidance in the kitchen.

Moments later, when Ugo, Pietro and Mario arrived, they found their dining room full of strange desks and makeshift shelves stacked with beans and spam.

"As you can see, things happen here, not just in the city," Alda sighed, telling them about Giovanni's close call. When Mario explained about the bridges, Alda pulled little Aldo close to her, trying to cover his ears from the news. "We can't stay here. We have to move back to the city," she said, looking down at her son, who held her hand tight.

As Mario read Aldo the adventures of *Sandokan* by Emilio Salgari, Alda spent the day packing. Then she walked through the entire villa, checking everything. In the last room at the end of the corridor, she found a solitary young American soldier sitting by the window, smoking a cigarette. He sat up when Alda entered. Without the language, she could only smile at the man, so young for the horrors of war. Then she noticed something scribbled in pencil on the flat part of the shutter just above him. She pointed to the scribble, annoyed by his disregard for her property.

"That's my name and address in America!" he announced proudly, talking loudly, hoping to be understood. "My home, signora."

Her anger melted at the word. *Home.* She figured he must be marking his journey, recording his stay in case something happened to him, as if his family would ever discover this scribble. She wanted to embrace the shabby young American.

Turning down the corridor, she felt her jaw tighten thinking of all the homesick young men far away from family, trained to kill. As twilight crept into darkness, Alda walked over to the glass doors facing their once manicured, wooded park behind the house. Deeply disturbed by this invasion, her face flushed in anger seeing all their furniture out there, left on the dirt, vulnerable to the elements. She was furious about the disregard for their possessions but sighed. "None of this is important," she said to herself. Looking out, she prayed to the saint of the lost, Saint Anthony, about what did matter. "Please, please just keep Floro safe and bring him home." Her prayer was interrupted by a shadowy figure heading towards the house along the path of laurel bushes. She recognized the woman as a neighbor from Grassina. *Perhaps she heard the tank blast earlier and is coming to check on us...* As Alda was about to open the door to greet her, she watched the woman pick up one of the family's antique chairs and slither away. Alda, at first too stunned to move, snapped out of her inertia. Grabbing Elvira's cane, she flung open the door, shouting and shaking the cane, rushing after the woman, who dropped the chair and raced off, calling out, "*O signora, e' la guerra.*" As if war excused stealing.

She watched the figure rush under the umbrella pine and disappear. Retrieving the chair, Alda carried it closer to the villa and sat down, reclaiming possession of it and her nerves. She returned inside and gave a last look at their transformed dining room, now a war office. As Americans scurried about she thought, *Peace will come. Floro will return. We will all be here together soon.*

Mario appeared with Aldo. Taking his little hand, just before leaving their home to the occupiers, Alda gave one last glance outside at all their forlorn belongings: tossed tables, armoires, dressers and chairs. She recalled how every late autumn before the family moved back to Florence, she and Elvira would lay sheets over the furniture for protection. Now she envisioned one enormous white sheet, sailing in the air, hovering above the exposed furniture, a linen shroud, falling in slow motion.

ENGAGED

1976

Under a cloud of white linen we built mountain peaks with our elbows, plowed fields and forged rivers with our naked bodies. With the temperature rising under cover, I imagined floating on the ceiling, hovering above our white sheet like some astral voyeur, to witness our moving topography. Yet… the experience was far from unadulterated abandon. I needed to muffle my liberating waves of repeated rapture since Alda often sat in the parlor just below our room. She might even be down there now, threading her pink glass rosary beads with her thumb, praying for our souls. At the moment I was thankful that she was a little deaf.

Recommencing our corporeal exploration, I discovered a minuscule hole above Aldo's ear. "What's this?" I whispered, but before he could answer I'd moved back under our linen tent. No more interruptions! Then Aldo, breaking from the heated moment, emerged and sat up. Wrapping the sheet around his waist, he suddenly sounded serious and chaste.

"It's time," he pronounced. I lay there imagining what he meant before curling up next to him, my hair going every which way. "I can't face your family back in New York this summer without telling them my intentions," he continued.

I caught my breath, "Your what?"

"My intentions," he repeated.

We exhaled together, surrendering abandon and freedom. Did I misconstrue? Was he proposing? Had he been fretting about my family's opinion about our living together, unmarried, this whole past year?

I sighed. "And what about my intentions?" I said, staring at him. "I face your family here every day. Should I worry that your mother or your sisters might think I'm taking advantage of *you*?" He didn't get my reverse logic, didn't share all my concerns about my sojourn here. "Anyway, I thought you were a sworn bachelor?"

"I was. Until now," he insisted. I rested my head on his rising and falling chest. Was this the moment, not over a glass of wine or gazing at a blazing sunset? He'd thankfully refrained from the hackneyed falling down on his knee! Hackneyed! Hah! I laughed at my ridiculous pun before staring at the hair on his chest.

"So, whaddya say?" he spewed in his best New Yorkese. His question in English with the accent sent me wondering about who belongs where. Was I just another temporary foreign occupier here, like that American soldier? What if I'd remained home, forged another path, gone for a masters in fine arts, or explored that brief New York relationship that'd left me breathless? Aldo and I hailed from two different continents and cultures. We spoke different languages. There was an age difference of nine years. Were there too many obstacles?

I finally said, "Aldo! You're so unconventionally conventional. You feel the need to tell my family your intentions, but you haven't really asked me yet."

"Can't you see I'm asking?"

Lunch under the loggia - Aldo, Camilla, Alda, with Sue and Marcella visiting, 1976.

I looked into his soulful brown eyes and slapped his shoulder affectionately before settling my head back on his chest, stealing more time for perhaps the most important yes or no of my life. Lying quietly, I recalled his efforts to lure me here and make me feel at home. We even joked that he'd set a trap for me. Yet… his love and kindness prevailed. I thought of all the things I treasured about him: the way he cultivated land and his curious mind, how he talked about everything from astronomy and archeology to agriculture, from politics to physics. So what if he grew up rubber-leg dancing to Elvis and didn't comprehend my beloved Beatles? He'd absorbed much of American culture, and we shared the most basic values. I imagined the richness of our life together, of loving and learning. Aldo was a generous, unselfish lover. I felt lucky and hoped this was no anomaly, that equal opportunity lovemaking was the norm going forward, that neither men nor women would assume that male ecstasy sufficed to satisfy both.

What about children? Now this question also included that possibility. I'd seen Aldo be playful with my sister Carol's children when we visited them on Long Island, before he spoke a word of English. And he'd been so tender this summer with Marcella, my sister's two-year-old daughter. Sue had needed a break, was in the middle of a divorce, so she'd come to visit us. We'd driven to Zurich to pick them up. Aldo had even offered to watch Marcella so Sue and I could have an overnight in Venice, but my sister wanted her daughter to see the "city on the water." Having witnessed my sister's brief marriage and the pain of her divorce gave me pause. I finally focused on my man. I could tell him anything. There was mutual trust and respect. My whole body relaxed around him. And… *he's such a great cook!* After all my serious pondering, this classic role reversal made me laugh out loud.

"What's so funny?" Aldo asked.

"Oh nothing, I'm sorry. Give me another second, okay?"

He waited patiently for my response. I finally said: "There's an ocean between me and my home. Could either of us be happy when one of us is bound to live on a continent far away from family and friends?" This question made us both pensive. It was a stopgap, not my answer.

I thought about how overwhelmed I'd felt the first day I'd walked into the apartment he'd created for me, restoring all the old broken antique furniture I'd seen lying around the summer before. He'd returned those war-torn pieces to their former beauty, waxed and glowing. And how much more he'd done for my arrival. His generosity and thoughtful kindness were seductive.

And I recalled a month earlier, as we'd sat on the beach, with an expanse of Mediterranean behind me. He'd kissed me and said: "*Trovo il mare nei tuoi occhi!*" I find the sea in your eyes. I'd smiled and taken his hand and coaxed him into the real sea. How can I resist a man who sounds like our favorite poet Pablo Neruda?

And what about his long-ago vision of me looking out the window of this bedroom? Perhaps I really was destined to be here. This is my home now. *He feels like home.* How could my answer be anything but yes?

I swallowed. There was a larger issue. I needed to find a job. I'd come here to write but I wrote more in New York with a full-time job. I hated relying so completely on Aldo. I remembered the word that surfaced one morning after he'd gone off to work. With all the shutters closed, I'd risen thinking that I'd been *kept in the dark*. Kept. That was the lingering word that made me shudder. In some circumstances, marrying only institutionalizes a kind of keeping. Sure, I helped with harvests, taught Aldo's nephews English for a brief time and was still making some money translating for catalogues, but my writing was in limbo. To feel good about my yes, I had to emerge from feeling so dependent.

"Well?" Aldo whispered, patiently stroking my hair. I couldn't leave him hanging any longer. I would address these things later.

"Of course, Aldino," I said, lifting my head and kissing his mouth. Our silent, thoughtful embrace endured a long while.

When we finally dressed and headed downstairs to spill the news of our engagement, his mother exhaled with relief. Raising her hand in a joyful gesture, she said, "About time." I felt a sinking sensation, knowing that despite her good humor and acceptance, she was born a half-century before me, the year before Queen Victoria died.

That night, as I peeked into the parlor to say *buona notte*, Alda asked me to sit down. She opened a little box. "Here," she said, displaying a large, round diamond that gave off a yellow tinge in the light. "It belonged to Ugo, my father-in-law."

"This was your father-in-law's ring?" I gasped. It seemed unbelievable that the infamous patriarch would have worn something like this. Perhaps she meant it was Elvira's?

"I want you to have it," she said, smiling.

"This family heirloom…?" I choked, my eyes already stinging, wondering if she was trying to compensate for Aldo's lack of formality. It's okay, I wanted to assure her, I'm not attached to tradition. But I looked at her – all sincerity, trust and love. This was her way of welcoming me into her clan.

"Alda, it's beautiful," I smiled, wondering why she hadn't given the ring to Aldo to give to me. He clearly hadn't confided in her beforehand. Regardless, the gift felt like such an honor. "I will cherish it always; it will get passed down..." I felt overwhelmed by that thought. Who will I pass this on to? All this living in the blissful present ignored future questions. Marrying meant a lifetime of commitment. I wasn't just marrying Aldo – I was marrying his family, his history, his culture. We would be combining our genes to make other people. I looked at Alda and relaxed. This person will be my *mother-in-law*, a cranky word. I felt lucky that negative connotations didn't apply to this stoic yet witty woman. The soft sound of the Italian word *suocera* seemed much more apropos.

FLOWER SHOP AND WEDDING

1976-1977

Aldo's sisters Flora and Anna seemed delighted with our news. Anna took me to La Casa del Tessuto, an elegant fabric shop in Florence near the *Duomo*, owned by classmates of hers, the Romoli brothers.

"We'll get the fabric there, and my dressmaker can make your wedding dress," she said. I hadn't thought about the dress, or any wedding details, but loved the idea of the Rafanelli tradition of tailored clothing, and the thought that it would be unlike any other. Once inside the beautiful fabric shop, we examined bolts of gorgeous white fabric. My eyes landed on a beautiful gossamer material with tiny appliquéd flowers. I held it out, and Anna approved. "Franca can easily make a bodice for this," she said, holding the sheer crepe material up against me.

"Okay. *Perfetto,*" I said, and it was done.

The wedding would be a fleeting moment; it was the marriage that counted. A knot grew in my throat as the decision began to sink in. Being so far away from home, and assuming we would be living in Italy, I was afraid to find myself completely enveloped in Aldo's life. That night I thought about giving up my name and taking on Aldo's. I knew for some women it was more than symbolic, this relinquishing of identity. Even if Camilla Rafanelli had a more melodious ring than Camilla Calhoun, before we fell asleep I asked Aldo, "Would it bother you if I kept my name?" After all... I felt attached; it explained something of my ancestral mix of Scots, Irish, English and Dutch blood. I noted that his mother used her maiden name, Degli Innocenti, on all formal documents, alongside Rafanelli. Italians seemed more advanced than Americans in this regard. But more and more women in America were retaining their names, and this really resonated with me.

Aldo responded without hesitation. "Not at all; whatever you want." I loved him even more for his absolute confidence. Keeping my name didn't threaten him whatsoever and made me even more certain of my yes. Still I felt panic looming. I had to acknowledge my dreamy nature that mirrored the impractical side of my father. I needed work, I told him, a schedule. When I got a job, I would carve out time to write.

Just as I began my search, Aldo's dear friend Filippo called with news about a business opportunity: an old woman was selling her flower shop in Florence for a very reasonable price. I could run it. Although I had no experience as a florist, I was eager to work and learn a new trade. The three of us met on Via Cavour, across San Marco Square. There was no sign that a flower shop existed on the street except for a few red geranium pots sitting on a stone bench outside. Inside, we greeted the woman, who explained that Le Belle Arti forbade signage, as the location had been Lorenzo dei Medici's

Camilla in the flower shop greenhouse, Via Cavour, Florence, 1977.

sculpture garden where a young Michelangelo had sketched. As we passed into a courtyard, a long greenhouse stretched out before us. Behind the greenhouse were offices of the Appellate Court, a source of customers, she said, and there was an officers' club next door too. We entered a little room with tall containers holding long stem roses and gladioli. When I confessed to little experience, she told me I could apprentice with her for a while before taking over.

A few weeks later, when the deal was made, Aldo and I awoke at four am to reach the early morning wholesale flower market located in the narrow corridor in front of the Uffizi Gallery. Tall lamps illuminated the dark as I chose the freshest flowers and tried to maneuver my way around the male market crowd. I couldn't help thinking we were continuing the Rafanelli tradition, like with Ugo's wholesale fish business, with Aldo's father and family rising for the early market. I agreed when Aldo insisted on accompanying me, as I was intimidated as the only woman there.

Even in the shop I learned the unavoidable art of haggling with customers. It was a cultural aspect I didn't find at all charming, the exasperating back and forth about the price of live houseplants. At the outdoor San Lorenzo market, it was expected to negotiate for discounts. But for plants? For flowers? I complained to Aldo, "Our price should be our price." He understood my frustration but just raised his shoulders, accepting fate like a true Florentine.

I relished making floral arrangements, even small funereal pillows, something I'd never seen in America. I'd cover skeletal wooden pillows with moss, then affix flowers, making a pattern of miniature pink roses with yellow mimosa. I found the shape and notion of the pillow endearing, rather than impersonal flowers stuck in vases or slung around wreaths that reminded me of equestrian trophies. Filippo's wife Rosanda, who worked for the prestigious publisher Olschki, gave me a wonderful large book, *The Garden of the Renaissance,* about botanical symbolism in Italian paintings. I already knew that lilies and chrysanthemums were classic *flowers of the dead.* I found them too obvious. When I learned that roses, among other flowers, were funerary symbols in antiquity, it validated my more atypical arrangements.

Except for holidays, the shop was too sleepy. Across the street was where all the action was, and they weren't buying flowers. While I watched from under my shop's arched portico, Piazza San Marco transformed into a hotbed of political activism. Crowds of leftist youth converged on the square. Muffled voices reverberated through megaphones. When I was a student in Rome,

I'd witnessed *Il Popolo*'s proletariat, anti-imperialist rallies and, like today, anti-Americanism. I tried not to take it personally. I found it amusing to see the communist youth arrive wearing tattered jeans, riding on enormous, slick motorcycles that their fathers had clearly bought for them. Was their solidarity with impoverished workers sincere? The irony was that they appeared just like we young Americans had a few years earlier during Vietnam protests. Despite my sympathy for their activism, I couldn't help my nostalgia for the elegant Italians I recalled from my days in Rome when I was the one donning jeans and Adidas sneakers. I wished American youth had adopted the elegant Italian style with their form-fitting shirts, skirts and sexy shoes, instead of the Italian youth now embracing the rebellious American shabby fashion, as if it were a statement instead of a fad.

Meanwhile, trains, government offices and museums were striking for better conditions. As months passed, the newspapers reported on frequent kidnappings and violent acts of terrorism by the Red Brigades. The Italian economy generally seemed to be tanking. With Aldo and his friends who spanned the political spectrum – communists, moderates and a few conservatives – we engaged in something so often avoided in America: political dinner discussions. As we sat around our table, everyone was full of heated concern and opinions about Italy's direction. Despite both our conservative family histories, Aldo and I leaned leftward. Yet he, after the consequence of his father's political involvement, remained independent of any party affiliation, challenging every slanted argument with an open mind. I glanced around the table, absorbed by the passionate discourse, loving Aldo, Italians and Italy. Despite the fact that many held anti-American sentiments, I gained a valuable perspective and was accepted and swept up in the dynamic, vital search for solutions.

In Florence, we often had dinner with Giovanni and Fernanda in Fiesole, and with Ghita and Alberto at their home in Settignano. I was now paying rapt attention to the conjugal lives of Aldo's friends. Fernanda was a tentative cook, looking to Aldo for tips, probably because Giovanni always raved about Aldo's cooking on the boat. Alberto stayed away from the kitchen. Ghita had total command in the most chaotic kitchen I'd ever seen, so packed with plates, platters and jars of ingredients. It was astonishing the way she managed a storm of pots and pans, like Alda, and served the most gorgeous multi-course meals for herds of people, with no drama or help from anyone. With Filippo and Rosanda, as well as with Simonetta and Eugenio, the man was in command of the kitchen. Eugenio's fish risotto and pigeon stew were unforgettable. And it wasn't just the cooking roles. I listened to how couples spoke to one another. It seemed that roles were being reinvented in this generation of Italian marriages. We were a generation playing it by ear; life went along without dictation. Except we did lay some ground rules.

In the summer of 1976 we returned to New York. Aldo took my mother and elder brother aside to ask for my hand in marriage. (I expected he wanted my other parts too.) The concept was so retro-old-fashioned, but I was amused. My fretting was futile, as my entire family adored Aldo, whose English by then had greatly improved. We decided to marry in America, a small, no-fuss wedding the next summer on Long Island. My mother did the essential planning, with scant input from me. I had the excuse of living in Florence. A year later we rented a lovely house near Oyster Bay, Long Island, where my family stayed, and our small, homespun reception took place. Hilary, having learned Italian, French and German as an au pair in Europe, had returned home to Seattle. She arrived days before our August date, to cater our wedding, her enormous gift to us. There was no rehearsal dinner. I went to the market for the flowers and created small table settings. The night before, while Hilary prepared a luscious strawberry and cream wedding cake, Aldo, my mother, brothers and sisters and I sat around the kitchen table peeling carrots and chopping celery for the crudités. Aldo assisted chef Hilary. It all seemed like déjà vu, like being together in Alda's kitchen in Grassina again. Except it was only my family this time.

There were no bridesmaids or best men, just my sister Sue's little daughter Marcella as the flower girl for the church ceremony. Both Aldo and I wore white. He stood tall at the altar in his bell-bottom white linen suit, without the tie that Sue had wanted me to encourage him to wear. We exchanged rings, our hands sweating with emotion. There was no dancing, but lots of cheer as we served champagne and two enormous bottles of our friends' Tizzano wine from their estate near the villa.

Holding a champagne flute, my dearest college friend Linda approached. "Maybe this isn't the best time," she said, "but I'd like to ask you a serious question."

"What?" I said, anxious.

"I want to study Italian." My nervousness turned to excitement anticipating her question. "So, I was wondering…Could I take up your invitation to stay at the villa with you and Aldo while I take an Italian course? Be totally frank."

"Are you kidding? Yes, absolutely," I said without hesitation, knowing Aldo would welcome the idea. I loved Aldo's friends, but it had been lonely without Hilary. I missed my own friends. Then I asked how her husband would cope with her absence.

"It's fine. Joe is totally supportive of my doing this," she said.

"Well, Italian is in your blood and, with your French, you'll pick it up in no time," I said. "When?"

"October?" she said.

"In two months! Fantastic." I beamed, squeezing her hand.

After a wonderful honeymoon in California and Seattle, visiting Hilary's family and traveling to the San Juan Islands, we returned to Florence.

Aldo and Camilla, wedding, August 1977.

A few days before Linda was due to arrive, Aldo and I were sitting down to lunch with his mother. As Milena placed a tray of roast beef on the table, I watched Aldo carve the red meat. Suddenly I felt inexplicable revulsion as he offered me a rare slice, my usual preference. I gagged and looked away. "Oh, no *grazie. Non posso!*" I excused myself from the table, my hand covering my mouth. Out of the corner of my eye, I saw Alda smiling from ear to ear. As I rushed down the corridor and up the spiral stairs, I felt both sick to my stomach and simultaneously upset by my mother-in-law's smile. I sat on the bed and another wave of nausea hit as Aldo entered.

"I feel really sick. Why was your mother grinning?"

Aldo looked stunned, wide-eyed. "Because she thinks you're not sick, *amore*," he said. "She was smiling because you are *nello stato interessante*."

"What?"

He jested, touching his belly, expanding it outward as if to explain the meaning.

"*O Gesu*, Aldo, I know that *stato interessante* means pregnant," I blurted, "but it can't be. So soon! My doctor told me with my being so irregular it would be difficult for me to conceive. I know we've relaxed about it, but we wanted to wait a year or so," I insisted. "Besides, how can your mother tell? How does she know it isn't some stomach virus?"

"Being repulsed by red meat is a sign."

"What? How do *you* know that, Signor *confirmato* bachelor?"

"It happened to my mother. It's a known thing here."

"Oh God, you're serious?" I said, now in a panic. "I'll go this afternoon to the pharmacy. There are home pregnancy test kits available now."

"Maybe you should lie down." He took my hand and sat beside me. Woozy, my eyes wandered along the beautiful old worn terracotta floor to the half-written page sitting in my typewriter. I swallowed the knot in my throat.

When the shops reopened, I greeted the village pharmacist, pulling in my gut and making sure I bought other things I didn't need, like soap and lavender-scented lotion. I sneaked the pregnancy test off the shelf, praying that gossipy girl Pupa wasn't at the counter. A wonderful thing about Grassina was that shopping was personal, the way it used to be in my mother's time. Here the bread maker, Valdamaro, the butcher Franco, and Romano Piccini, the greengrocer, were all accountable and took great pride in their products. They knew all of us by name. It was always *Buon giorno, signorina*, now *signora*, and how are Aldo and his mother doing? Naturally they always saved you the very best. Everything was easily examined, package free, and Italians were supremely discerning about quality and everything they bought was carried away in their own mesh bags. But if one needed to save time, or pined for anonymity, Grassina was not the place to shop. My aversion to malls and supermarkets trumped my impatience or need for privacy. Standing in line, unlike orderly British or Americans, you had to watch with your elbows so nobody cut in front of you. But that day I was in no hurry. I whistled to feign nonchalance, as I dug out lira and paid for the one item I needed and the two I didn't. Slithering out of the pharmacy, I was anxious to get home. Holding my satchel tight, I sprinted defiantly past the post office, past the little stream, but slowed down at the bottom of the hill towards the villa. It was hot. Maybe I should be taking better care of myself? I shuddered. This was the hill where Floro had been ambushed during the war and where, years later, Uncle Mario, who'd been like a surrogate father to Aldo, had collapsed and died of heart failure at forty-five, while walking with fourteen-year-old Aldo, out for a day of hunting.

I ambled pensively up the hill, along the wall that marked the villa's sloping boundary. The glass shards encrusted on the top of the stucco and stone wall were inhibiting. But I was no intruder, I told myself. I belonged here. Turning right into the long, open driveway, I passed my hand over the succulent caper plants cascading from the dry wall, then gazed down at the perpendicular rows of grapevines and scattered olive trees. Breathless from anxiety, I entered the villa and tiptoed through the corridor, avoiding questions. I ran, dizzy, up the spiral staircase. With my heart pounding in my ears, I tore open the package and read the instructions in our bedroom. If positive, a circle would appear after ten minutes on the petri dish. I exhaled as I washed my hands, studying my face in the mirror for any telltale alterations. Sitting on the toilet, I captured my urine and placed the dish on my dresser. I couldn't just stand there watching it decide, so I moved to the window and pushed out the shutters. I sat on the Savonarola chair staring down at the terrace, the lemon trees, the *loggia*, the cypress trees and the fields beyond. I hummed the words to John Lennon's song *Imagine*. After five minutes I got up and took a look at the petri dish of my destiny. A distinct circle stared up at me. At that moment Aldo appeared on the threshold, just in time to witness my jaw drop.

"Are you alright?"

"*Guarda, guarda,*" I said. "Maybe something's wrong. It's supposed to take much longer. It's already a very clear circle – positive." We both gazed dumbly at it.

"*Gesù,* Aldo! You and your mother were right." Our wide eyes blinked.

"*Un bambino!*" I finally said, a wave of chills passing over me. Clasping both his hands, I felt both thrilled and scared. We smiled at each other. "Are you okay?" I said. Not yet married two full months, it was a surprise.

"Of course," Aldo said, taking me into his arms. We embraced a long while, incredulous.

"Your mother will be thrilled... A little Rafanelli! When should we tell her?"

"She already suspects. It'd be torture to make her wait."

We headed downstairs and found her on the phone in the parlor, donning her serious negotiator voice, crochet work on her lap, books on her side table amidst, as always, bursting piles of newspapers and catalogues. Aldo and I quietly sank into the old sofa, holding hands, waiting. It sounded like she was trying to sell off her last property.

"This is my life," she shrugged as she finished, "borrowing from Peter to pay Paul."

"*Mamma*," Aldo interrupted, "we're having a baby."

"*O Dio*! I knew it!" she cried, her hands rising, beckoning us to her. As we encircled her, she looked into our teary eyes, gently patting our faces.

That evening after dinner I sat down with Alda, eager to learn more of her war experiences. Being pregnant now and working at the flower shop, I wanted to carve out the time to record as much as possible. Before long a new life would be demanding my attention. So, with notebook in hand, I asked Alda to start again from where she had left off.

PIETRO AND THE SNIPER

Florence, 1944

Giovanni loaded the family's belongings onto a donkey cart before lifting Aldo on top of trunks and sacks. The Americans occupying the villa forced them to return to their home in Florence, where they hadn't lived in over a year.

"Hold on," Alda said to her son, who felt like a little prince perched on high. He smiled down at his mother and two sisters. Flora and Anna found little adventure in walking the nine miles back to Florence.

Meanwhile, in the city, with the only car that hadn't been confiscated, Mario and Ugo were checking on their unoccupied house in Florence. At the door, they were surprised to find it unlocked. Ugo opened it slowly and found broken glass and their possessions scattered all over the floor. Every piece of furniture had been overturned. They walked through the house. Paintings, vases, dishes – all smashed. Nothing was in one piece. The place reeked of human feces that someone had smeared around. Ugo leaned on the wall, holding his hand to his chest. Mario stood behind him.

"*Babbo*, this is political vendetta," Mario said, shaken by the hatred reverberating in their ransacked house.

"I bet I know who did this – neighborhood youth who've threatened us before for being a fascist family," Ugo said. "We have to wait here for Alda. We can't let the children see this."

Four hours later Alda arrived with the children, exhausted. She waved when she saw Mario and Ugo standing guard at the front door.

"Look in the house with Mario, but keep the children out," Ugo said.

She cried when she saw the chaos. "We can't live here. We'll have to go to my friend's empty apartment on Via Niccolini. She gave me the keys in case of an emergency. And this is an emergency."

Although the quarters were tight in the apartment, they were grateful for a safe haven. Alda worried aloud, "How will Floro find us when he comes home?"

"He'll go to the office," Mario said.

From the apartment window, Alda pulled the curtains aside to look out. Seeing German soldiers milling around across the street, she wondered once again when Florence would be free.

Later that week, as the adults gathered around listening to a Mozart concerto in the sitting room, Pietro, in a cloudy mood and still convalescing from stomach surgery, left the room without saying a word. Alda sensed he was up to something, so when Anna appeared to bid everyone goodnight, her mother called her over and whispered, "Would you check if your uncle is in his room?" She made Anna promise to search no further and to let her know immediately if she didn't find him there. "He likes to defy the curfew, so I want to be certain he isn't on the roof."

"Sure, *Mamma*," Anna said.

When Anna knocked on her uncle's bedroom door, there was no answer. She peeked in. *Il professore* was perpetually lost in his own world. He wasn't in his room, so she closed his door. Forgetting what she had promised her mother, she searched other rooms. "*Zio?*" Anna exhaled in exasperation, seeing the door to the roof terrace ajar. She realized he was up there, ignoring the curfew. *I'll just tell him to come down*, she thought, *without bothering Mamma*. She climbed the spiral stairs up to the roof terrace and poked her head out. Pietro was sitting on a bench, his face hidden by his straw hat.

"Ah, there you are, *Zio*," Anna called to her uncle. "I've been searching for you!" He ignored her. *You really are aloof*, she thought and walked onto the roof. Reaching him, she tugged at his sleeve. "*Mamma* says you shouldn't be up here!"

"Oh Anna," Pietro sighed. "We've lost every shred of freedom. What a bore! I'm just taking in air and sky."

She lifted her gaze to watch a cloud pass. "It is peaceful up here," she admitted. They talked a while. *He's right*, she thought, *they'd been cooped up for so long, she wished she could just sit there forever*. Their peace was interrupted by loud banging from downstairs.

"We'd better go down," Pietro said, putting his cigarette out on the ground. Anna followed him to the roof door. The banging had momentarily ceased, and she lingered for a last glimpse at the sky before stepping on the spiral stairs.

Meanwhile, downstairs in the parlor, as the thunderous banging continued, Mario and Ugo stared at each other. Alda stood up.

"Don't open that door!" Ugo insisted.

"If I don't, we'll just be in more serious trouble," Alda said.

When she opened the door, two irate soldiers pointed their rifles at Alda's face. Shouting and pushing themselves through the threshold, they motioned for the family to line up. *My God*, she thought, *they're going to shoot us*. Her throat clutched. She prayed the children would stay in their rooms. "*Per favore!*" she blurted. Mario and Ugo approached cautiously, trying to understand the Germans' angry rant. The soldiers' faces distorted in anger as they gestured upstairs. But the family didn't understand German and the soldiers didn't understand Italian.

Ugo repeated, "*Cosa?*" loudly, as if the young soldiers were deaf. Alda noted his attitude only escalated their anger.

"Please, Ugo!" she demanded, gesturing *calma*.

The soldiers continued pointing their rifles up and then at them. When Pietro and Anna appeared, the soldiers motioned for all of them to step outside, menacing with their weapons. Alda was terrified that they were about to be shot. Just then, out of the corner of her eye, she noticed a Franciscan friar in a brown robe slither across the street, clearly avoiding the situation. She remembered that he spoke German, so she cried out for his help.

"*Padre! Per favore, venga qua!*"

As the friar approached, the soldiers directed their guns at him. He pleaded in German, raising his hands in surrender.

"They kept pointing up!" Alda implored the friar. "What were they ranting about?"

The friar waited for the agitated explanation to end. "They say a spy is on your roof, signora. They have rooftop snipers, so you must tell them," he translated.

Alda, incredulous, said, "That's absurd! We have no spies here!" but suddenly she turned and looked at Pietro. She was livid but stayed calm. "Please explain," she said. "It was no spy, only this feeble man was up there, my old brother-in-law. He recently had an operation and needed some air!" When Ugo heard this, he clenched his fists but closed his eyes to hide his fury.

"I was minding my own business!" Pietro interjected.

The soldiers snarled at him. "Curfew! Stay off the roof!" When the friar translated, Pietro nodded curtly. Alda smelled the young men's filth and fear from soldiering too long. She noted their soiled jackets and missing buttons. Finally the soldiers put their rifles down by their sides, too tired even to check the roof. Alda felt relief. When they turned and disappeared down the street, a trace of their acrid sweat remained.

Alda sighed, thanking the friar, who made the sign of the cross. "God was with us this time." She watched his brown robes sway and heard the large wooden rosary around his waist click as he walked away.

Exhaling in relief, Alda glanced at her daughter's face. Anna looked as if she'd seen a ghost.

"Are you alright?" Alda said.

"I'm not sure."

She'd found her uncle on the roof, she explained, and described that when she was stepping down, she'd heard a whizzing noise pass above her head, and then a strange snap, or a thud. The hair on her neck had prickled. It felt as if something had grazed her hair. Maybe she was just imagining things.

"You were on the roof? I told you not to go there." Alda, now terrified, grabbed her daughter, examining her head.

"She is imagining things," Pietro insisted. "I stepped down right before her and heard nothing."

Anna followed her mother who headed to the steps leading to the roof. While standing on the top rung, Alda swept her hand on the wall and found a bullet lodged there. She collapsed on a step.

"It must have passed over my head just as I stepped down. *Mamma*, I must have a guardian angel," Anna said calmly. Alda realized that if Anna had lingered a moment more, the bullet would have struck her in the head.

"*Mamma?*"

Alda was furious. "Don't ever, ever go on the roof until the war is over, do you understand? You could've been killed!" she shouted, pulling Anna towards her.

"But I wasn't, *Mamma*," she said.

"Go to bed. And don't tell Aldo what happened," Alda gasped.

"*Mamma*, I didn't want to bother you," Anna said, heading off.

Alda stormed into the sitting room and found Ugo, Mario and Pietro listening to Albinoni to quieten their nerves. They looked up at Alda as she picked up the needle on the record. She stood inches from Pietro, who sat there ignoring her steely presence.

"What is it, Alda?" Mario said.

She fixed her eyes on Pietro. "There's a sniper's bullet embedded in the wall that just missed Anna's head," she said, her voice livid. Alda had the patriarch's attention.

"What?" Ugo shot up. Alda continued to glare at Pietro.

"There are no entitled exceptions here. Do you understand, Signor Rafanelli?" her voice rose to a shout. "Nobody goes on that roof, day or night, until the war is over."

Pietro smirked, said she had a lively imagination, that he'd heard nothing. Since his father had already left the room, he followed him and headed for the roof steps to see for himself. Moments later they returned, looking pale.

Alda gritted her teeth. "Promise."

"*Va bene,*" Pietro said, contrite.

She left the room without saying goodnight.

In her bedroom, her fury was directed towards her missing husband. *Why did you take such a risk, Floro, and leave me with your family? Where are you?* she cried to herself. *Why did you dismiss my warning?!* Alda knelt on the kneeler every night praying for her husband's safe return. Tonight she thanked God for sparing her daughter. She prayed to let the bitterness she felt towards her brother-in-law go, not just for this evening's recklessness, but for the past. It was hard to forget the time she had suggested that she and Floro live in a separate house with the children. Pietro, nonplussed, had responded with a shrug. "Fine. We'll just get another maid."

MARIO AND PIETRO'S RESCUE

Florence, 1944

A week after the sniper incident, the family sat in silence around the dinner table. Floro was still missing and the Germans soldiers who occupied Florence seemed increasingly agitated. As Alda heard commotion outside, she left the table and peered out the window. Neighborhood families were pleading with Nazis who were lining up their husbands and boys next to a truck.

"What are they doing?" Alda cried as Mario joined her at the window. A moment later they heard a loud banging at their door. Alda and Mario looked at each other.

As the rest of the family sat immobilized, Ugo said, "Do not open it! You saw what happened last time!"

"Ugo... they'll just knock it down!" Alda said as the furious banging escalated. She insisted the children go to their rooms before she opened the door. Two soldiers pushed their way in. One pointed a gun at Pietro, indicating he should stand. Pietro remained at the table. The other grabbed Mario and pushed him out the door. The one with the gun headed towards Pietro, shouting in German. Knocking his shoulder with the barrel, he insisted Pietro stand up and shoved him out the door. The soldiers ignored the patriarch as he demanded to know where they were taking his sons.

Alda implored, "They're both sick; leave them!" but it was no use. They watched as Mario and Pietro and hordes of men and boys were jammed onto a truck. As it sped off, old men, women and children poured onto the streets, in a daze, wondering where they were taking their men.

"This is their final vendetta; they'll shoot them just for the sport of it," one woman lamented, and Alda reproached her.

"Be quiet! You don't know that. There are children here."

"I know where they're taking them!" one elderly man said. "To Villa Triste. Tomorrow they'll be sent on trains to Germany for hard labor. This is their last stand."

There was a hush in the crowd as families speculated and conferred before dispersing. Everyone knew how the 'Villa of Sadness' on Via Bolognese had gotten its name: from the desperate cries of those being tortured inside. It was a renowned place of torture led first by fascists, then by Nazis.

"Where are Pietro and Mario's medical records?" Alda asked when they were back in the apartment.

"In the desk," Ugo said. She found them in a drawer and waved the papers.

"This is proof. I'll be on the first tram in the morning to Villa Triste. I'll convince them your sons are unfit to work, with their stomach ailments and recent surgeries. They will release them."

"You stay here with the children. I'll go," Ugo said.

"No, signore, you are needed here," she insisted. "What if they take you too, then all the Rafanelli men will be gone, and who will protect us?" She knew if they'd wanted the old man, they would've taken him, but she appealed to his pride. Ugo lacked diplomacy; she believed she had a better chance of getting them free if she went alone.

"You know how persuasive I can be," she said.

"That's a given, Alda." He shook his head, thinking about the time before the war when she'd convinced him to buy the complete set of *Ginori* china along with the heavy silver and crystal glasses at *Poggi*, doling out a sum in one minute that exceeded any property he'd ever purchased. He hadn't spoken to her for days afterwards.

Suddenly there was another knock at their door, this time gentle but urgent. Alda opened it to find their old housekeeper, shaking.

"Marta, come in."

"Signora. They've taken Eduardo. You know so many people. Have you heard anything?"

"Only that they've been taken to Villa Triste."

"*O Dio*, signora." Marta clutched her chest.

"Someone suggested they're sending them to Germany, to labor camps. Tomorrow morning I'm going to bring Pietro and Mario back. They're sick, as you know, of no use to them."

"Signora, would you inquire about Eduardo as well? He has a heart murmur. He cannot do hard labor."

"Of course, Marta. Can you bring me some proof?" she said, but she knew it would be difficult getting him released since he was young.

"Signora. Yes. You are an angel. *Grazie.*" The woman squeezed her hand.

Early the next morning with a *salva condotto*, permission to travel around the city, Alda stepped onto the dangerous streets. Boarding the tram she clutched the medical records, heading to the place of sadness. She recalled Floro describing Villa Triste, had felt his sense of shame and powerlessness about the harrowing screams reverberating from that ungodly place. Could he, could they, have done something to stop that abuse then? As she peered out the window at the destroyed fringes of her beloved, unrecognizable Florence, Mozart's *Laudate Dominum* played over and over in her head. She watched as soldiers and a few residents passed by, looking too tired to be frightened. "Where are you, Floro?" she whispered, praying for strength. As the music reached a crescendo in her head, she arrived at her destination on the Via Bolognese. She whispered the last musical phrase aloud: "World without end, Amen."

Knocking at the huge door, Alda stepped back as a soldier opened it. Clutching papers under her arm, she braced herself and asked for the person in charge. The man laughed. She tried to look around him, to get the attention of another man at a desk behind him.

"Who is it?" the man inquired, but she didn't understand.

"No one," the German answered.

Alda forged ahead. "I've come to save you some trouble."

"*Vai via,* signora! No place for a woman," the one sitting at the desk said before she could explain. "Go back where you belong!"

Where I belong? she thought. "I belong here, signore," she answered, undaunted, skirting around the soldier, waving the medical reports. "You have two men, Mario and Pietro Rafanelli, and a young neighbor's son. They are of no use to you. These medical papers prove they are incapable of physical labor." She opened their files. "They've had stomach operations. This boy has a heart murmur." The man sniggered, pushing the papers onto the floor. *At least he speaks Italian,* Alda thought as she bent to pick them up: "Please. They will just be wasting space. These men cannot work."

"It's not up to me!" the man finally said as a tall German official approached from down the corridor.

"What is it? Why are you here, signora?"

"You have Mario and Pietro Rafanelli, and my neighbor's son," she implored. "I have medical records that prove they are unfit for hard labor. They won't survive the trip to Germany." She handed him the papers, adding, "Is Captain Schmidt here by any chance? We hosted him and other German officers at our villa a while ago."

"Oh signora, I am in charge here," he said. She had hoped he could help, and she wanted to hear that Schmidt had gone home to his family. But there was no sharing of information, and she wasn't sure she should have brought him up. Moments passed while the official examined the records.

"Please," she whispered. "They cannot possibly work."

"Release the two," the official ordered.

"*Grazie...*" she whispered, adding, "And Eduardo Borlotti – my housekeeper's only son?"

He looked askance at her, shaking his head. "Borlotti is gone." The man perused the list in front of him. "On the first morning train. Name's at the top of the alphabet. Half the alphabet is already gone."

"Oh dear God!" Alda wondered how she would break the news to Marta.

"Get the two Rafanelli men out here."

Minutes later they appeared, speechless to find Alda standing there. The official looked at them. "Get going," he warned, waving his arm and telling Mario and Pietro, "You are forever in this woman's debt." As they walked out the door, Alda turned for a last look and shuddered.

"*Santo cielo!* You did it," Ugo cried as the three staggered through the apartment door. The children rushed to embrace their mother.

"I have to sit." Her knees ached. She felt older than she expected at forty-four. She collapsed on a chair, thinking of the horrible place she'd just been. If she prayed for Floro's safe return now, would she be greedy? She knew, if he'd been home, that his arthritic back might not have been enough to have had him released. Not to mention his pride. For the first time in the months since he'd left, Alda thanked God he had been away when the soldiers came for all the men. She was convinced he would be on his way to Germany. Maybe he's already there, corralled from up north? Mulling over these thoughts, there was another knock at the door. Ugo opened it.

"Is la signora here?" Marta implored, standing at the threshold.

"She's resting, Marta," Ugo said.

"Does she have news of my son?" she urged, seeing Pietro and Mario standing in the foyer. "Oh signori, you're home! How wonderful! Did you see Eduardo?"

"No, Marta, we were packed like sardines," Mario said as Alda stood up and walked towards the foyer, her heart sinking.

"Signora! Any news of Eduardo?" she approached.

"Oh dear, Marta!" she sighed. "I tried to get him released, but they'd already put him on a train to Germany, early this morning, before I even arrived."

Looking at Mario and Pietro, the woman stiffened. "But of course, signora, you had your priorities. I'm not a relative, just a former servant. There was no urgency." Her voice was cold.

"But Marta, how can you say that? They sent the men off by last names, and Borlotti is at the beginning of the alphabet."

"Oh of course, the alphabet. Even the alphabet smiles on those who have!" she cried, turning and storming out.

"Oh Lord," Alda whispered, watching her back as Ugo closed the door. "How can she think that of me?"

Ugo raised his two hands in the 'lascia fare' gesture. Let it go. Mario escorted Alda back to her chair where she sat in silence. He pulled a chair near her, patting her hand. "Poor Marta, poor Eduardo. I've known him since he was a tender boy. Will he survive the trip?"

"Oh Alda. Those men won't be in Germany long. The war will be over soon," he said. "You were very brave to come to Villa Triste. You did everything in your power. Don't let that woman's accusation bother you."

When she looked up, Anna and Flora came and sat by her.

"Where's Aldo?" Alda said. "Please go play with him."

They told her he was alright, that he was playing with blocks. Pietro assured her he would go to his room and read them all poetry. "Come with me, girls," Pietro said, and they followed him out.

Mario leaned towards her. "Listen, Alda. Last night while we were in that godforsaken place we heard news. The Germans have left the last fascist stronghold up north. The partisans have taken over, blocking the way back and forth to Tuscany, hoping to round up all remaining fascists. That must be the reason Floro isn't back. There's a blockade. He can't get back home without a pass. He's probably hiding, trapped somewhere avoiding arrest."

"Oh Mario, let's pray he's found some kind soul to harbor him until all this is over," Alda said, and he nodded, squeezing her hand.

LINDA AT THE VILLA

1977-1978

Under the archway of my flower shop, I looked out the door onto Piazza San Marco, fretting about Linda's arrival from Rome by train. There was always the expected delay, but I didn't want the threatened strike to ruin her perception of Italy. I wanted all travelers here to experience Italy's marvelousness, not be deterred by inconveniences. I turned and entered the greenhouse, discovering the gardenia buds carpeted with aphids. Having just learned of my pregnancy, I was even more adamant about not using pesticides. Grabbing a wet cloth, I removed the insects manually, bud by bud, over and under the leaves. Then, in the musty silence while waiting for Linda or a customer to appear, I rearranged the greenhouse plants with complementary colors in mind: succulent clusters of red kalanchoe flowers next to green dieffenbachia, then yellow chrysanthemum aside purple dogbane. With my favorite *capelvenere*, maidenhair fern, I created a soft edge around the colorful plants. Observing the overall pleasing effect, I walked back into my office, popping a few saltines to stave off nausea.

A woman finally entered, wanting a funereal pillow for her aunt. Offering condolences, I suggested seasonal flowers to adorn the wooden pillow. Uncertain, she walked into the greenhouse. As we examined other options, Linda appeared in the doorway. Relieved, I excused myself to greet her, suppressing a scream of delight.

"Thank God, you made it!" I said. "How was your trip?"

"*Perfetto*," she smiled.

"I have a customer. It should only take a few minutes."

After the woman agreed, I took her order. She would return in the evening hours to pick it up.

I approached my friend, hardly believing we were going to have a sojourn in Florence together. Linda rarely talked about herself. Brilliant, witty and always curious, she possessed heightened powers of observation and an astute understanding of human nature. I didn't want to swamp her with my news, so decided to hold off on revealing my pregnancy. She had to focus on her language studies without preoccupation.

"Is everything alright?" she stared, already sensing something was up.

"Of course!" I blurted, wondering if my face was green. "Tell me your first impressions of Italy."

She'd reached Florence without seeing Rome and had traveled in a compartment on the train with a family who'd wanted to share their food. As the countryside whizzed by, she'd tried to understand the little children sitting across from her.

"We'll visit Rome," I said. "It's my first love."

"Right now, I just want to settle in."

I showed her my shop and greenhouse. At the midday closing time I locked the enormous wooden door and linked arms with Linda as Italian friends and family do when promenading on the streets. "*Andiamo*. I'm taking you to the cafe across the street," I said. We were quite the odd pair. With my tall frame, broad shoulders and blonde hair, I stuck out. Linda, with dark hair, perfect thin frame, narrow waist and Italian ancestry, belonged.

She pulled out her map to get oriented. I pointed out the monastery, museum and church of San Marco across the street.

"That's where the infamous 'bonfire of the vanities' monk Savonarola held court. Fra Angelico's gorgeous paintings are in the monk cells there, and there's an interior courtyard in the monastery that's a great place to sit and meditate."

After we went to the corner cafe for a Campari soda, I looked at my watch. "We'd better move. I'm sure Aldo's mother will have prepared a welcome meal. I hope you're very hungry!"

"*Andiamo*," she said, grabbing my arm, asking if I got along with her.

"Absolutely. She's fifty years older. Maybe that's why. Seems more like my grandmother than a mother-in-law." I re-opened the arched door to my shop where my car was parked alongside the greenhouse.

"What's this?" Linda asked before climbing into my tiny car.

"A very old *cinquecento* Fiat," I said; "driving it feels like wearing a glove." We laughed and she, unlike Hilary, easily folded in.

Driving up Viale Michelangelo, I pointed out Villa Hotel Liberty, the city house where Aldo grew up, now a hotel. As we passed sycamore trees lining the avenue, I stopped by the ancient church of San Miniato al Monte.

"Where are we now?" Linda asked.

I explained it was the best panorama in Florence, a good way to get oriented. Out of the car, she looked up at San Miniato's early Christian façade.

"Magnificent," she said as we walked up steep steps.

"The interior is layers of centuries. The oldest part is a crypt where monks chant at five pm. We'll listen another time. Today I just wanted you to view the city from up here." I added that tourists usually went to Piazzale Michelangelo for the panorama, "but I prefer this perspective." I pointed out the Arno River, the *Duomo*, the Signoria, the Uffizi museum, the bridges and churches, and the great national library, flooded in 1966. I explained about the plaques all around Florence indicating the level where floodwaters had risen in the 1966 flood and in other past hundred-year floods.

On our way out I showed her the cemetery below the church, midway down the stairs. "Aldo's father was buried on this hill, but when the terrain shifted they had to relocate many graves. His mother got a call to come identify his remains. Can you imagine, after more than a decade? Aldo, a young man by then, offered to accompany his mother, but she wanted to do it alone. She still protects him." I turned. "The whole family is buried in a mausoleum over there in the newer section, in marble compartments, one on top of the other." Then I showed her the solitary, more personal graves and headstones with faces of the dead embossed on oval enamel.

We stared, then I took a detour up a few stairs to another tier.

"Look over here. It's eerie." I pointed to an image of Aldo's uncle.

"Oh my God, he looks just like Aldo."

"That's what I mean. This man, his uncle Mario, was like a second father to him. When Aldo was seven his father died. Seven year later his uncle suddenly died, and Aldo was with him."

"Poor Aldo," she said, trying to read the elaborate inscription on the stone.

"It says Mario was prematurely taken from, among others, his adored nephew Aldo," I read. "He was only forty-five."

"What happened?"

"He was taking Aldo to hunt in the fields. They were walking up the hill towards the villa. At a certain point Aldo realized his uncle wasn't walking alongside him. He turned just in time to see him collapse in the middle of the road, cradling his rifle. When Aldo reached him, he mistook his death rattle for snoring. He couldn't understand why he couldn't wake him. He ran up the hill to get help. The farmers carried his body onto the terrace and laid him on the chaise that's still under the *loggia*. It took Aldo a while to realize he was gone."

"Poor dear," she sighed.

I showed her another image on the grave next to Mario's, the face of his brother, strong Danilo. "He was only twenty when he died. Aldo's mother never knew him, but apparently he was a formidable young man."

It was getting late. We would visit more of the cemetery and the church another time. Twenty minutes later I pointed up the hill in Grassina.

Aldo was waiting at the top of the terrace steps as I parked.

"*Benvenuta, bella*! I was getting a little worried," he said, coming down to greet Linda and giving us both a hug. Aldo's two English hunting dogs, D'oro the old powerful champion and his lazy son Tom, emerged from their lair under the *loggia* to sniff the newcomer as we stepped onto the terrace.

Linda turned 360 degrees to look around, ignoring the dogs. As Aldo opened the front door, she smelled the aroma from the kitchen. She approached Alda, who dropped her wooden spoon and gave my friend a smile. "Signora, *molto piacere*," Linda said perfectly.

Alda had made *ravioli gnudi*, one of my favorite dishes, a delicate mix of cooked spinach and ricotta flavored with nutmeg, rolled into thick sausage shapes and gently covered in a thin layer of flour. Linda watched as she tossed the 'nude' ravioli into the boiling water. When they floated to the surface, Alda announced: "*Si mangia!*" suggesting we go wash up. At the table, I watched everyone delight in the ravioli drenched in browned butter and sage, covered generously with freshly grated *parmigiano*. Alda had also prepared a tomato sauce, to try the ravioli two ways. After a few tentative bites, I stopped eating, trying to calm my agitated gut. Roasted guinea hens were the next course, served with potatoes and porcini mushrooms. As Linda savored each bite, I excused myself and rushed upstairs to my room, just making it to the bathroom in time. Looking at my pale face, I wondered why they called it morning sickness, as my retching occurred every time I tried to eat and at other random moments. I drank a sip of water and went down to the table where everyone looked up at me. Linda frowned suspiciously and asked if I was okay.

"Fine," I said. "What did I miss?"

"Linda was already inquiring about Italian phrases and recording our answers in her notebook," Aldo said.

I laughed. "*Naturalmente!*"

After lunch I took her outside onto the sunlit terrace.

"These huge vases and lemon trees are gorgeous," she said. I led her to the terrace's edge, pointing down to a small oval pool with a fountain at its center.

"Rainwater has been running off the villa's roof and terrace for about five hundred years. It drains and collects in a cistern below us. The overflow runs into this oval fountain. Aldo and his farmer Gigetto still use the collected rainwater to water his vegetable garden, the geraniums and all these lemon trees," I explained. "During the war, German soldiers bathing in that oval pool broke that bronze fountain spout."

"I thought the villa was occupied by Americans?"

"It was. They came here after the German officers left. You can still see remnants of their visits," I said, motioning towards the long façade. "Aldo and I live on the second floor. Next to our quarters, we share a wall with that attached farm building. When the Americans arrived down in the valley, their tank fired a warning shell that blasted through the façade all the way through the back wall. See how the wall is different? The blast killed a cow in the stall below. The poor farmer, who was washing his hands at the sink when he saw the tank, nearly died of fright. The sink was pulverized, but miraculously he was fine."

We noted how spoiled Americans are, two hundred years free of foreign invasion. Linda asked how they'd survived and I told her it was thanks in part to what they'd grown on this land.

"Aside from vegetables, they have fruit trees — apricots, cherries, pears and peaches. There is nothing like eating apricots and pears ripe off these trees. Nirvana! I've discovered my senses here. It's beyond a dream," I said. "And you're here to share a part of it."

We moved under the *loggia*, where Linda pointed to the Bentwood chaise. "May I move that out under the sun?" I stared at the chaise, thinking of Uncle Mario lying on it after he'd collapsed dead, but I didn't want to alter the elated mood. "Aren't you going to sit?" she asked, breaking me out of my reverie.

"Of course," I said, grabbing a wicker chair. When I sat down she squinted at me suspiciously.

"Okay, so what's going on with you?"

"Geez, Linda, I can't hide anything from you!" I said. "Okay… it's really early. I haven't told anyone. I'm pregnant."

"Oh my God! Why didn't you tell me right away?" She jumped up, giving me a hug. "I knew something was wrong. Well, not wrong," she laughed, "but that you weren't yourself."

"We only found out a short time ago." I smiled.

"Oh God. Are you thrilled?"

"Thrilled and scared. That's normal, right?"

"Are you kidding? I'd be out of my skin!" she said. "While I'm here these next few months, we have to make every minute count. We'll cherish this precious, carefree time. *Carpe diem*! Life will be complicated soon enough."

"*Assolutamente*! Let's just sit here in the sun!" I said, thinking of all the times in the college dorm when we'd talked all night about boyfriends, lust and the tragedy of Anna Karenina's demise. When I came to the villa, I told her, I was determined to live in the blissful moment but that being pregnant altered my orientation. I was still finding it hard to believe a person was incubating inside me. I confessed to wondering if throwing up was my subconscious mind rejecting this new daunting responsibility.

"Oh, stop it! Morning sickness isn't your fault. It just happens."

I changed the subject, asking her what she wanted to accomplish while here.

"Immerse myself in Dante and Petrarch. If all goes well learning Italian, I'll apply for a PhD program back home."

With her love of language, her knowledge of French and her passion for Plato and classical literature, it seemed a perfect fit. "*Brava*," I said.

An hour passed like seconds as we soaked in the heat of the sun. Suddenly I bolted up. "*O Dio!* I've lost track of time. I have to get back to the flower shop to make the funereal pillow!"

The next day I had off. Aldo disappeared early for work, consulting for a Chianti vineyard. I could hear Linda banging around in our little kitchen.

"I've made you some French toast!" she called cheerfully, hoping her efforts would settle my stomach.

"How'd you sleep?" I asked her, shuffling tentatively in.

"*Perfetto*," she smiled, serving me breakfast. She was dressed for exercise, raring to go out for a jog. She watched me eat.

I told her to go, but that she shouldn't be surprised if people stopped and gawked. Nobody jogged in Italy.

"Are you sure you're okay?"

"Please, I'm not sick, I'm just pregnant."

As she headed down the spiral staircase, I ran to the bathroom to lose my breakfast, longing to feel normal again. By the time I ventured downstairs, I heard Milena's agitated voice in the kitchen telling la signora that she'd just seen a young woman with a dark ponytail running so fast up the hill beyond the villa that she was worried the girl was being chased. But when she turned and began running backwards, Milena figured she must be the new American visitor. I entered the kitchen smiling and found Alda laughing, her shoulders shaking.

"*Americani*," she said affectionately, looking at me, and I joined their laughter.

The next week Aldo and I showed Linda our favorite places around Florence, including the Osteria Albergaccio where Machiavelli had played cards while in exile. When we visited his home across the street and saw the desk where he wrote *The Prince*, I wondered if the solitude of exile had served as a catalyst or stifled his writing. I thought of my various aborted attempts, the unfinished stories. Maybe true exile, not voluntary exile, is best for writing.

We drove Linda up to Montemorello and had a wonderful meal at Anna's summer home with her husband Nico and their two boys Federico and Luca. Linda's Italian was impressive after just a few weeks. When she heard me say a phrase or proverb she didn't know, or saw me make one of the million Italian hand gestures, she wanted to know the meaning. I had learned by listening and watching and living the language, the way children learn. I'd gathered Tuscan proverbs and absorbed funny colloquialisms, gestures and phrases that she wouldn't learn at the *Scuola di Dante*. She was a perfectionist who insisted on learning the pure and complicated Italian grammar. I was certain Linda caught mistakes I still made in grammar, but she was too gracious to correct me. When I said I had begun to think and even dream in Italian, she sighed. She was a long way off from that, she admitted.

The following weekend Aldo was invited to a boar hunt in Maremma. Our friends had included us in the weekend at their beautiful estate. I was excited for Linda to see another part of Italy, but as we headed to the coast Aldo had to stop at every curve so I could throw up onto the road. After sticking my head out the car door five times, I knew we had to turn around. Once home I insisted he and Linda go back without me. She decided to stay, but Aldo felt oblidged to go.

Linda studied hard, got to know Florence and visited Gubbio and other small cities. She won the hearts of Aldo's family and friends. When her semester was up in December, we had a goodbye meal at a wonderful countryside trattoria, *Omero*, in Pian di Giullari. I fought back tears and insisted she return. We hugged and cried until we laughed, which was par for the course for us, always mixing laughter with tears.

As winter set in, I missed Linda's energy and encouraging presence. At six months' pregnant, my morning sickness persisted unabated. My great bear-hug obstetrician, Augusto Battisti, Anna and Flora's dear old friend, encouraged Aldo to take me away to the mountains where the air might help calm my nausea. Some women with morning sickness had to be hospitalized with IV fluids, my doctor insisted, and he didn't want that to happen to me. Why would higher altitude help? The head honcho of the hospital of Prato just shrugged. "We don't really know." I wondered how we had traveled to the moon, yet morning sickness remained a medical mystery.

Linda on the terrace with D'oro, autumn 1977.

A few days later Aldo drove me to Abetone in the Apennine Mountains, only a little over an hour from Florence. Again I had him stop at every other curve, but once I got to the mountain hotel, I had three miraculous, nausea-free days. I prayed the cycle had been broken, but on the winding road back to the villa, it started all over again. By mid-March, still looking for relief, Aldo took me on yet another mountain trip, this time to the spectacular Alpine mountains of Cortina d'Ampezzo. Once we left the straight autostrada, the routine repeated itself. I hoisted myself back in with the car door just ajar, but I felt depleted.

"Too many curves. Maybe this wasn't such a good idea," I sighed, holding a handkerchief embroidered by Alda to my mouth.

"All mountain roads have curves, *amore*," Aldo said. "Just hold on. Once I get you there, you'll be fine again." I chewed slowly on multiple saltines, staring at the horizon. But when I glanced at Aldo, I sensed he was preoccupied about something else.

"What's up?" I asked. "Was it the roof? You never told me about the estimate you got this morning for fixing it?"

"I don't want to talk about it."

"Uh oh. That doesn't sound good. Is that what's bothering you?"

He finally spilled what he'd pent up. "So, the roofer can't just fix the leaks or replace a few tiles. The whole terracotta roof needs replacing." Aldo quoted a number in many millions of lira. Translating the amount to dollars in my head, I realized it was astronomical, the price of buying a small apartment in New York.

"That's outrageous," I said. "Can you get another estimate?"

"No. Next week I'm getting another estimate, for rebuilding the collapsing vaults under the *loggia*." He'd already cordoned off the area, as walking there was now dangerous. Why was the villa suddenly falling apart under his watch, he wondered angrily? His grandfather Ugo, the wealthy fish importer, deferred maintenance!

"God, the vaults — that'll be a huge sum too," I said. "What are you going to do?"

"I think I have to sell it," he said, matter-of-factly.

"Sell?" I gasped. "What?"

"I refuse to spend my life juggling debts like my mother did."

I thought of the medieval buildings in Italian cities with the boarded-up doors next to main entrances that were used long ago for transporting family members out after they'd died.

"Oh Aldo, you can't sell! Your mother told me she expects to leave the villa *feet first*. This is terrible." After a long silence, I blurted, "Our baby will be the fourth generation of Rafanellis living at the villa. We can't go!"

"*Cristo di Dio*. You know what it's like there in the winter. It's okay for adults to be cavalier, even joke about wearing heavy sweaters and coats while watching television. But have you thought about how it'll be having our little baby there next winter?"

"But we're in Italy, Aldo. It doesn't get *that* cold in Grassina. I figure we'd keep the stoves and heaters roaring. I don't know. Let's not get all wimpy. People, even babies, survived like that for centuries." As I said this, I thought of all the stove stoking and of the time I'd tucked Alda's pink blanket into the electric blanket and nearly caused a fire.

"Both the terracotta roof and the vaults absolutely have to be fixed. Central heating would be another enormous expense. Do you understand my reasoning? It's endless. The villa reminds me of the *Maristella*. Sure, it's a beautiful sailboat, but it's so old and huge, requiring so much maintenance that we've never actually been sailing on it. Giovanni is like my mother, an eternal optimist, always making light of things that need fixing. Not me: I would've been happier working on a small boat, so we might have actually gotten out on the water and sailed!" he sighed. "It's the same. Twenty rooms and four outbuildings? I don't enjoy tinkering, fixing things. If I paid it the attention it warrants, there'd be no time for anything else! And the expense of it! What's the point? I want a life."

I stared ahead at the road as he turned into another curve. "Pull over!" I cried, thrusting my head out the door to empty my stomach on the side of the road. When I hauled my sorry self back in and closed the door, I faced my side window, using my sleeve to wipe the tears I didn't want Aldo to witness. Linda's prophetic words of a few months ago came to mind. We should *seize the day*, enjoy our relatively carefree time together at the villa while we could. With new responsibilities, life would be complicated very soon. What I had imagined for the future would never be: sitting under the *loggia* with our baby, singing Italian lullabies, eating next to the hearth, watching *Nonna* Alda delight in this new generation at the villa. The place that had anchored me, and us, had fulfilled my longing for continuity and community, was no longer going to be home.

"God, this is awful. Where will we all go?" I sniffed.

"We can buy a smaller, more manageable *casa colonica*, preferably on a hillside outside Florence."

"With your mother, right?"

"Of course."

"Good," I said. "This is going to break her heart."

"Now you know why I didn't want to talk about it," he said.

Poor Alda. Poor Aldo. It was easy for me to be romantic about the villa. I wasn't paying those bills.

"Okay, *amore*. Let's discuss it later."

Once we arrived in Cortina, I forced myself to forget about our conversation. Buoyed by the fairy-tale memories of the majestic jagged rose mountain, I recalled the untracked runs we'd skied on the winter before with our friends Alberto and Ghita and their two adorable daughters.

Aldo parked near a condominium complex, and we settled into our little weekend getaway apartment. The next morning, I opened a window to the hushed whiteness of deep snow. The air smelled fresh and metallic. Large icicles hung from the roof like menacing translucent swords catching the sun. Behind them shone a cloudless sky. We listened, looking out on the pure white that buffered all noise. Aldo broke the silence by yanking down the dangerous icicles. "Let's go," he said. "With this virgin powder, I'd like to be the first one down the slope."

I was amazed to be feeling fine for the first time since Abetone. Trying to remain in the moment and not think about the villa, we drove behind a snowplow toward Cristallo, that glorious pink mountain rising sharply against a pure cobalt sky. The limpid landscape took my breath away.

When we got to the bottom of the slope that early morning, we were alone. It was magical, just the two of us. Holding a little camera, standing at the bottom of the mountain, I filmed Aldo, solo skier on virgin powder. I was awed by his graceful zigzag and envied his abandon, wishing I could learn to ski like it was a dance, fearless and free. Since I was too pregnant to ski downhill this time, later that afternoon we learned to cross-country ski for the first time. It was a new experience, sliding horizontally through a glistening wooded wonderland.

We returned to the little apartment, exhausted but elated, glad for our day of fresh air, sun and brisk weather. I continued to feel fine despite the underlying angst about the villa, which we still avoided discussing.

I was hungry without worrying if I'd keep food down and began dreaming about the cheese fondue we planned to order at the local restaurant. Before we left for dinner, Aldo turned on the television for news. We stood watching, expecting nothing extraordinary. Instead an image of the former Italian Prime Minister, Aldo Moro, appeared on the screen. A grim voice announced that he'd been kidnapped in Rome. The reporter said he'd been on his way to vote for his *compromesso storico*, the historic compromise that Moro had coordinated, a plan that included communists in the Christian Democrat government. "Five of his bodyguards were murdered," the newscaster announced. "The terrorist organization, the Red Brigades, has taken responsibility."

"Oh my God!" I cried.

"Why Moro of all people?" Aldo whispered. "He's a good man."

We stared at the screen. The Red Brigades got their inspiration in part from Marx, Mao and World War II partisans. But why would they kidnap Moro, who wanted to include the left in the government?

Aldo gave me a fierce look, making a gesture with his hands: taut fingers of his right hand striking the left palm. I knew this gesture meant: 'Let's get out of here.'

"You want to leave Cortina already?" I said, understanding it felt strange to stay on vacation after this horrible thing had happened.

"No," he said. "Italy."

"What?" I was shocked. This was too much to consider all of a sudden.

Once we'd returned to the villa, we discussed for weeks if we should sell, stay or move elsewhere. Aldo had talked about living in Quito, Ecuador when I first met him, but I thought it was just talk. We didn't want to upset his mother with our indecision, so we tried to settle our best course before involving her. As we struggled, we wondered about Aldo Moro, still held hostage by the Red Brigades who were making demands on the government in exchange for freeing him. The Italian government remained obdurate. They would not release terrorists in exchange for Moro. Pope Paul VI offered himself in exchange.

Nearly two more months passed. On May 9th, five days after celebrating Aldo's 37th birthday, we sat on the big Victorian couch watching the news in the parlor with Alda. A Renault flashed before the screen as a solemn voice said, "Prime Minister Aldo Moro's body was found in the trunk of this R4, near the Christian Democrat headquarters in the center of Rome."

"*O Dio!*" Alda cried. I grabbed her arm. We both burst into tears at the fact and indignity of the assassination. Aldo stared at the television.

BRINGING BACK FLORO

Spring 1945

Alda was perpetually anxious about Floro's whereabouts but relieved that her children were now living in a city no longer occupied. Allied troops - South Africans, New Zealanders and the British - had liberated Florence from the Germans the summer before. Still, Alda took nothing for granted as she freely walked hand in hand with Aldo down the street. She couldn't help remembering the warnings posted by the Germans: Anyone caught walking in the streets without permission would be shot. She opened the gate to their Florence home, holding a little package for Aldo, whose fourth birthday was in less than a week.

Mario arrived at the gate right after them. Alda turned and watched her agitated brother-in-law roll his newspaper under his arm. Seeing his face, she asked, "What is it?"

"In a minute," he said, "when we're alone." When they entered the house Alda sent Aldo off to find his sisters. She turned as Mario lay the paper on the piano. As the news unfurled, she read aloud, "Partisans caught Mussolini heading to the Alps, shooting him and Clara Petacci."

Alda stared at the photograph showing Mussolini's corpse upside down, like a scene from a butcher shop, alongside his mistress and other henchmen in front of an Esso station.

"They chose that station as revenge for all the partisans that the fascists hanged there," Mario said.

Despite all the suffering Mussolini had wrought, it was an ugly scene. Alda stared at the woman's upside-down corpse, her skirt tied around her legs, wondering why they'd killed his mistress. She folded the paper and laid it on the table. "Did they really have to publish that photograph? Will they also show us Hitler's corpse when the time comes?" She thought about herself at Anna's age, during the First World War that sowed the seeds for Mussolini's ascent to power. What would her children's generation face? She told Mario to hide the paper where they wouldn't see it. "With their *Babbo* gone so long, they already have nightmares." Her brother-in-law looked pensive as she said, "Maybe with Mussolini gone, they'll lift the northern blockade and Floro will be free to pass."

"We'll know soon," Mario said.

Over a year had gone by without a word from Floro, but Alda shuttered her despair to maintain some semblance of normalcy. She put meals on the table with limited resources and followed her children's tutored lessons. She insisted Flora continue her vocal lessons. These tasks helped distract Alda from her deep distress. She never gave up faith that Floro was alive. Prayer and hope were her best allies. She looked at Mario. She knew he loved and admired his older brother. He'd been so kind and attentive this anguished year. He'd enraptured Aldo by reading him *The Black Corsair* by Salgari and Kipling's *The Jungle Book,* instilling his nephew with a passion for reading.

"We would've been lost without you, Mario."

"Alda, you are family." She heard his voice crack as he walked away.

As she entered the kitchen with a sigh, Ugo walked in. "Is lunch ready?"

Alda unfolded the newspaper, splaying it on the table, saying nothing as he picked it up. "Ah, now I've seen everything. *Imbecille,*" Ugo growled, looking down at the table. "Maybe we can really get back to work now." He slammed his hand on the paper before exiting. "And we still have to eat."

Two days after Mussolini's death, Hitler committed suicide. "Coward," Alda said aloud. His death reminded her of *Canto XIII* of Dante's *Inferno,* the circle of hell reserved for suicides. Bodies turned into thorny thickets while knees and toes morphed into roots like Apollo's *Daphne.* Spirits of lost hope were entwined in branches, their blood spilling as they struggled for release. Alda was certain that Dante would have invented an even more hideous circle of hell for Hitler.

With Mussolini and Hitler gone, everyone knew the war would finally be declared over. On the second day of May, two days before Aldo turned four, nearly one million German troops in Austria and Italy surrendered to the British. Yet throughout Italy violence and anarchy persisted; the city streets and countryside were rampant with vendettas. The partisan tide swept against fascists, Italian versus Italian, in the yet undeclared civil war. Alda kept her children close. Days earlier a stunned neighbor had witnessed a group of young boys in downtown Florence. Pointing to an old man, one of them had shouted: "I know that man! He's a fascist!" The next moment she'd heard shots and watched the old man crumple, dead on the ground.

Alda prayed that the revenge would end soon, that she would again recognize Italians as generous, peace-loving people. She understood that war brought out the worst in people but sometimes also the best. She believed someone was hiding Floro up north. Later she discovered her optimism to be true. All the time he'd been missing, he'd been harbored by a farmer's family, hiding in a small, dusty *fienile* constructed for wheat storage, biding his time. With no real windows, he'd spent most days peering through the little half-moon brick wall slits, taking in air and watching for movement. They gave him straw bedding. The farmer's wife brought him soup and bread. The farmer told Floro about Mussolini's death but urged him not to leave. The situation was even more chaotic and dangerous now, with partisans all over Italy retaliating against fascist families. That was all Floro had to hear. He was frantic to get through the blockade to protect his family who still didn't know he was alive. He stuffed his pack and embraced the farmers who'd risked their lives sheltering him for the long months. As nonchalantly as possible, he ventured into town to request a passage out, pretending to be a local who'd lost his papers. But they immediately discerned his Tuscan accent and threw him into a makeshift partisan prison.

"*Mamma*, if the Germans surrendered, why isn't *Babbo* home?" Anna asked one night before bed.

"Soon, dear, soon," Alda insisted, feigning courage as she kissed her daughter's forehead.

The next morning Alda and Palma were in the kitchen making *salsa verde*. Alda held both hands firmly on the *mezzaluna* handles as the blade swayed back and forth, slicing the parsley and garlic, greening the block of wood. As they heard eager tapping at the door, Palma wiped her hands and walked to open it. Their old farmer Giovanni stood immobile at the threshold, hat in hand. "Is la signora home?" he asked nervously.

"*Certo*, Giovanni," Palma said, quickly leading him in.

"Signora," the farmer said, stopping at the kitchen doorway, hesitant to deliver his message to Alda.

"Oh Giovanni, what a surprise! Come in," Alda exclaimed. "How is everything in Grassina? No more tank blasts, I hope?" Alda washed her hands. Her smile faded when she saw his grim expression.

"Is your family alright?"

He wrung his hat with his hand, still quiet. Finally, he spoke. "Signora," he swallowed, "my family is fine, but I have news from the *circolo a Grassina* about Signor Floro. I found out he's in a partisan prison near Brescia."

Alda steadied herself, looking at the pots of steaming beef about to boil over. "But Giovanni, he's alive!" she cried happily. "They'll be releasing prisoners soon. The war is over."

Giovanni's face darkened. He shook his head. "Signora, the partisans are in control up there. They've got scores to settle. It's not like there's real law," he repeated, still fidgeting with his hat.

Alda thought of Mussolini hanging upside down. "But no one has a score to settle with Floro! Where is this prison, Giovanni? I'll travel up there and have him released. It worked for his brothers. Can you tell me, exactly?"

Seeing the farmer's clouding eyes stirred her emotions. He'd known Floro since he was a young man. Afraid Giovanni would dissolve, Alda patted his arm, reassuring him that she'd get documents vouching for his character, perhaps a letter from the priest saying he'd never been part of the *squadristi*, that he only engaged in charitable acts.

"Signor Ugo has a lawyer friend and knows people high up in the partisan pool. He'll contact whoever can help," she added. "Don't worry, Giovanni. We will bring him home."

After the farmer told her all he knew, Alda thanked him and rushed to Ugo's room, knocking but entering without waiting for his permission.

He scowled at the unprecedented disturbance, but when she explained why and what she was about to do the patriarch jumped to his feet.

"You can't go to a prison alone. I'll go with you."

She was afraid his irascible character would be a detriment to her mission. "Please stay here, protect the children. Get word to any contact you have from the left, partisan or communist, anyone who might help. They should have no quarrel with Floro," she insisted. "Tell them I intend to bring him home. I'll need a vehicle to drive me there."

Ugo said, "If I'm to stay, then I'll ask Signor Chiotti to accompany you." The lawyer, who was Ugo's close friend, was also very fond of Floro.

"That could be helpful, if he's willing," Alda said.

Ugo, Mario and Pietro conferred with Alda as she made plans to travel north, finding a driver to take her and contacting their lawyer, who immediately agreed to take the journey. Alda was anxious about telling Anna and Flora about their father.

"Be brave and pray," Alda said. "I'm leaving very early tomorrow. You'll stay here with your uncles and grandfather. Palma will be in charge. Take care of your brother. The trip will take days, but I promise I'll return soon with your father."

"But *Babbo* promised over a year ago that he'd be home soon!" Flora cried, and Anna nodded as their mother sighed and hugged them.

"Don't worry. Nothing will keep me away long."

She left their room and tiptoed in to see Aldo. "What are you building, *amore*?" she asked her four-year-old who was playing with his father's old wooden blocks.

"Ponte alla Trinità," he said. "I'm rebuilding one of the bombed bridges." Alda leaned over and hugged her son, heartbroken.

"Good idea, Aldino. We have a lot of rebuilding to do." Sitting on his bed looking at her son, she saw a face that must have been the image of Floro long ago.

"The bombs have stopped. We've found your father, and I'm going up north to bring him home," she said, feigning cheerfulness. He looked at her with a knitted brow. "Why do you have to go?" he asked. He hardly remembered his father.

"I just do. Be a good boy. Pay attention to Palma, your grandfather and your sisters." She kissed him and slipped out the door before he could ask any other questions.

The next morning the lawyer arrived moments before the lorry appeared on the street. Tipping his hat, the driver opened the back cab before introducing himself to the family. Alda insisted she sit in the open back, thinking that the only seat inside the truck should be reserved for the old lawyer. She had packed food, a flask of wine, some first aid and a thick blanket.

"If anyone can bring Floro home, it's you, Alda," Mario said. She gave him a half smile, insisting that Ugo's contacts could be even more crucial. Mario placed the blanket on the rusty cab and gave Alda a hand as she climbed up. Ugo looked hopefully at the lawyer as the lorry's motor hummed. Alda waved from the open back as they drove off.

Despite the scarf tied on her head, the wind whipped Alda's hair as they left the city and headed north towards Brescia. Wrapping herself in the gray blanket, she closed her eyes and pretended she was back in those courtship days with Floro, driving around the Florentine hills with the top down in his little *Ballila Coppa D'oro* Fiat. She remembered the sensation of air on her face and the scent of perfumed hills in May, an association of joyful expectation. As the lorry sped up, the landscape became a whir. The war had damaged everything, including Mussolini's improved roads. The jarring trip on the cold metal bed would take longer than a day with the remaining blockades. They would stop somewhere overnight. Bumps in the road and the fumes of petrol forced her mind from pleasant past thoughts. Chilled to the bone, she prayed that Ugo would pull through with his political contacts. All day and into the blackness of the night she sat swaddled in the blanket, dozing on and off, lost in dreams, until she awoke with a start. She had a sinking sensation that something had happened to Floro.

Her intuition was deep. Only a day before her journey began, the prison had lined up fascists for execution. Floro, standing in the line, rose above everyone else in the courtyard.

"When your name is called, step forward," a guard shouted. As they read out names alphabetically: Albieri, Brancusi, Cantini, Donetti… each man stepped forward. Listening to the alphabet, Floro began to sweat as the roll call continued. But when they passed the Rs, his name was skipped. He was bewildered as he stood along the wall with two other men. They looked at one another. Towering Floro appeared like the tip of a pyramid between them. The two men were shaking by his side. He assumed the three of them would be executed. He wondered how his family would receive the news. Would Alda ever forgive him? She had been right, once again. He should have listened to her, never should have left home. A partisan serving as a guard motioned for the three of them to follow him.

Floro nudged them with his elbow. They shuffled towards the door while the other men observed, confused. Floro turned to see the other prisoners shoved against the wall. As they passed the door's threshold, from the corner of his eye Floro saw the partisans pick up their rifles. Pushed down the corridor, Floro froze when he heard the order. "*Face forward!*" Then another order and, a second later, synchronized shots rang out. His long legs buckled. This wasn't just a scare, they'd just killed those men. No trial. Nothing. Hot pain blazed up Floro's spine as if he'd been shot. The guard continued to push him and the other two men back to their cells.

"Rafanelli?" his cellmate cried seeing him, slapping Floro's shoulder as he collapsed on to his cot.

"I have no idea," Floro whispered, muttering something about a sick game of roulette.

***

Alda figured they must be near a boarding house where they'd find a place to stay. She prayed, trying to rid herself of the foreboding she felt, shivering in the impenetrable night. The driver pulled over on the shoulder of the road and approached the cab.

"Have we arrived?" Alda asked.

"Just needed to make a stop," the man said and walked off in the dark. When he returned, he asked if there was anything she needed.

"No," she insisted. "How much longer?"

"A half hour and we'll be there, signora."

She pulled out a *panino* as the driver moved back onto the road. You're going to need all your strength, she told herself, biting into Ugo's favorite sandwich, roast beef and *salami*. She'd made one for the driver, one for the lawyer and three for Floro.

Finally they arrived at the boarding house. Their lawyer friend opened the back. "I'm so sorry, Alda," he said, "it wasn't very cavalier of me to let you sit back here."

"Please don't worry," she insisted; "you're here." He held her hand as she descended stiff with cold. The driver knocked on the door to the boarding house and a gaunt man welcomed them. Entering a dingy bedroom, Alda noticed the bed's four feet were resting in small buckets. Bedbugs, she thought. She smelled alcohol. Forget it, she told herself shivering. Resigned to get rest, she climbed in.

***

A guard called Floro out of his cell again the next evening. Prodding his back with a rifle butt, he was headed down the same corridor. Floro wondered, what was going on as other prisoners gathered around that same courtyard. He looked down at the ground. The dirt was crimson. Fear engulfed him. How would Alda ever know how sorry he was? One man was sobbing. Floro's heart pounded, his throat constricted. Someone read out names – the excruciating alphabet again. He felt anger rising. Just how far did these partisans intend on going? If they were executing people just for being fascist, they'd have to exterminate half of Italy. How had it gone from building something to destroying everything? An inordinate number of names were read that began with P. An image surfaced of his mother sitting in a long linen dress on the villa's terrace, with naughty Yusk lying at her feet. He felt the breeze of Grassina, smelled the sweet scent of lavender. But his mother's face was stern, her back rigid on the chair. The memory was from a photograph taken the day his family moved to the villa in the '20s. Was she chastising him now? He trembled as he heard the name *Romolo* called. Floro stood, feeling sick to his stomach, bracing himself to step in line, but the next name he heard was *Suozzi*. He looked down at the bloody ground, incredulous. How could they make the same mistake twice? Once again, he was left standing by just a few other men. He was summoned out with the few others. What he couldn't have known was that this time his name had been on the list but that it had been struck out with a pencil just an hour earlier after a call from a high-ranking communist member.

"Take Floro Rafanelli off," the capo had ordered. "No complaints. Never a *squadrista*."

***

When Alda knocked at the prison door the following day, Floro was no longer there. He was nearly dead, lying in a hospital bed nearby. Amidst rows of wounded and dying men, he peered up at a flaky ceiling through slits in his beaten, swollen eyes. Strains of Puccini's *Turandot* flooded his head. *If the determined suitor guesses the riddle before dawn, he can save his own life and win the hand of the ice princess. Vincero'! Vincero'!* But the sublime tenor's voice came to a screeching halt. Floro was overwhelmed with pain and regret. How many times had Alda warned him that his size might get him into trouble! He struggled to recall what had happened. He had faced the firing squad twice and for some reason been led back to his cell.

He remembered lying in his cell and feeling shame that others had lost their lives while he'd been saved twice. Then he'd awoken to the loud drunken partisan youth screaming, *"Maledetti fascisti!"* The guards always let the prisoners out of their cells, for exercise they'd insist, but Floro knew the drunken men were there to beat the prisoners. Because of his size they usually kept Floro locked in his cell, shoving the others far enough away so he heard nothing.

As he lay there in pain on the hospital cot, Floro struggled to recall what had happened next. The guards had entered, grabbing his skinny cellmate and locking the door behind them. Floro remembered them laughing unmercifully. Disturbed by the unfairness of the fight, he lunged forward.

"Why not take me?" he banged on the cell door. The guards acquiesced, calling to the drunken youth. Four jeering men descended upon him. He recalled swinging, knocking the partisans down. At first he'd had the advantage, until one snuck behind him and swung a rifle, striking him behind his knees. Floro buckled, a toppling tower. They converged upon him with the butts of their rifles, repeatedly hitting him, cracking his ribs.

"Want to be the Savior, eh?" one had smirked, pressing his boot hard on Floro's back while the others administered brutal blows, over and over, smashing down on his lungs and kidneys, his head, his face. His cellmate had looked on aghast.

"He wants to sacrifice himself!" one partisan had shouted. "Let's put him on the cross." They'd hauled his limp body up against the wall, tying his arms parallel to the floor as if crucifying him.

"*Vai vai, Cristo!*" another had mocked, "you want to die for our sins?" Then they'd renewed their assault. His cellmate, at first dumbstruck, had finally screamed that they were killing him. One reasonable guard had stopped the fight.

"You idiots! That man is to be released!" the guard had said.

Floro vaguely remembered being cut down before slumping unconscious on the ground. How could he ever have dreamed that at that moment his wife was only a short distance away, driving towards him to bring him home?

***

Standing next to her lawyer, Alda composed herself before she knocked on the prison door. As she peered at whitewashed walls and boarded-up windows, she imagined desperate eyes looking out at her. Like Villa Triste this was a makeshift prison, a place about revenge not justice. Alda knocked again. Finally a man opened the door, and the two entered.

"We've come for Floro Rafanelli," she insisted, fearless.

The man shuffled. "You should've been here yesterday. He got himself involved in a fight."

"What?" the lawyer said.

"But he's alright," Alda said with confidence, knowing Floro's strength. The man looked at her.

"Signora, your husband is in the hospital, a kilometer down the road." He pointed in the direction.

"Hospital?" she nearly collapsed. *Pay attention*, she thought. She turned and held onto the lawyer's arm as they walked back to the lorry, explaining the situation to the driver. If only they'd driven through the night, Alda thought.

They found the hospital and rushed in. The lawyer followed at a slow pace. A nurse ushered Alda into a room that smelled of death.

She finally found Floro, passed out on a bed. Her heart pounded. She could tell he was badly bruised but saw his chest rise. He was still alive.

"Oh Florino," she cried softly, bending over her husband to kiss his forehead. "What have they done to you?" With her voice and touch, he stirred slightly.

"Alda?" he whispered almost imperceptibly. Tears rolled down his cheeks as she stood over him. "No," he uttered, wanting to stop her as she began to pull back his sheet.

"Floro," she whispered, seeing how brutally he was beaten. "I'm taking you home."

As he fell again into unconsciousness, she asked the lawyer to stay by his side. She found a doctor, who recited his multiple wounds, internal and external: broken ribs, kidneys, compromised lungs. "He won't survive long if he stays here, with the risk of infection. His best chance is if you take him home."

The doctor handed Alda tincture of laudanum to give Floro for his pain — it would help him sleep through the journey. Alda found a telephone and called home. When Ugo answered, she explained Floro's situation and said that they would arrive sometime before dawn, that he should alert their doctor. She hung up before he could ask any more questions. Then Floro, still unconscious, was carried out on a gurney. They laid him on Alda's blanket. She sat behind him on the cold metal, and picking up his head she rested it on her lap. Her only covering was her woolen shawl. For several hours he was in and out of consciousness. When the medication wore off, he screamed with every bump in the road. Alda administered the last remaining medicine, praying. All through the night they traveled without stopping.

At dawn, when they heard Alda at the door, Mario, Pietro and Ugo rushed out onto the street, struggling to get Floro onto the makeshift stretcher. Breathless and freezing, Alda was relieved the children were asleep.

"Down here to my room," instructed Ugo. As Floro lay listless in his father's bed, his infection raged. Alda undressed him, wincing at the physical evidence of cruelty. His brothers grimaced and looked away. Alda cleaned his wounds and washed his body before the doctor came in and examined him. With his instructions she applied bandages as Palma assisted. The brothers stood aghast. Ugo walked out with his lawyer friend, thanking him for bringing his son home.

"I just took up the more comfortable seat. Alda did everything, everything," Chiotti replied, shaking his head.

The doctor said nothing else could be done. They would have to wait. "Keep Floro comfortable, clean his wounds, pray his inner organs heal, that his fever abates and the infection passes. Contagion is a concern," he warned. It was best to especially keep little Aldo, the most vulnerable, away from his father. One never knew, with the threat of tuberculosis or some other infectious disease. Alda stiffened, thinking of their baby Ugo's meningitis. She would not let anything happen to Aldo. Her jaw hurt from clenching her teeth.

After everyone had returned to bed, in the early morning hours she sat by Floro's side on a low yellow slipper chair, the same chair where she'd nursed her babies. Clutching her rosary beads, she kept her weary eyes on her husband. He was home at last.

CRUMBLING VAULTS AND DREAMS

1978

Alda had revealed so much about the man who would have been my father-in-law. I had let her reminisce without interruption. Left suspended were the harder questions surrounding fascism and the war.

Now my preoccupation was with Aldo telling his mother about his plan to sell. Why was this house, steady for almost five hundred years, suddenly falling apart under his watch? Yellow is the color of caution. He had placed wooden barriers and strung yellow sashes to keep people away from the unstable vaults under the *loggia*. It was no longer possible to delay the inevitable with the potential of collapse. Yellow also seemed a metaphor for beleaguered Italy and the uncertain direction of our lives.

I didn't want to muck up matters with my tears. However heartfelt, my connection to the villa was so minor compared to their lifetime of memories. The night Aldo planned on facing the issue with his mother, I sat on an upright log by the fireplace waiting for him to come home. I looked at the log seats placed there by Aldo, one of his anti-bourgeois gestures that I'd once found appealing. Now, far along in my pregnancy, they seemed more like another youthful avoidance technique. At times, living at the villa had felt like camping. But we were young and free then, never pressured to transform it into a *casa borghese*.

When Aldo entered, I kissed him. Seeing his face, I decided to be with him when he told her. We walked silently down the corridor lined with the same trunks that'd been parked there since I first visited five years ago. As he opened the green glass parlor door and peeked in, Alda looked up at us, smiling with a brave face. I sensed she already understood. When he kissed his mother on her forehead, I couldn't help thinking of Judas. *Oh, just cut the drama,* I chastised myself as Aldo sank into the overstuffed velvet sofa next to her. I sat next to him.

"*Mamma,*" Aldo said slowly, leaning forward. "This time I'm certain. We have to sell. There are too many costly repairs. I will not go into huge debt."

Alda put down her knitting and exhaled. It was strange for her, this long-suffering breath. She usually stood up to challenges, spouting the appropriate Tuscan proverb to give any situation meaning. The silence was painful as we listened for her reply. She sat up and turned to her son with focused, tense energy. "This is your decision since this place is in your name. But selling now is terrible timing with the market way down. You really should wait."

I kept my mouth shut. She was right. The question was how much longer could we wait, ignoring the exorbitant repairs of the terracotta roof and the collapsing vaults that already devalued the villa? How long before real estate might rise in value to make it worth the risk?

"Why don't you let me see what I can juggle?" Alda said.

"No!" he shouted. I'd never witnessed such an outburst by him and was startled. He continued, thankfully calmer but still tense. "You've done that my entire life. There's nothing left to juggle!"

A while ago Aldo had insisted that I dispel my romantic notion that his mother had been home making meals for them every day growing up. She had told me that after the war she was absent for endless hours every day or on the phone with lawyers, meeting with bankers, trying to rent, sell or buy time, bit by bit. Even though it was exhausting, she was determined to keep as much of the patrimony together as possible so that her children could have a decent life. But because of the way this struggle had consumed his mother, just the thought of debt produced in Aldo an angst he couldn't abide.

"I can't force you," Alda said. She'd always found a way but, looking at her son, she relinquished the fight. I imagined her thinking: *He's stubborn, intractable, just like his father.*

Aldo didn't mention we had considered the possibility of leaving Italy, as in truth we thought we couldn't leave Alda. Instead he said we were going to look around for some manageable place outside Florence. She got up from her chair, grabbing her cane. I choked at the sound of her slippers shuffling on the tile floor, the finality of this decision weighing heavily on her. I felt culpable. If I hadn't come and wasn't expecting a baby, she and Aldo probably would've stayed at the villa even with it falling down around them – at least until the end of her days, until she got her wish.

"That seemed so harsh," I said as his mother left the room.

"I had to seem decisive, couldn't let her latch onto false hope," he insisted. "She's always the hard-headed optimist convinced she can resolve everything."

We entered the kitchen as she prepared a meal. Her exaggerated clanging of pots felt like a personal protest, a tolling that sounded the way her heart felt. I swallowed hard, pained by the ensuing silence. I wished her son would just embrace her.

Instead he cleared his throat, stood up and said, "I'll be back." *Good escape artist*, I thought. I asked Alda if I could do anything, but she dismissed me.

"Don't worry. Go." She probably now wished she hadn't convinced her father-in-law Ugo to leave the beloved villa to her only son.

After Aldo put it on the market, we looked around the countryside at charming, small, manageable farmhouses. We decided to stay near Florence. Leaving would be so hard on Alda, so living with us would soften the blow. We fell in love with a little *casa colonica* in Cerchina, not far from Montemorello, where Anna and her husband Nico and their boys had their summer home. It was just big enough for us, our baby and Alda. The house overlooked an olive grove, with Brunelleschi's *Duomo* visible in the distance. There was a tiny old church just steps away. But everything needed a lot of work, and we didn't know if we wanted to get involved in gutting a place. We decided to make an offer, but the villa had to sell first. A month passed and there were still no buyers. Finally, Aldo complained about the market to his friend Simonetta, and she decided she wanted it. Before long the deal was done. Simonetta and her husband Eugenio became the new owners of Villa Rafanelli, taking possession in October. There was solace in knowing they would honor and restore it. And it meant we could visit them there.

Then something happened that changed our intention to remain in Italy. One morning, at eight months pregnant and barely fitting into my Fiat, I arrived at my flower shop surprised to find a crowd milling on Via Cavour. Stretching my neck, I saw an urban police officer standing by my shop door and a yellow band of caution blocking the building next to mine. My first thought was: *Oh no, not more crumbling vaults!* As I got out of my car I discovered a gaping hole in the wall that my shop shared with the officers' club and appellate court. Queasy, I unlocked the large wooden door and the policeman allowed me to drive in. Once parked inside I was overcome by nausea and retched on the ground by the greenhouse. Composing myself, I ventured onto the street again to assess the damage and ask the policeman what had happened.

"*Una bomba*," he said, matter-of-factly, "during the night. No one was hurt." Instinctively my arms surrounded my swollen belly, as if protecting my unborn from aftershocks.

"Thank God no one was hurt," I said, but repeated, "*Una bomba*? Why?" What was the target: the florist shop run by the American, the officers' club or the appellate court? When I asked the policeman, his shoulders lifted high.

"*Chi sa!*" His glib answer, *who knows*, didn't satisfy me, but then he mumbled something about *i giovani terroristi*. Could it have been the Red Brigades? I recalled the *Nazione*'s cartoonist Fremura illustrating the long ignored *Brigate Rosse* threat. His cartoon showed Italians sitting around, ignoring a stream of little bombs blowing up in the distance. As the bombs get closer and closer, Italy only wakes up after an enormous one explodes. Was this our wake-up call too? I knew being pregnant amplified my sense of vulnerability. Looking for peace and a moment to think, I locked the shop and walked across the street to the museum and monastery of San Marco.

I stood in front of Fra Angelico's painting of the *Last Judgment*, drawn towards the artist's sweet *Paradiso* panel where delicate angels and blessed souls ascend, hand in hand, in a shimmering dance. Christ sits on high in the center, flanked by angels and his mother, as saints float on a cloud shelf surrounded by a lapis lazuli sky. The opposite panel depicts the friar's version of *inferno*, a hell of flames, cauldrons and grotesque demons dismembering and devouring the damned. Despite my Roman Catholic upbringing, or perhaps because of it, I reject this afterlife damnation scene. Everything unfolds right here on earth as we all move in and out of a state of grace.

This monastery, like this city, has had its share of tumultuous history. Savonarola, the fanatical head prior here at San Marco, was burned at the stake in 1498. Some Florentines consider him a saint for fighting the rise of hedonistic humanism. Just this past May, numerous people entered my flower shop wanting *un mazzo di fiori* to honor the anniversary of Savonarola's death. It was hard to fathom making money off a righteous monk martyred half a millennium ago. After my customers had paid me for their bouquets, I remember feeling mystified as I watched them head towards Piazza Signoria to lay the flowers on a commemorative medallion embedded in the pavement. I'd wondered if they just considered Savonarola a holy martyr promoting the sacred, or if they actually supported his overzealous *bonfire of the vanities*.

I moved towards San Marco's interior courtyard, my treasured place of meditation. Sitting on a Savonarola scissor chair, I gazed at the tall Cedar of Lebanon tree across the way, ingesting the silent, airy space. How was I to interpret the bomb next to my flower shop? Was it a sign, a warning? I began to pray the same way I had since I was five years old. "Dear God…" which always sounded like the beginning of a letter, "should we wait to move to America or leave now?" As I looked up at the thick needles cascading from the cedar's branches, I pondered Aldo's point. *If we buy a house around Florence now, we'll probably never move to America. What were we waiting for?* He was well into his thirties; his English was still rudimentary. The longer we delayed, the harder it would be to find work in New York. We had to focus now on our baby's future. I knew little about Italian schools. I'd been living in a bubble that'd burst first by the Red Brigades and the Aldo Moro assassination, then by the daily news of kidnapped children. And now this bomb. Where was Italy going?

The awful death of Aldo Moro had really shaken us. I couldn't help drawing the parallel to another kidnapping and assassination that had deeply disturbed Alda when she was also in her twenties. The socialist politician Matteotti was killed in 1924 because he publicly denounced election fraud, fascist violence and Mussolini. If Matteotti had endured and fascism had been overthrown, the unholy alliance with Hitler would never have happened. But history is history. The point was the uncertain present and going forward.

Pensive, my hands stretched over my front. I felt the determined life flutter inside me and pondered the decision. We eventually hoped to move to America, but with the current political and economic situation in Italy I was now convinced it should be sooner rather than later. My biggest concern was leaving Aldo's mother, his sisters, nephews and dear friends.

I rose from the scissor chair and returned to my flower shop, staring again at the bomb blast before climbing into my little car. I drove up the villa's fateful hill with tears clouding my eyes. The sound of the first gear grinding reflected my mood. I found Aldo on the stone bench, looking out over his vineyard. His chin was propped up on his fist, in that familiar pose reminiscent of Rodin's *Thinker.* Had he come to the same conclusion?

As he turned towards me and saw my face, he guessed something was up. I stared at him before making the same hand movement he'd made in Cortina, the gesture meaning: *let's get out of here.* Swinging my stiff fingers back and forth, I tapped the side of my right hand with my left palm. It seemed blasé, this Italian gesture, but it was laden with anguish.

CHESTNUTS

1947-1948

Floro napped as Alda sat nearby focusing on the rhythm her fingers made looping an intricate crochet pattern. She paused to listen to her husband's labored breathing, worried about this new infection, longing to be in Grassina where the country air might purify his lungs. *If only we could get back in.* The villa, occupied first by Germans and then Americans during the war, had been inaccessible to them in the three years since the end of the war, sequestered by the government's campaign to house Italians made homeless by the conflict. Alda had compassion for those who'd lost everything, but what about fresh air for Floro's lung disease? What about Floro's homeless spirit? Alda imagined them sitting under the *loggia*, finally gazing down on the valley without fear. Was it too much to ask to relish the simple pleasures of the countryside? She also knew her little son needed to get out of the city. Because of the war he had been confined the first half of his life, surrounded by anxiety and fear. It had been over three years since that August in '44 when the Germans had bombed the bridges and left the city. Yet being around his sick and dispirited father since then had taken its toll on Aldo. No six-year-old child should have such sad eyes. Alda was afraid not only that her husband's disease was potentially contagious, but that his despair was as well.

Alda got up and stood by the window. Aldo was out on the sidewalk standing near the older boys, longing to be a part of their gang as they placed coins on the tram tracks. The boys would wait for the tram and cheer as it passed. She'd found flattened coins in her son's drawer and wondered if her vulnerable boy would take risks just to impress the gang? He was a constant concern.

She turned to Floro with a sinking feeling. This past week he could hardly move. Although some months he seemed on the mend and was out of bed, he'd tempted fate too often during his convalescence. Now it had been weeks since he'd collapsed in bed, and he hadn't gotten up since. Palma knocked and peeked into the room.

"Do you need anything, signora?"

"No, thank you, Palma," Alda said, suddenly having an idea. She worried that the accretion of sorrow in her son's tender years would define the rest of his life.

"Actually, Palma…"

"Yes, signora?"

"I have a question," she said, motioning her outside the room. "It's Aldo," she whispered. "He should be carefree at his age, but with this latest infection the doctor says there's new risk of contagion. How can I tell my little boy that he has to stay away from his father again? He doesn't understand; he takes the restriction as a punishment. He wants to be close to me, but I have to attend to my husband. So, I just had a thought…"

Palma leaned towards her.

She asked if she would consider taking Aldo to her family's home in the mountains. "You've spoken so fondly of the place. I think the distraction and the mountain air would do him good. You've said there are children there? He seems lost here. He isn't eating. He tags along with older boys who are not a good influence."

"But signora! You need me here."

"We'll manage somehow, Palma. You haven't been home since last Christmas. The change would be good for you too," Alda urged. "Would the children play with him? Are they a welcoming bunch?"

Palma explained there was not much time for play, as it was the season of the chestnut harvest. A band of children was always in the woods, gathering all day long.

"Could Aldo help with the harvest? It would be so good to engage him in something constructive. He's so sensitive, so withdrawn, Palma. I'm really concerned – unless you think he'd be in the way?"

"My sweet Aldo in the way? No, signora, it isn't that." She paused a moment before reassuring her that he would be welcome.

"Then it's settled," Alda said, relieved.

When the time came a week later for Palma and Aldo to leave for their sojourn, Alda gave her son a tight squeeze, stifling her tears. She told him to mind Palma, assured him he would have a wonderful adventure in the mountains and that he would be back home before he knew it.

Aldo had no idea why he was being sent away or for how long. What had he done wrong? Ugo accompanied Palma and Aldo to the bus stop, making sure that Aldo was settled in his seat. Standing outside the bus, he looked up at his grandson through the window. Aldo had two hands splayed on the glass, a desperate goodbye. Ugo's eyes filled with tears. When the bus took off, Palma put her arm around Aldo as he leaned on her.

"In all my years with your family, I've never seen your grandfather cry," she said. "But there's nothing to worry about, Aldino. You'll be with other boys and girls helping with the chestnut harvest."

Aldo stared out the window as the bus wound its way up around mountain roads, taking hours to reach Palma's stop. Once off the bus, they walked hand in hand into the woods before reaching a clearing with a cluster of four or five small houses. Despite her kind, encouraging words, Aldo was taken aback when Palma opened the door to her house. The floor was dirt; the only light emanating from the room was the hearth fire. Aldo grasped Palma's hand tighter as she brought him into the dark room, directing his attention to the boiling cauldron filled with chestnuts. "You can eat as many as you want!" she exclaimed. His eyes opened wide with surprise. He'd always been limited to very few, and only after he'd finished his plate of vegetables, meat and fish. His stomach growled as he stared at the roiling chestnuts.

"Go on, there's the ladle. Take a few." She handed him a thick napkin, and he scooped up four chestnuts. He attempted a smile as Palma showed him his little room. "You'll sleep in this bed." As Aldo stared, he was startled by someone entering the house. Dropping his napkin, the chestnuts rolled on the floor. "Don't worry! It's only Pa," Palma said as Aldo picked up his treasures and put them in his pocket. A burly old man appeared, resting an axe by the door.

"Palma!" the man cried, approaching his daughter who fell into his embrace. The man winked at Aldo. "So, you must be the boy!"

When they finally sat down to eat dinner, Palma served soup. Aldo was amazed to see the bottom of his bowl with only a few strands of pasta floating in a watery broth. He left the table with a stomachache, having eaten five more chestnuts to fill himself up. That night, missing his mother, he cried himself to sleep.

The next morning Aldo drank hot milk and devoured another plateful of warm chestnuts. As a band of children gathered outside Palma's house, she greeted them and introduced Aldo, who hadn't said a word since he'd arrived.

"Nino," she called to the eldest boy, the leader of the group, "show Aldo here how to harvest. He's a good boy." Aldo was terrified to leave Palma, but she insisted. Nino told him to stay close as twelve children all walked into the woods.

The chestnut trees, rising in such majesty all around them, took Aldo's breath away. He had never seen such tall and wide trees. As he gazed up at them he prayed silently that his *mamma* would come to see them too. She adored trees, would introduce each kind to him whenever they took a walk together. "Good morning, Mr. Umbrella Pine," she'd say.

Aldo was mystified by the band of children fanning out with purpose into the wondrous woods, joking while harvesting. All day he followed Nino's instructions, adding to the pile of thorny chestnuts. When he found the ones freed from prickly pods, he followed the other children's lead and dropped these hulled ones onto a growing pile. In the afternoon Nino opened a tiny paper package filled with salt that he added to a pot of water filled from a nearby stream. Although Aldo barely understood the dialect, the eldest boy told him to gather twigs for the fire. He watched the pot full of chestnuts above the sticks. Nino took two matches and struck a fire.

The next day Palma took Aldo to the market to buy a pair of boots like the other boys wore. Signora Alda had given her the money, as she wanted her son to be properly dressed for the harvest. She imagined he might be teased wearing his city shoes. Aldo wore the new boots all day long while he harvested, but it was agony. He limped all the way home. When Palma saw his face, she knew something was wrong.

"Sit down on the bench." She took off his boots and his bloody socks. "*O povero Aldino!*" she exclaimed, fetching a bucket of water to soak his feet. After, as he suppressed his whimpering, she wrapped his feet in towels and had him sit down. Palma returned holding a needle, lifting his foot towards her, then the needle to his foot.

"What are you doing?" he cried.

"I have to drain that blister, Aldo. It's only dead skin, it won't hurt."

"Oh noooo! Please, Palma." He had no clue what dead skin meant but it didn't sound good. After numerous tries, she gave up, bandaged his ankle and let him run around barefoot. In a few days he and his feet had toughened.

He relished being useful and loved the freedom of harvesting all day long with boys and girls of all ages. Soon he understood their accent and dialect and felt like he belonged. Although they worked hard, they were a team, their camaraderie unsupervised by hovering adults. He particularly liked to play after dinner with a girl named Lucia. She even taught him needlework, something his mother and sisters said was only for girls. It would have been the most ideal place in the world if he hadn't felt hungry all the time.

Over a month passed in the sacred quiet of the woods before they returned to Viale Michelangelo. When a tram passed on the Florentine street, Aldo was shaken by the sound. As Palma opened the gate and stepped into the house, Aldo kept his hat on, looking around as if he was entering a stranger's place. He was struck by the familiar scent of strong pine soap, reminding him of his father's illness.

From upstairs Alda heard voices and looked down. There was Palma at the door with a boy she assumed was Aldo but who looked completely different from her son. He was taller, unkempt, wearing an odd hat and long pants. Aldo stared at his mother curiously, his chin jutting out. Alda's hand reached for her mouth to muffle a cry of disbelief. She hoped the gesture seemed more like surprise than desperation at her son's transformation.

"Aldo!" she cried. "Palma!"

"Ciao Ma," Aldo finally said, gruffly.

Alda's shoulders dropped. Even his voice had changed.

"Welcome home!" Alda said, rushing down, trying to hide her dismay. He was taller but thinner, yet his complexion was ruddy, no longer pale, thank God. She embraced her son and took his hand, which had lost its delicate tenderness. She stood back to take a good look at him. His hair needed cutting. "Aldo! How you've grown!" She then reminded him to remove his hat while in the house. The next moment Anna and Flora rushed to see their brother. They halted on the stairs at the sight of him, bursting into tears.

"*O Dio!*" Anna and Flora cried in shock.

Alda frowned at her daughters, not wanting to hurt Aldo or Palma's feelings.

"Look how tall he is!" Alda asserted, forcing gaiety.

"Pa?" Aldo said, ignoring his sisters as they stared in astonishment.

"*Babbo* is still in bed, Aldo," his mother said, patting his head, looking at his unruly hair, wondering if her son would welcome another hug. He made a forlorn face and turned towards the door, saying he wanted to go outside. His chin seemed to lead him there.

Palma said, "I hope you didn't get a fright not expecting us. There's no telephone at home."

"Oh no, just surprised," Alda swallowed. "It's been so lonely here without you both. Thank heavens you're home safe."

"*Grazie*, signora," Palma said, excusing herself. Alda, Flora and Anna eyed each other as Palma left the room.

"Even the way he walks is different!" Flora cried.

"Maybe I shouldn't have sent him away," Alda whispered, clutching her chest, before going to prepare a bath for him.

The next day Alda summoned Aldo's tutor. Late in the afternoon, Anna played the piano as Flora sang.

"Do you recognize this, Aldino?" Flora begged. The response was a disinterested shrug. "Of course you do! It's Puccini's *Madama Butterfly*," she cried.

At dinner Aldo devoured everything on his plate for each course. Alda, Anna and Flora blinked in amazement at his appetite. They had spent years running after him with forks full of food.

"Are you sure you're Aldo, or have you been switched?" Flora asked. At the table his grandfather asked if he enjoyed picking chestnuts. Aldo nodded, again leading with his chin and holding his fork with his fist.

"*Nonno*, I ate so many chestnuts that I don't care if I see another one in my life!" They all burst out laughing. He had always begged for them. The laughter brought on a flashback for Aldo, of one time his father had piled a mound of chestnuts on his plate. He remembered his own glee and his eyes widening at the pile, before his father took all but one away. "Just teasing," his father had said. Aldo recalled his eyes swelling with tears. That time, even though he was a sick man, his mother had chastised her husband for his cruel joke.

After dinner Aldo approached his mother as she sat sewing. Holding something behind his back, he said, "I've got something for Pa." He pulled out a pillow cover, crocheted with a tree.

"That's for *Babbo*?" she asked, tears surfacing, as her son seemed to have forgotten the Tuscan word for dad.

"Yes, *Mamma*," he said gruffly. "Lucia and I made it."

"Well, son, you are certainly full of surprises." She motioned for him to sit next to her, wanting to kiss his forehead. "*Babbo* will love this thoughtful gift. How can we thank your friend Lucia?"

"*Mamma!*" he spouted, his chin jutting out. "One day I'll marry her!"

Alda laughed, putting her arm around him. Her boy was a sensitive chameleon. She understood his metamorphosis and hoped that, when he returned to the more familiar Aldo, he would retain this new hearty resilience.

"Well, Aldo! That's very good to hear. Shall we make an announcement?"

"No," he insisted, "it can wait."

When Alda entered her husband's bedroom later, Floro whispered, "This can't go on forever." As she opened the shutter to let light in, she wondered if he was referring to his illness or to his endless sense of guilt about his misdirected youth.

"*Lascia fare.* Let anguish go, Floro. Nothing is forever."

"Let me see my son. I want to sit at the table." His raspy voice was unconvincing. He pulled up his slumped self, waiting. She propped pillows behind him, avoiding his request. "Alda!?"

"We'll see, Floro." She put her shawl around his sunken shoulders and kissed his head.

"*Mio Dio,*" he uttered, "how can you stand it? All this time, as years pass."

"Oh Floro," she waved away his concern.

"Has Aldo asked for me yet?"

"Of course," she said. "In fact, he brought you something special."

"Good. Let me see him. Just one meal with the family," Floro pleaded.

"Alright," she sighed, "but we still need to be careful. He seems heartier, but he's still the most vulnerable at his age. You'll find him really changed. He's taller and not so painfully shy. He's even inherited your sense of humor," she smiled. "But most importantly, his time away in the mountains has lifted his spirits."

"I'm so sorry. You all should have had a break after the war. I've dragged everyone down," he said.

"Oh Floro, stop that useless talk."

As he struggled to lift himself, she shifted his gangly legs to the floor. Seeing his skin this white pained her, recalling how dark he used to get sitting under the sun. From the armoire she chose a crisp blue shirt to perk him up.

"Alda," he sputtered, looking up at her with remorseful eyes as she dressed his emaciated body.

"Floro… conserve your breath." She was impatient with his need for forgiveness. "I'll have Mario come get you when lunch is ready."

"Lucky brother," he said, wrapping his long, scrawny arms around her waist. "And Pietro?" Floro asked.

"He's probably writing..."

"My eulogy," Floro blurted. "He finds death intriguing – another subject to hover over and write about. Life is all academic to him."

Alda frowned. "You know it's his way."

Mario accompanied Floro into the dining room. Alda was relieved the children weren't there to see his shuffled entry. When Anna and Flora appeared, they cried, "*Babbino!*" rushing towards him at the table. Aldo hesitated, then followed his sisters. Their mother quietly cautioned them to keep a certain distance, as Floro wrung his own hands and grinned.

"How handsome you all are!"

Aldo stared at the ghostly figure of his emaciated father who bore no resemblance to the once formidable man who was a shadow of a memory. The three children sat by their uncle Mario, across the table from their father who shifted to sit up straight. After long moments of silence, Aldo remembered the pillow cover. He ran out with no explanation. Everyone assumed he was upset, but a minute later he returned looking proud, holding something behind his back.

"Oh, Aldo, of course!" his mother cried. "Hand it to me."

Aldo frowned. He'd wanted to give the gift to his father directly. As his chin jutted out, asserting his will, his mother hoped this aggressive affectation was temporary. She intercepted him with a smile, took the pillow cover and handed it to Floro, who touched it gently.

"Is this a chestnut tree? Who made this?" he asked, catching his breath.

"Well, mostly Lucia. But I helped with a few stitches."

"Thank her," he uttered.

"And my dear daughters – *tutto bene?*" Floro asked, clearing his throat.

"*Tutto bene, Babbo,*" Flora said.

Anna nodded, always feeling she was the only one who understood her father's anguish. *Can't they see how he suffers?*

"So, Aldo... tell me... the mountains?" Floro struggled.

The little boy swallowed the knot in his throat. He hoped to provoke some levity again. "I ate an avalanche of chestnuts."

Floro's shoulders shook, but his laugh provoked a tubercular cough. Covering his mouth, he wiped his forehead with a handkerchief that his mother Elvira had embroidered long ago. When he looked up, his vacant

251

eyes were the color of slate.

"I'm fine," he gasped, feeling pain with each breath.

Ugo, who entered with Pietro, nodded, looking tense. "Ah Floro! You're here. Well, let's eat," he bellowed. Palma served *ribollita*, the hearty Tuscan soup Alda had made that morning. Aldo stared at the thickness.

"I can't see the bottom of the bowl!" he cried, thinking of Palma's watery soup. Then he looked around, worried Palma might think he was complaining. His father smiled, but everyone was quiet. Floro realized his own presence made his family uncomfortable. He should have stayed in bed. His eyes rested again on Aldo, whose appetite seemed to have greatly improved since being away. Looking at him was like seeing himself as a child.

Aldo, sensing his father's gaze, blinked at him. Hoping to break the tension with a little playfulness, Floro stuck out his tongue. Aldo glanced in disbelief at his mother for guidance. Alda, so happy to see Floro's playful spirit re-emerge, smiled and raised her eyebrows with a look of encouragement. When Floro repeated the antic, Aldo responded by sticking his tongue out at his father. Everyone laughed, hoping that they could still have lighthearted moments. But a second later Floro's laughter turned into another fit of interminable coughing. He gasped for breath, bending towards the floor. Everyone sat immobilized. Floro grabbed his handkerchief and covered his now bloody mouth. Alda rose and rushed to him, her hands on his shoulders. His hacking subsided.

"Come, Floro. You'll be more comfortable in bed."

"*Dio... mi dispiace tanto*," he struggled. As Alda attempted to lift her husband off the chair from behind, Mario and Pietro supported him. Ugo sat frozen in his chair. Floro smiled apologetically at his children. Aldo watched his father hobble down the corridor, with his uncles acting like crutches on either side. Alda rushed into the kitchen to fill a jug with water. *Thirsty*, she thought, nearly crying.

Alda pursued her husband down the hall. Looking to his sisters for guidance, Aldo observed tears flowing down their cheeks. He felt guilty he couldn't cry. He got up to move to the space just occupied by the man who'd stuck his tongue out at him. On the floor near his father's chair, Aldo noticed a bright red splotch. Palma entered to clear the soup bowls. When she noticed Aldo looking down, she saw the blood.

"*O Dio!* Aldo, girls... go outside immediately."

They obeyed as Palma ran into the kitchen for a rag and disinfectant.

Once outside, Aldo shook himself free of his sister Flora's hand and ran into the field behind the house. He was used to finding refuge there so they wouldn't witness his tears. When he finally emerged, he found his sisters standing by the makeshift front gates, staring silently out onto Viale Michelangelo. A man passed by with a heavy satchel. Across the street a neighbor walked arm and arm with his wife, conversing happily. Their two little boys followed, side by side, poking each other. *How can they laugh and joke just outside our gates, as if everything were normal?*

A trolley passed, interrupting his melancholy with the lightning buzz of its electrical connection. How Aldo wished he could travel far far away on that trolley.

FLORO

May 1948

Floro, under a wide-brimmed hat, slouched on a wheelchair as he waited outside in the lush garden of the sanitarium outside Florence. When he spotted his family arriving, he struggled to sit upright. Alda bent to give her husband a kiss. She had instructed the children to keep their distance from everyone in this place filled with patients with serious lung diseases. Aldo fidgeted on one of the wicker chairs placed in a semi-circle around his father. With forced levity, the girls recounted normal things to their father – their school work, the choral music Flora was singing, the piano pieces they were both learning. Growing impatient, Aldo jumped to his feet and left the gathering, running like crazy around the garden. In fast circles, getting dizzy, he finally bumped his elbow so hard on a tree that he nearly fainted. In terrible pain, he returned to his family circle, casually holding his hurt arm and trying not to cause a scene.

"What's wrong, Aldo, did you hurt yourself?" his mother asked as he shook his head vigorously.

"He did, look at his eyes," Flora said. Tears finally streamed down his face.

"Come sit by me," his mother said as Anna got up to examine Aldo's arm, giving him her chair.

A few days later a doctor at the sanitarium told the family there was nothing more they could do, so Floro was sent home. Once or twice Aldo, who had just turned seven earlier in May, was allowed to stand at the threshold of the bedroom where his father lay dying. Life was eclipsed by this languishing march towards death, with wailing females in every corner of the house. This behavior sharply contrasted the demeanor of Pietro, who sat at his desk, calmly writing in his notebook, as if oblivious to the swirling emotions around him. No one understood that Pietro was writing his brother's eulogy.

Aldo was longing to play outside with the older neighborhood boys. Sometimes he seemed almost accepted by them, but mostly he felt like an observer. One afternoon one of them found a box of long bullets from the war. Excited, the boy even showed Aldo the shiny stash in the box. He helped them line a row of them on the trolley tracks in front of his house, just like they'd done many times with coins. As one shouted to take cover, Aldo watched from behind his gate. When the trolley passed, the sight was spectacular, the sound louder than fireworks. Sparks flew, bullet parts shot off in every direction. As they realized someone passing could've been killed, the boys were stunned and chastened. The eldest boy took the box of remaining bullets and buried it in the woods. Aldo ran into his house, relieved that his mother was too busy with his father to even notice.

The following day, May 19th, Alda sent her son out behind the house. As usual, she urged him not to play in the bomb crater near the garage. Aldo nodded, *"Certo, Mamma,"* not wanting to give her another reason to be upset. He sought his solitary refuge behind the bushes.

In the bedroom, Alda stood by Floro, wearing an oxygen mask, fighting for his last breath. When Pietro came in to the room, she heard his compassionate whisper to his brother, assuring him that his family would be taken care of: *"Stai calmo, Floro, stai calmo."* She was relieved that in the end he wanted to calm his brother's spirit.

When his mother appeared and stood by the back door calling with a shaky voice, Aldo remained hiding a long while. He watched her sit quietly on a wicker chair, keeping the door open. "I know you're out there, Aldino. Please come here." Her voice was firm. He finally inched towards her. As she took his hand, he noticed his mother's bloodshot eyes.

"Corraggio, Aldino," she said, pulling him close to her, smoothing his hair. "Babbo's spirit has gone to heaven. Come, see him one last time." She ushered him towards the sick room, holding his shoulders, still forbidding him to pass the threshold. He was immediately struck by the enormous soles of his father's shoes staring at him, out of proportion to the rest of his body. Uncle Mario, sitting by the bed, turned towards his nephew with a forced smile. *Nonno* Ugo stood shaking his head. Leaning to one side of the doorway, Aldo observed his father's very long body stretched out on the bed.

Why is Babbo wearing a suit? he wondered. After seeing his father for so long in nightclothes, why was he now dressed, as if going to work? Where *was* he going next? What surprised him most was the white handkerchief tied from above his father's head down to a big knot under his chin. Did his father also have a toothache in the end? He didn't understand it was to keep his mouth closed.

As *Zio* Pietro straddled the threshold, he patted Aldo's head and said "*Povero orfano.*" Pietro's insinuation that her son was a poor orphan incensed Alda. *My son is no orphan,* she wanted to shout. Earlier in the day she had hoped her conflict with Pietro might be over. The next moment she had to comfort her girls, who came into the room crying.

When Palma appeared, Alda pleaded, "Take Aldo away." *Take me where, back to the mountains?* Instead, she took him into the kitchen and made him a snack of chocolate and bread while he searched for his father's childhood glass marbles, stored in a brown leather pouch. After his snack Aldo went outside and played with a small pile of dirt, forming the marbles into a kind of ziggurat. Soon Palma was by his side.

"I'm taking you to Ilario," she said, pointing up the hill to the old farmer's house. Looking past the cleared field, he stared at Palma quizzically before silently gathering the marbles. He stood up and looked at his dirty knees. He wondered: now that his father was gone, would he be allowed to wear long pants like he had in the mountains? Palma washed his dirty hands and knees before she took him away.

"We'll come for you tomorrow," she promised. Aldo bit his lip, refusing to cry in front of the old man who'd taken him into his dark house.

The following morning Aldo sat outside on the ground, cross-legged, repeatedly tossing his father's marble sack in the air, catching it, listening to the chaotic clatter of glass balls. *Why did Palma leave me here?* As if answering his question, old Ilario suddenly appeared and told him to stand up.

"Take a look down there," the farmer suggested. Through the trees Aldo spied a long train of people dressed in black, walking behind a black carriage. The dark procession slowly snaked up Viale Michelangelo.

"What's that?" the seven-year-old asked.

"That's your father's funeral cortege," Ilario said, taking off his hat. From that distance, everything and everyone seemed small to Aldo.

"Are my mother and sisters down there?" he asked, wondering why he wasn't with them.

"Yes," he said. "That's your mother up front, holding your grandfather's arm."

"Where are they going?" Aldo asked, looking up at the old man.

"To your *babbo's* funeral mass, then to the Porte Sante for his burial."

Aldo shrugged. *Basta! Enough!* As soon as the procession disappeared, he emptied his father's sack of glass marbles, threw the sack and ran off until he found a patch of grass where he tumbled, topsy-turvy, over and over, down the hill.

SEASIDE CLOSE CALL

Summer 1955

Alda sat cramped in an airplane next to Flora, who dozed on her shoulder. She looked down on her youngest daughter's shiny black hair, then gazed out the oval window, conversing with her dead mother-in-law. *We are gliding through the air in this metal behemoth, Elvira! Do you know the reason for our first travel through the air? We are flying to Palermo, to Teatro Massimo, the largest opera house in Italy! All those lessons have paid off! Your namesake, Flora Elvira, is going to perform at the Arena di Verona, a Roma e alla Scala! The opera world embraces her mezzo soprano voice!* Alda looked out at the clouds as they opened up to a bright blue sky. The humming sound was constant. Then she looked down and saw scintillating gold, orange and seething red. *The volcano Mt. Etna! Serene heaven up here. Down there, molten hell.* Suddenly she was traveling in her father's Lancia, on a narrow back road she recognized, near Fiesole. Her father pointed to Monte Cerceri, the cliff where Leonardo da Vinci had convinced that poor man to fly his apparatus. As her vision zoomed in, she was the one on that cliff wearing the wings of the genius. Descending fast, about to crash, Alda yelled and woke up.

Anna stood over her mother who had been asleep on the sofa, asking if she was alright. Her mother sighed, saying it had been a dream. She must be worried about flying with Flora to Palermo, she admitted.

Anna, such an elegant young woman, was wearing an orange chiffon scarf and the lovely dress that they'd made together. Alda was glad that wearing black wasn't required after a death, although it would mirror her current state of mind. She couldn't shake the thick darkness this past month since the unexpected loss of Mario. Anna sat down next to her mother. Their favorite *pensione* in Versillia had just called to say there was a cancellation. They could

Flora Elvira Rafanelli as Suzuki in Madame Butterfly.

finally escape the August heat! When Alda found excuses to avoid the seaside, Anna assured her that Aldo would be fine. She added that, at fourteen, it was high time he experienced the sea. Anna added that with the recent shock of Zio Mario, they all needed to get away.

"*Va bene*, Anna, you're right," she said. "I'll make arrangements with the *pensione* at Lido."

A week later Alda and her three children headed to the seaside. Long-legged Aldo was dressed in white linen pants. His sisters, in crisp sundresses with cardigans over their shoulders, climbed into a taxi. Alda asked her son to sit up front with the driver.

"*La stazione*," Alda said.

"What's your final destination, signora?"

"Lido di Camaiore."

The driver suggested he could take them to the *pensione* for just a fraction more. As Alda negotiated with the driver, Aldo's eyebrows raised in amazement. His frugal mother took buses and trains everywhere. Although she claimed to have driven her father's Lancia at a very young age, she'd never gotten a driver's license. As they sped towards the coast, Aldo dreamed of the day he could motor around on his own.

Over an hour later they reached the boulevard *lungomare*. Between tall pines, Aldo saw an endless stretch of blue.

"*Mamma*, can we stop a minute?!" he pleaded. The family poured out of the car to witness Aldo's first sight of the sea. Ambling towards the water, he stared in amazement at what seemed like an infinity of stars scintillating on the water's surface. Mesmerized, he wondered if it was a mirage.

Flora laughed at her brother. "You'll catch a fly with your mouth open so wide."

"*Dio*," he whispered and both sisters laughed. Observing his expression, his mother thought that waiting so long had merit. Seeing the sea for the first time at his age, he would never take it for granted.

At the *pensione*, Alda's trio followed her inside. The owner's daughter, who'd known the family since before the war, greeted them with a huge smile.

"*Benvenuta, famiglia Rafanelli*," she welcomed. "*Finalmente*."

As Anna and Flora settled in, Alda sensed that her son was reluctant to share the room with her.

"Aldo… during the week, I have to return to Florence. You will have this room all to yourself except on the weekend. I hope that's fine with you?"

"*Va bene, Mamma*," he smiled, relieved.

Once on the beach, Alda watched her son take off his sandals to experience sand between his toes. Drawn towards the water as if hypnotized, his mother grabbed his arm and directed him to the cabana to change.

Awkward Aldo finally emerged with a long towel around his neck, feigning nonchalance as he wore a bathing suit for the first time. He sat on the chaise, sifting sand through his fingers.

"Sand grains are the remains of seashells ground up by water and time," she told Aldo as he discovered shell fragments. A moment later a muscle-bound man passed, dragging a white boat towards the water.

"That's the lifeguard," Anna said, "and his *patino*."

"What's that for?" Aldo asked.

"Rescue. Sometimes, when it gets quiet, the lifeguards take people for rides. But mostly they use it to row around when they're bored."

"Bored?" Aldo said, gawking as bare-legged girls passed by. "That's impossible!"

Anna laughed. Picking up a book, she stretched out on a canvas chaise under the canopy. Flora peered towards the sea and recognized a dear friend approaching.

"*Guarda, guarda!* Look who's here!" Flora cried and rushed towards a robust young man, who embraced her. Anna looked up, a wide grin crossing her face.

"*Cara Signora Rafanelli,*" the young man said to Alda, kissing her hand under the shade. "*E buona sera, ragazzi!*" With an air of intelligent mischief about him, Augusto Battisti embodied the word *simpatico*.

"*O te!*" Anna laughed. After they talked a while, she said: "Augusto, let's take Aldo down to the water. It's his first time."

"*Andiamo,*" Augusto said, "with your permission, signora."

"Of course," Alda smiled, "but only up to his knees." She watched, elated that her children were now in the company of their dear friend and future doctor. He could help in case of any emergency, even if his specialty would be delivering babies.

After Augusto said goodbye, Alda allowed her family to go on the *patino* with the lifeguard. From the edge of the water, she watched them ride suspended in the small white catamaran-type boat. She could see that her son was happy, which meant she was happy. She'd do anything to take away Aldo's trauma of having been with Mario when he collapsed and died on the road as they walked towards the villa. His uncle had been more of a father to Aldo than his actual father, whom he associated with absence and illness, a man he barely remembered. Alda hoped this vacation would help distract her son and them all from that sudden loss. She'd experienced long illness with Elvira and with Floro, and Ugo's short illness before he died five years earlier, but losing someone so dear, without any warning, was an unbearable shock. There was some comfort knowing that Mario himself had said that a sudden heart attack, rather than a languishing death, was "*la morte del giusto.*" Yet at only forty-five, it seemed so unjust. She couldn't shake the image of him lying dead on the chaise under the villa's *loggia*.

Alda looked out and saw the lifeguard handing Aldo an oar. She picked up her camera. She would freeze this image of her only son rowing. The moment would be captured forever, of Aldo next to his beautiful sister Anna in her white bathing suit, hair so fair, and dear Flora, in a bathing cap, waving from the water.

After the weekend Alda reluctantly returned to Florence, giving strict instructions to her daughters to watch their brother. She made them promise to venture out in the water only to their knees, and only when it was calm. The sisters stood at the bus stop, reassuring their mother.

Flora and Anna, with Aldo rowing the patino, at Lido di Camaiore.

"*Mamma*, stop worrying," Anna insisted.

Stepping on the bus, Alda gave them another warning look. She'd never left them alone, but her daughters were now in their twenties.

The next morning in Florence, Alda sat in a waiting room at the city's administrative offices. She looked down at the familiar tiles on the floor. Their Grassina villa had been occupied now for over ten years. Trying to re-possess their own home was just one of the many tasks that filled her days. She waited an hour before her name was called, recognizing the man with the large bald spot sitting behind the desk. He looked like a judge, but he was just another man in the labyrinth of bureaucracy. She never could figure out who was responsible for the decision to let them back in. Ugo had never had the patience to petition these offices. It had always been up to her. She tried to make herself worse than an infestation of weeds. Someday her nagging would wear them down.

"Signora Rafanelli, how may I help you?" This falsely accommodating greeting annoyed her. But this time she had a different spin to her answer.

"Well, as you are well aware, we have not been allowed access to our villa in Grassina in over a decade," she sighed. "I understand the homeless need a home. I am a compassionate woman."

"Indeed," he nodded.

"So, I propose a fair solution. Have all the empty villas in our neighborhood take turns sheltering these unfortunate people for five years. Give us back

Aldo in the sea.

our home. After all the others have done their share, I will be more than happy to host them again."

She felt that, whatever his response, their villa had been chosen as a refuge because of Floro's fascist association. It was another political vendetta.

The man slumped. "Signora," he admitted, "you have a good point."

Staring at her thick file he promised to pass on her suggestion. She thanked him and took her leave. Exiting the building, Alda's natural optimism was renewed. She forgot she always left there with the same rush, only to have her hopes dashed.

Her next appointment was with the tax attorney. So many things yet unsettled, even the unpaid back taxes, thanks to her cavalier father-in-law Ugo. Maybe he had refrained from paying because he'd been unfairly compensated for all the land the government had taken from him. Even after five years, there were still some issues to resolve.

While Alda was exiting the tax attorney's office in Florence, her children were wading through endless shallow Mediterranean water, remembering the promise to only go out up to their knees. Flora, a little slower than her siblings, turned around to gaze at the Apuana Alps rising in the distance behind them. She imagined the white Carrara marble carved out of the mountain range as a vast amphitheater even grander than Verona, where she was programmed to sing. Opening her arms wide, as if embracing an audience populating the mountains, Flora belted out a Verdi aria. She was interrupted by a wave hitting the back of her legs. Turning, she heard a cry and saw splashing. Anna? Aldo? Where did they go? Clutching her throat, her voice momentarily lost, she saw a hand appear in a vortex of roiling water.

"*O mio Dio!*" she cried, rushing towards them. As Flora plummeted into a deep hole, she understood what had happened. She knew how to swim so she pumped her legs to the surface. This new liquid world completely disoriented Aldo, who was trapped underwater, swallowing water while attempting to breathe. He couldn't tell if he was up or down. Wave after wave sloshed them around. Underwater, Anna was in a panic. The two were drowning. As Flora reached the surface, she took a huge breath into her formidable operatic lungs and screamed "*Aiuuuuuto*," flailing about to get the lifeguard's attention. The white point of the *patino* suddenly appeared. Dragged onto the boat, Flora knelt, breathlessly sputtering, her brother and sister, still down there. The two lifeguards dove in. Moments later Anna was hauled onto the boat, coughing. Flora, in hysterics, cried, "*O signore!* My brother! You have to save my brother! This cannot happen again at the sea, not to *Mamma!*" She prayed fervently to her mother's favorite saint Rita.

Aldo's limp, gangly body was hauled onto the boat. Anna, now revived, looked on horrified. She and Flora clutched each other's hands as they watched the lifeguard try to resuscitate Aldo. He finally stirred, vomited water, inhaled and fell back in exhaustion. The lifeguards rowed the stunned siblings back to the beach. When Anna stepped onto solid ground, first she thanked the lifeguards for saving them, but then she shouted, "You should flag those holes. That sudden drop is extremely dangerous. We all could have died!"

They sat wrapped in towels and silence under their canopy, grateful to be alive. They returned to the *pensione* and dressed for lunch. As they headed into the dining room, the phone rang at the main desk. The proprietor motioned to Anna, giving her the phone, "It's your mother."

As Aldo and Flora stood by, Anna said: "Of course… We're all fine, *Mamma*. It's sunny and hot, not a cloud in the sky," she added with wide eyes. "How's it going? Did you get the villa back?"

Anna covered the receiver. "Go on," she said. "I'll take care of this." Aldo and Flora shrugged and walked into the dining room.

Anna listened. "*Va bene, Mamma*. I will give them a hug for you," Anna reassured her mother before she hung up. She entered the dining room and sat next to her brother and sister, adjusting the white linen napkin on her lap. Aldo and Flora looked at her, incredulous.

"You didn't tell her, did you?" Flora said.

"Absolutely not, but I didn't lie," Anna insisted. "She asked how we are and I told her the truth — we *are* fine! You know how anxious *Mamma* is about us being here," she shuddered. "She'd end up like *Zio* Mario if she knew. At the very least she'd have rushed here just to see us all in one piece. I didn't want to disturb her. She has all these appointments. I'll tell her tomorrow when she arrives."

"I guess you're right," Flora said as she dug into her seafood *antipasto*.

"I always am," Anna insisted.

That afternoon in Florence the *geometer* knocked at Alda's door with a tube of maps under his arm. "*Buon giorno*, signora," he said. When Alda welcomed him, he unfolded the velum and she placed stones around so that the survey map would lie flat on the dining room table.

"If my calculations are correct," Alda asserted, "the parcel I want to sell is two hundred square meters of land." The man measured out one of Ugo's properties, exactly as Alda had with her own property map. He was amazed. La signora was precise.

"The price is per *ettaro*. I know the rate, and I'm sure that these hectares, in their location, will get a good price," she added. When they finished, he told her it was a pleasure working with her, as always, so well informed, saying she hardly needed him.

"*Grazie*, but you know it wouldn't be legal without your work," she said. He bowed slightly and she thought of all the costs associated with the sale of every property. She was determined to maintain as much of Ugo's patrimony as possible, but with paying back taxes, inheritance taxes and maintaining properties with such low rent her only recourse was to sell to survive. Little by little, she thought. She had to make sacrifices to give her children a good life.

Later that afternoon, on a bus to meet her lawyer about her tax case, she passed some villas she'd rented. Seeing such fancy cars in the driveway, she felt a bitterness that was unusual for her. It seemed unfair. *With such low rents they can afford to buy those cars, while I struggle and have to sell off properties to make ends meet.*

Stepping off the bus at Le Cascine, Florence's largest park, Alda watched as children and families gathered around carts full of crickets sold in little cages. She'd forgotten about the *Festa del Grillo*. Years earlier, while Floro was still missing up north, and once just after he'd died, Mario had accompanied Aldo to the festival, carrying a special cricket cage for him. Aldo, then seven, had been embarrassed that his cage was fancier than the others. Returning home, he'd wanted to free the cricket. She had to explain that farmers took crickets to the festival to remove them from the fields, to avoid devastating their crops. He would have to feed his cricket lettuce and never let it free. She had a clear memory of the cage by Aldo's bedside and her relief hearing her son giggle when he heard the *grillo's* scratching sound. It had been the first sign of delight since his father had died.

That night at the *pensione*, as Aldo lay alone in his dark room, still shaken from the experience of nearly drowning, he thought about his dead uncle, about his voice and the stories he'd never hear again. Then he remembered how terrified he'd been of the dark as a child, and another early childhood memory surfaced. He saw his mother in the kitchen commanding, "Close your eyes!" Obeying, he'd heard the shutters clatter before she'd said, "Now open them." In complete darkness, she had held out a tray that was shimmering with light. It was the shrimp that *Nonno* Ugo had brought home that day. His mother explained the mystery of their powerful luminosity. "It's bioluminescence, Aldino." Filled with wonder, he'd felt that moment as something magical and, after the experience, was never again afraid of the dark.

GENERATION FOUR AT THE VILLA

July to September 1978

Already two weeks past my June due date, I sat like a beached whale on the cool tile parlor floor, waiting impatiently for instructions from my mother-in-law who was subjecting me to some old wives' tale test to ascertain my baby's gender.

"Lean sideways," she said. I obeyed and shifted my inflated front. After eight months of vomiting, in this last month things had finally settled down. As if making up for lost time, I ate everything Alda cooked and my belly ballooned. Months earlier she'd declared that my baby was a boy by the way I was carrying. But today I made the mistake of teasing her.

Camilla on the terrace, pregnant, summer 1978.

"Alda, couldn't my new balloon shape mean I'm carrying a girl?" The experiment she was now subjecting me to was penance for that sarcastic comment. My mother, who'd arrived at the villa on my due date to help, sat on the big sofa giving me a cautionary look. Although my mother and mother-in-law couldn't communicate directly (I was the official translator), between them there already existed a sweet affinity. They had a lot in common – they were both kind, unselfish and devoted to their families. These two were daunting, nagging models for someone about to give birth in a time when roles for women and mothers were in transition.

"Stand up," Alda said. I exhaled while pushing aside the endless collection of her craft magazines piled in mounds on the floor. She was a packrat with an excess of excuses – *The Depression, Two World Wars, Every Little Thing Might Come In Handy*. Aldo had told me that when his mother moved to the villa she'd hired an entire truck to transport old newspapers and magazines from their house on Viale Michelangelo. As much as I admired the attentive re-use of objects in our increasingly disposable society, Alda's attachment reached a level of obsession. We were moving soon. We had to convince her to let go of certain things.

"*Certamente un maschio,*" Alda said, watching me rise.

"Really? A boy? How can you tell?"

From the sofa my mother gave me another warning glare.

"The way you got up," Alda insisted.

Camilla home with newborn Marco, under the loggia, July 1978.

"Uh huh."

I changed the subject and asked Alda to show my mother her handiwork for the baby. She lifted up the delicate bright white, crocheted, scalloped top and shorts suit. "Isn't it gorgeous?" I gushed. I could barely sew a button on a shirt.

My mother smiled, leaned over and shook her head in amazement. "*Bellisima*," she remarked, her favorite Italian word.

"*Bellisimo*," I corrected her, explaining that the word for suit in Italian has a masculine 'o' ending. I gave my mother two examples of why it was so important to be attentive to the Italian male/female noun endings. Years earlier Aldo's American artist friend Ellie attended a cocktail party with Florentines. She so wanted to express how their city was the "cradle of civilization." Instead of using the female noun for cradle, she said Firenze was "*il culo*," the ass, of civilization.

The second faux pas was mine; it happened shortly after arriving in Rome as a student. Our class went on a field trip to Siena with a group of Italian youths. We had lunch at the *enoteca*, a wine-tasting museum. We'd sat around a harvest table raising our wine glasses toasting to "*Americani*" and "*Italiani*." Since I'd just tasted fresh figs for the first time, I wanted to celebrate the luscious fruit. Enthusiastically raising my glass, I toasted, "*Alla fica!*" The response had been clamorous. Young Tuscan men leapt to their feet and cheered. I thought what a clever and original toast I'd made! As we

Flora, Alda holding Marco, Aldo, back terrace.

left the tasting, every handsome Italian from our table asked for my number. Months passed before I discovered what my toast really meant. In Tuscany, *il fico* means fig. But I'd unwittingly used the female ending and toasted to *la fica*, which in slang means vulva. My mother put her hand to her mouth, suppressing a laugh. I then had to translate the whole story to Alda. When she erupted in laughter, the three of us burst into hysterics.

Alda, realizing it was time to prepare lunch, grabbed her cane and headed to the kitchen. We followed. My mother watched as I helped make thin incisions in the zucchini blossoms, just harvested in the cool morning. I carefully removed the stamens and the little green tendrils near the base of the stem, while Alda mixed flour, water, salt and olive oil into a pancake batter consistency. Alda took over, dipped the male blossoms lightly into the batter and then dropped them in to sizzling oil. When both sides were golden, she drained them on brown paper, adding lots of salt. I adored Alda's fried zucchini flowers, so crisp and light. *Someday*, I thought, *I'll make zucchini flowers in my own kitchen.* Alda seemed to read my mind. She gave me a melancholy look. These were the last days of our being in the kitchen together. There was newness ahead for me and a hopeful beginning, but for Alda, leaving the villa was more like an ending. I turned to avoid crying.

We sat down to a sybaritic lunch of fried zucchini flowers and rounded medallions of *gnocchi di semolina*, baked and browned with butter and Parmesan cheese. The second course of fried meats and vegetables, *frito misto*, was followed by *radicchio*, arugula and bib lettuce, green gifts from the garden, seasoned with the Rafanellis' own vinegar and olive oil. Tomatoes picked an hour before were garnished with *nipitella*, a wild herb that Aldo and I had gathered that morning from the fields. I savored everything slowly, so relieved to be keeping food down.

Tasting our fresh tomatoes my mother moaned, "This is heaven." The flavor carried her back to her upstate New York childhood farm. After she'd escaped that place for married life in a Long Island suburb, she finally, in her sixties, felt nostalgia for it. Savoring juicy, lush apricots and freshly picked peaches for dessert was an experience I'd never known before moving to the villa. I raved on to my mother about the cherry season and the yields of delicious figs, plums, pears and persimmons. My mother complained that fruit in America is never harvested ripe anymore, that shelf life wins over taste, that peaches get mealy from refrigeration.

After lunch Aldo and I escorted my mother to the terrace. July was so scorching that he jokingly suggested we could cook an egg on the terracotta pavement. We moved under the shade of the *loggia*. She'd arrived on my due date for two weeks to help me out, but her time was already up, and I was still waiting to give birth. She could only extend her departure date another week. Her husband, who'd never had children, suggested I had deceived my mother about the due date, just to have her with me longer. I was furious. I wasn't even sure our baby would be born before my mother had to leave.

As we sat on the bentwood chaise, my mother wondered aloud how we could leave the villa, so I pointed to the area next to where we were sitting, cordoned off because of collapsing vaults, and reminded her of the untenable cost of replacing the terracotta roof.

"It's still sad," my mother sighed.

It was a relief, I told her, to think of Aldo's dear friends Simonetta and Eugenio restoring it. "But it's awful for Alda… This villa is her last link…" I stopped, choking on my words.

"Let's take a walk," my mother suggested. As we reached the *fieniele*, where hay was usually stored and where the olives were kept until they were pressed, we peered in through the half-moon brick slits. I explained it was the kind of farm building up north where Aldo's father had been sheltered for a year during the war. I wondered, since this building was going to be transformed into someone's home, where the harvested olives were going to be stored. Gigetto and his family had already left for Gubbio. Their departure, and the division of this property, meant the end of this small farm.

The walk wasn't helping my mood. I looked towards the field, to the rows of Aldo's grapevines laden with big green leaves and thought, *No more grape harvests, no more drinking his wine, no more eating fresh fruit or artichokes from these fields, no more hunting mushrooms with Alda in the boschetto.* When we reached the entrance to the garden park, I held my breath standing under Aldo's dilapidated treehouse. I didn't even look up. As we silently ambled towards the back door, pebbles on the path crunched under our feet.

There was a little levity that afternoon when Aldo's friend Pier Luigi discovered our baby would be born not in Florence but at the hospital in nearby Prato. "You mean, for the rest of his life, your child will have *Prato* on his documents as his place of birth?" I laughed at the proud Florentine-centric *campanellismo*. All Italians believe that no other city compares to their own, just as no meal beats home cooking.

The next day Aldo, my mother and I drove to the Prato hospital, as we'd been doing all week, to check on my overdue baby. My *primario* obstetrician Augusto Battisti, Anna and Flora's dear old friend, gave me my first sonogram with clear, cold jelly rubbed over my belly.

"Listen," *il dottore* said. Aldo and I were astonished by the steady loopy sound of the baby's heartbeat. This new technology reassured us that the baby was fine.

A day later, labor pains finally started. As I was wheeled into the delivery room, the attending doctor placed his hand on my enormous belly. "So… you first came to Italy to study art history, eh?" I nearly choked laughing between spasms of horrible back pain.

"Yes, it's true," I cried, adding a proverb I learned from Alda: "*I nodi vengono al pettine*… we reap what we sow." Taking deep breaths, I told him I might want to rethink that deal I made about no drugs. My obstetrician had yet to arrive, but before too long the formidable face of softhearted Augusto smiled down at me.

"Here we go," I said, and he laughed, holding my hand with his enormous one.

"*Cara*, everything will be okay."

Aldo was not allowed in the delivery room in this pre-Lamaze Italy. The hospital prided itself on its strict rules, attributing the lack of outside contact to its having one of the lowest infant mortality rates in Italy. I shuddered. Infant mortality? Up until that moment, the thought hadn't entered my mind. But with Augusto, I felt confident that my baby and I would be fine.

Aldo and my mother sat in the waiting room with Augusto's wife Marisa. Having researched Lamaze techniques, I focused on a picture on the wall and my breathing. I was told to push. My focus went from my own excruciating pain to getting this child safely out of the birth canal. A beautiful infant boy (yes, Alda) was finally laid across my belly. His body and fingers were astonishingly long. Tears of relief and elation streamed down my cheeks. After all these months of this life occupying my womb, we were now separate beings. I touched his exquisite hand, examined his long, delicate fingers, his perfect little fingernails, his tiny toes, his miraculous face.

Augusto looked down at me. "*Bello, eh?*" He patted my drenched head and told me he'd let Aldo know the good news. Acting like a version of Jackie Gleason (he actually looked like a mix of Alberto Sordi and Jackie Gleason), he made a comical face and exited, *stage left*, into the waiting room.

"*Un bel maschio di quattro kili!*" Augusto announced.

I was told later that Aldo, my mother and Marisa jumped up, gleefully hugging each other. Then my mother tugged on Aldo's shirt.

"I didn't understand! Please translate."

"Of course," he laughed and said in English, "It's a boy, almost nine pounds." Even though it was against the rules, Aldo sneaked in to kiss my forehead and glance at our baby. He wasn't allowed in again until I left the hospital four days later.

After the flood of emotion and exhaustion, I was wheeled to my room. Our *bambino*, Marco, was taken off to the nursery. Sleep was impossible with a woman next door in the thick of labor. Every minute she moaned a cavernous moan and shrieked *Aiii!* I waited and hoped for sleep, but the moaning got worse. I pulled my weary body out of bed. Although I was a self-taught convert to Lamaze, I pretended to be a guru.

"*Mi scusi,*" I said, knocking at the laboring woman's door. She looked bewildered to see a haggard American stranger peek in. She was alone with her pain. Her hair was wild. I forged ahead in Italian, explaining I'd just had my baby. "*Non ti preoccupare,*" I said. There really is an end in sight. I told her to breathe deeply when the pain hit and to focus on the picture on the wall, not on the pain. I offered a quick, slow breathing demo as she stared at me with wide eyes. (Do we really need breathing lessons?) Wincing, I wished her well, waved *ciao* and waddled off, hauling my deflated but still sore, misshapen body back into bed. The next minute I heard exaggerated breathing, but no more screaming or moaning, only gigantic loud inhales and exhales. She was in control, feeling better, a win-win situation. I fell asleep smiling.

After the first peek, Aldo only got to see his son on a small screen outside the nursery. He would push a button to ask for *Bambino Rafanelli,* and then a nursery camera would focus on our baby. Aldo's friend Fabrizio said that Marco looked just like photographs he'd seen of Aldo's *nonno* Ugo.

For four days I was in heaven, alone with our infant. Once healed from a painful bout of mastitis with fever, I adored the connection I felt while nursing. Before my baby fell asleep, I sang him a song by the popular Italian singer Mina. "*Quando ero piccola, dormivo alla luce di una lampada, per la paura della solitudine…*" I knew it was the first of countless lullabies I'd sing to my little captive audience, in Italian and in English.

Returning home with our miracle, Alda quickly scheduled his baptism since my mother had to leave. The villa's tiny chapel under the *loggia* was being utilized as D'oro and Tom's doghouse, something that Aldo's irreverent uncle Pietro would have appreciated. Restoring the chapel had been one of Alda's unfulfilled dreams. (A year after we left, Eugenio restored the chapel and discovered all sorts of bones buried in the walls. He and Simonetta swore that the villa was occupied by ghosts.)

The priest appeared at the front door wearing a long white robe. Alda, Aldo, my mother and I were joined by Anna and her boys, along with Flora, the only Rafanelli actually born at the villa. We stood by the piano in the dining room for the baptism as Anna held six-day-old Marco, standing in for his godmother, Linda, back in San Francisco. Anna's teenage son Luca, our nephew, stood next to his mother as Marco's godfather. As the priest poured a stream of water over his tiny forehead, our infant passed a trumpeting, endless *pernacchia*. I wondered if that string of formidable gas foreshadowed some kind of irreverence for religion. All our lips tightened to suppress hysteria, but when I observed Alda's laughing shoulders I was so relieved. However devout and however sorry she was about our looming departure from the villa, my mother-in-law's sense of humor transcended all. How awe inspired I was by her deep well of resilience.

Since we were moving in two months, once my mother left we began packing up the fifty-year multitude of possessions. Along with furniture, pots, pans and dishes, personal things would travel on our container to America. I watched Aldo gently wrap his father's brown leather motorcycle cap and black leather fascist boots. I knew how bitterly Aldo felt about fascism, I knew he would never wear those boots, yet how could he throw them out? They were an undeniable part of his father's story. All these belongings would travel across the ocean, then sit in storage until we anchored somewhere in New York. We would take the massive wooden kitchen *madia* that opens at the top to store flour, a place where Alda had kneaded bread; two nineteenth-century walnut *cassoni* carved with mysterious heraldic symbols and mythological creatures grasping a crescent moon in their talons; a tall antique terracotta vase with a six-ball Medici crest carved amidst swirling grapevines, a gift to Aldo from his mother's friend Rina; the harvest table and benches that Aldo had made with the wood from the obsolete chestnut wine barrel; the antique walnut oval dining table that graced my upstairs apartment; Alda's *prie-Dieu;* the breakfront Ugo had commissioned with a frieze of two open-mouthed griffons (Ugo had teased Anna, Flora and Aldo when they were babies with this frieze, sticking their little fingers in the mouth of the gaping griffons); the narrow, low slipper chair where Alda had nursed her children and where I was now nursing Marco; a spindly desk with gouges from Floro's making shotgun shells for hunting; and finally, the reproduction Savonarola chair where I'd sat contemplating sunsets over the villa's terrace, desperately longing to unblock my writing.

Before leaving for New York, Aldo and I would remain a few additional months in Fiesole with Giovanni and Fernanda, hoping it would be less of an abrupt break. Alda would live with Anna for a while. Maybe later she'd move in with Flora. I avoided thinking about the next uprooted, uncertain weeks for her. I focused on our establishing new traditions in our new world with my friends and relatives in America. Yet, when I thought about what created a sense of belonging, I couldn't imagine a place where I'd felt happier or more at home than the villa.

In the days before our departure, Alda took me aside to say that when her time came, she didn't want Aldo to come back to Florence for her funeral. She reminded me of his trouble with death, having experienced it so early in life. I dismissed her excuses, saying he was now a grown man. "Of course he'll come. You're his mother!" That's when she also told me about the visitation from a white moth.

On the last day at the villa, Aldo slowly opened the glass doors to *il boschetto*. Teenagers Luca and Federico were sitting in the open carriage of

Aldo with nephews Federico and Luca, with Alda and Anna sitting.

his truck laden with the furniture and terracotta vases that Anna wanted. Alda passed through the back door so she wouldn't have to walk over the terrace and down those front steps. No matter which way out, the fact weighed heavily on us.

Shuffling through the dining room, Alda stopped to lean on her cane. Her breathing labored as she paused, but she didn't look up at the rafters, as I did, at the little planted arrow, at the hearth with traces of ash from the last fire and bird roast. When she passed the threshold and stepped out onto the garden's pebble path, Alda turned and glanced up at the villa's back façade, up at a broken railing. What was she thinking? I couldn't ask, but her pain was palpable. Passing the truck with his nephews aboard, as Aldo gently guided his mother towards his blue Peugeot, I watched her slowly climb in.

EPILOGUE

Westchester, NY, 1986

My sleepy eyes settle on the pink and white blanket that once covered my bed at the villa. There's the round web Alda wove to repair the burn hole I caused that first winter when I tucked in the electric blanket. I remember feeling mortified that I might have burned the villa down, but Alda, without drama or lecturing, taught me another lesson in resourcefulness. She simply cut out the smoldered section and crocheted a web reminiscent of a dream-catcher, a spiderweb, a lovely snowflake. *No matter how tattered this blanket becomes, I can never throw it out.*

I check my bedside clock. I have spent most of the night reading notes from Alda's life, writing an outline. Looking at the notebook full of her stories, I can't help wondering: *In the end, Alda, as you lay dying, did you long to be back at the villa?*

When my own mother died a year ago, my then seven-year-old Marco asked me why people had to die. As we walked together in the woods, his younger brother Alessandro listened. "Every living thing has a limited time here." I turned over a rotting log and pointed out decomposers, explaining how they recycle life from what's dead and make soil. "Imagine if all the leaves on all these trees fell to the ground every season for a hundred years and never turned to soil. We'd be walking through leaves a mile high," I said. "Same with people. It's a great big cycle that makes way for the generation that follows." Attempting to reassure them, I added, "Nothing here on earth really goes away, it just changes form."

A gentle knock shakes me from my reverie. My two boys open the door. "You okay, Ma?" my four-year-old Alessandro says as he peers in.

"I'm fine," I lie, gesturing for him to climb under the covers. I tussle his straw blond hair and pull him close, patting the other side of the bed for Marco to join us. I can tell they are both eager for me to be my old cheerful self and get out of bed.

"We're hungry, Mom. Can you make pancakes?" Marco asks.

"Sure," I say without moving.

Wanting to rouse me, Marco goes to the window. "It's dark in here; I'll pull up the shades." Snapping it hard, it flaps up. We laugh. Light streams in as Marco looks down. "There's a white moth on the floor."

I'd already forgotten. "Oh dear. Bring her to me… carefully."

Clasping the delicate white wings between two little fingers, Marco places the moth in the palm of my outstretched hand and climbs into bed. The three of us examine it. My eyes sting, announcing tears.

"This is a particular visitor moth," I whisper, the punster in me wanting to say *moth-er*. I pick up my notebook and carefully bury the creature between the pages of Alda's story.

I smile at my boys. Their features have elements of long gone family from both sides.

Squeezing my hand, Alessandro says, "Come on, Ma, get up."

The strength of his grasp conjures up the memory of the tiny, tenacious infant Anna holding her mother's finger, coaxing Alda back to life after Elvira's death. *How can little ones be so wise?*

I return the squeeze and finally get out of bed, kissing the top of his head. "Okay," I say, pulling on my bathrobe. Marco grabs one hand and Alessandro holds the other. As my two darling boys lead me through the doorway, I long for this tender empathic moment to last forever. But as soon as they know I am okay, as if illustrating the point of all things cyclical and ephemeral, my sons let go and bound down the stairs, out of sight.

Pietro, Danilo and Floro Rafanelli, circa 1906.

Danilo, born 1899, died in Palermo military hospital, 1920.

Floro with young Flora, al mare, circa 1937.

Flora and Anna.

Aldo's Treehouse, in woods behind villa, 1975.

Cinquecento Villa Rafanelli, formerly Il Boschetto, 1975.

ALDA'S FLORENTINE RECIPES PASSED DOWN TO ANNA, TO ALDO AND TO ME

Antipasto
Fiori di Zucchini Fritti
(my version of Alda's fried
zucchini flowers + fried sage leaves)
Serves 10

24 male zucchini flowers
1 cup of white flour
water
olive oil
corn oil
salt
large sage leaves

When picking your own zucchini flowers, it's important to snip the male flowers which have a long stem with no zucchini attached, or you prematurely harvest your plant. If possible, cut the flowers when they are closed rather than splayed out under the sun. In the kitchen, carefully remove the stem and pointy tendrils at the base of the blossom. With a small sharp knife make a length-wise slit in the flower and remove the stamen without damaging the blossom. Lay blossoms on a platter.

In a shallow bowl mix the flour, adding enough water little by little to make a creamy/pancake consistency batter, neither too thick nor too thin. Add a drizzle of olive oil to the mix.

Cover the bottom of a pan with abundant corn oil and heat without burning. Check with a drop of the batter to see when the oil sizzles. When it does, pass a zucchini blossom over the batter until the blossom is coated. Drain off excess. Carefully place into sizzling oil. Repeat until the pan is full without crowding the blossoms. If sizzling too much, turn flame down a bit. When golden underneath, turn the flowers with a fork to fry both sides. When golden remove flowers with slotted spoon. While the blossom is on the spoon, take a fork and drain residual oil into the pan before placing the blossom on a platter covered with a paper towel. Remove paper and replace when needed to absorb oil. Salt all flowers and serve hot.

Fried sage, for a crispy addition, to use up remaining batter: Take wide sage leaves and dip in the mixture to thinly coat leaves before dropping into the frying oil. Turn with fork, same as the blossom recipe above, and add to a platter covered with paper towel. Salt and serve hot.

Antipasto
Crostini di Fegato
della Mamma
(Florentine liver canapes)
Serves 15

½ kg chicken liver
heart of 1 onion
5 sage leaves
40-50 juniper berries
olive oil
40g butter
chicken broth
anchovy paste – optional
caper
vino bianco
baguette, toast or grill both sides

Chop onion, sage and juniper berries. Saute in 30g butter on slow fire. Wash and chop liver into small pieces. When butter takes on a walnut color, add liver and cook slowly. Add a bit of broth and white wine as it cooks for a creamy consistency. Once cooked, pass soft liver through a *passa tutto*, metal food mill. Add 4-8g of raw butter if needed, and anchovy paste if desired. Serve creamy liver pate on a long slice of toast and top with a caper.

Primo
Ravioli Gnudi alla Fiorentina
(called 'nude' ravioli as this dish has no pasta cover.
Also called 'Malfatti' as they are uneven in shape)
Serves 8

1 kg of fresh spinach, removing largest stems
1kg of fresh ricotta
5 eggs
flour
200g of freshly grated Parmigiano – Reggiano
grated nutmeg, salt and black pepper

Butter/sage sauce:
12 fresh sage leaves
100g of butter

Tomato and garlic sauce:
5 chopped San Marzano tomatoes
4 garlic cloves sliced length-wise in quarters
olive oil

Wash the spinach numerous times before throwing in boiling salted water. Cook and drain very well in a colander and let cool. Once room temperature, pick up in sections and make a ball of spinach, squeezing in palm to get all liquid out. Once squeezed dry, place on a cutting board and chop to semi-fine pieces. Place a paper towel over to absorb remaining liquid. (It's important that the spinach is well drained or the ravioli will unravel in the boiling water.)

Put a pot of abundant water on the stove to boil, adding a fistful of kosher salt.

In a large bowl add the ricotta, eggs, half of grated Parmigiano and mix well with a generous amount of grated nutmeg. Add salt and pepper and the chopped spinach and mix again. Mixture should not be too thick or too liquid. If too liquid, add some flour.

Take a few tablespoons worth of the mixture from the bowl and gently form into a sausage shape that should remain whole. Pass/roll and cover the form lightly in flour. Place on a tray covered with parchment or wax paper so they don't stick. Repeat until all mixture is finished and the forms are side by side but not touching. (Figure about five ravioli forms for each person's pasta bowl.)

For the tomato sauce, put a small pan on a medium fire. Cover bottom of pan with virgin olive oil. The garlic should be sautéed until softened before adding the chopped tomatoes. Cook gently for ten minutes, adding a bit of water or olive oil when needed.

For the butter/sage sauce: in a small pan melt the butter and add sage leaves. Cook carefully until butter is brown, but not burnt. Keep hot while the ravioli forms are cooking.

When the water is gently boiling, carefully immerse one ravioli and then another into the water and continue, keeping in mind how wide the pot is, as the ravioli should float to the surface when ready, without crowding. Add forms in stages. As each ravioli rises to the surface, remove with a slotted spoon. Place 4-5 directly in each person's pasta bowl. Pour a few tablespoons of butter sage sauce or the tomato sauce, or a combination, over each bowl. Add abundant grated cheese and black pepper. Repeat the process and serve immediately.

Secondo
Alda's Fricasse di carne:
(chicken, rabbit or beef stew with béchamel sauce)
Serves 4

carrot
parsley stalk
celery

whole red onion
chicken, rabbit or beef chunks
flour
2 egg yolks
½ lemon
112g butter (1 stick)

Put carrot, parsley stalk, celery, whole red onion into pot of water (enough to cover vegetables and meat) and bring to a boil. Add chunks of chicken, rabbit or beef to the pot. While water boils, gingerly melt a stick of butter in a small pan over a low flame. With a wooden spoon, gradually stir two tablespoons of flour into butter pan. As stew boils, add ladle full of the broth to the butter/flour mixture, stirring so it (the béchamel) doesn't curdle. Remove the parsley from the pot and add butter/flour sauce to the stew as liquid reduces.

Minutes before serving, add two egg yolks (already stirred) with juice of ½ lemon to the pot. Serve.

Contorno
Faggioli all' Ucelletto (cannellini beans in tomato sauce)
Serves 10

454g of dry cannellini beans
garlic
bunch of sage leaves
extra virgin olive oil
300g ripe tomatoes for sauce
salt and pepper

After soaking overnight, cook dried cannellini beans in boiling water. When beans are cooked and soft but not broken, turn fire under the pot off. In a pan covered with a bit of olive oil, add sliced quarters of garlic cloves and a bunch of sage leaves. Once sautéed, add chopped tomatoes (without skin - use the food mill) and cook for fifteen minutes. Stir in drained boiled beans, keeping some of their liquid, and add to tomato sauce. Cook for additional 10-15 minutes. Season with salt and pepper and serve.

Dessert
Cantucci di Prato (almond biscuits – served with vinsanto)
Yields 40 biscuits

Preheat oven at 350 degrees/moderate temp.
500g of '00' white flour
400g of granulated sugar
250g toasted almonds, with skin
3 whole eggs
2 yolks
1 egg, beaten
50g melted butter
2 teaspoons of baking powder
salt
Another option: add 2 teaspoons of anise seeds, 2 teaspoons of vinsanto, grated lemon rind.

In a large bowl create a well in the middle of the flour. Add the three whole eggs, two yolks (leave aside the beaten egg for afterwards) and sugar, and blend with baking powder, melted butter and salt. Add almonds and mix quickly. Knead and form mix into long flattened strips, two fingers wide, 1cm thick. Lay on a baking pan lined with parchment or other oven-proof paper. Allow to rest for an hour. Brush strips with beaten egg and put them into the oven at a moderate temperature for about 30 minutes. When hot and crunchy remove and cut into oblique slices about 1cm thick. Toast again in the oven for a few minutes if needed.

Allow to cool. May be stored for a week in an airtight container once cooled. Serve dipped in a little glass of vinsanto.

ACKNOWLEDGEMENTS

I want to thank so many people for their enduring interest and encouragement over the years. Such love and generosity often remedied the isolation and frustration of writing. Sincere apologies if I have left anyone out. Initially the story was entirely focused on the life of my mother-in-law, Alda. I shared a first draft with a young friend, Morgan Keay, who strongly suggested that I include my connection to Italy, to Aldo and to Alda. Her recommendations inspired me to expand the scope of the book into a multi-layered story that bridges three generations. Thanks Morgan! In later, but still early, iterations, I was buoyed by the enthusiasm and notes from dear friend and business partner Nancy Bloch, who shared the first draft with friend Kathy Reno, who then introduced me to her friend, the author Kathleen Kent, who gave me some thoughtful insight into marketing. I was also moved by the early, excited read by Maria Fama and Dawn Watson. Over the last four years it has been an enormous support to meet regularly with two authors who are now friends, Valerie Matthews and Margie Winslow, as we shared chapter by chapter of our books and made comments on countless drafts. Thanks also to Renata Rosati, who astonished me with her rapid, enthusiastic read and introduction to her literary agent friend whose editor, Julie Mosow, later read and reviewed my book. Since I had never met Julie, her ebullient reaction to *The White Moth* encouraged me to launch it into the world beyond family and friends. A big thanks goes to dear Susan Schwarz, whose cheerleading and notes on two versions of my manuscript are dearly appreciated. *Mille grazie* also for the invaluable input and enthusiasm from dear friend and author Hilary Horder. She participated in the Italian sojourn so could check the accuracy of my memory, as well as countless other details in two separate drafts. It's impossible to express enough gratitude to my dear college friend, Linda Armao, who also lived at the villa with us and is found within these pages. After reading an early draft, more recently Linda combed through every line of every page. Her command of English grammar and the Italian language was a great gift as we discussed her editorial comments and suggestions over and over for hours on the phone. Her meticulous and generous guidance, sometimes erupting in hysterical laughter, throughout every detail of this journey has been astonishing. I am also deeply grateful for the unflagging interest I received from author and friend Christine Lehner, who read an early version and recently the most final. Twice she invited me to read sections of my book to her writing group (thank you, Becky, for coming up with the title!), and her ardent support extends to hosting a book launch party that will include Alda's recipes. When I lacked feedback from a male perspective, I was heartened by John Scribner's comments, especially when he said he'd read the last two hundred pages in one riveted sitting. Thanks also to Bette Valdre who translated four chapters of my book into Italian. And a thousand thanks to my Florentine family, especially to my sister-in-law Anna Bencini, who filled in so many essential blanks with her astonishing memory. And to her son Federico Bencini and his wife Lucilla Pezzuti for their dear support through this process and for introducing me to Chiara Vismara, and to Luca Bencini and his Eleanora Franchi for their enduring interest. Thanks also to my sister Carol Kelly, and friends Reneé and Jordan Kalfus for their design sense, and to Robin Price and Carl Weber for their comments. To my spiritual gurus Jane Cameron, Charlene Paden and Dawn Watson for constant support and listening to snippets of this story. To Marianna Houston for her introduction to a small press, and to Kate McGloughlin for the same and much more. And to all my dear Italian and American friends who have been waiting to read it, thank you for sustaining me with your curiosity and patience! My son Marco read a draft early on, and then again both he and his younger brother Alessandro read the almost finished version during the week of their father's funeral in Florence in 2016. Their emotional response was heartbreaking, treasured and reassuring, as was the insightful feedback from Marco's wife Christine Gibadlo and Alessandro's wife Sarah Russell. I will forever be profoundly grateful for the day in Carrara that I met Aldo, for our transformative life together in Italy, and for nearly forty years of marriage. Initially a skeptic who wondered why I wasn't writing about my own family, after numerous readings Aldo became my dearest champion. His steadfast love and support over the decade it took to complete this work was essential. Aldo: I'm so sorry I never bought you that Norton Atlas English motorcycle many decades ago. It's heartbreaking that you are not here to finally see this book in print. As I write this I am humbled, blessed and so grateful for all the people who have contributed to this long process. Thank you. Lastly, many thanks to production manager Rosie Lowe and all the kind, professional staff at Matador.